Fatherless

A Memoir

Phil Barber

Published in 2014 by **Hallow Press**

Cover design: © 2014 Steve Shaw

ISBN: 978-0-9928994-0-0

To my older brother Dave
1951 - 2007

"He Ain't Heavy, He's My Brother"
One of his favourite songs

The above song title was a slogan taken from Boys Town,
a children's home in America

Contents

Part III

Introduction

Emotions persist, transporting me back to the boys' homes. The dormitories go quiet. I lay on my back staring at the ceiling. A deep longing hovers, *someone will come for me soon*. With my father gone, that someone could only have been my mother, and I could hardly remember what she looked like.

Really there was no clear wish; it was more a faint wave of feeling or expectation waiting in silence in the wardrobe of my mind. The reality of my mother coming to collect me was non-existent. But my pipe dream insisted, surely that must be true. To compensate, my mind made up beliefs.

Beliefs are like writings in the sand; only lasting till the tide of experiential truth washes the lies out of them.

The belief that those born out of wedlock or from broken families were of bad blood was still prevalent in the 1960s. I know that, because I believed it too.

Being raised in an institution, exiled from the cleansing touch of wise elders, it was easy to feel like a reject, permanently weathering an invisible storm. Children crave faces that smile, hearts that melt, people who know how to dance. No institution can match the power of a wise elder, a man or woman seasoned by their life storms, saved and spirited by the wings of their unique gifts. Such elders look for and validate the delicate cargo of beauty, the unique genius, in every child. This, I did not know.

The health of a society can be measured by the state of its institutional care. As far back as the 1600s private landlords were paid to care for the poor and destitute. The Industrial Revolution then created more of, and tried to help, the poor and vulnerable. In 1834 the Poor Law Amendment Act instigated the widespread building of *Workhouses*, where paupers were housed in exchange for work. Workhouses were mostly harsh places, places of last resort. Inmates were bedevilled with shame, as if they'd belonged to a forbidden society.

Charles Dickens published *Oliver Twist* in 1838, a fictional novel about an orphan born in such an institution. The novel lifted the veil on the abysmal treatment of children in a parish workhouse.

In 1870 Dr Barnardo, a medical student studying in London, became a philanthropist and opened the first of his homes for destitute children. Boys were given tradesmen's skills or raised in Barnardo's naval training schools. Girls were raised to become domestic servants. The *Dr Barnardo's* organisation grew and went on to run 188 homes throughout the UK.

At the turn of the century the *Cottage Homes* organisation also housed children suffering in the parish workhouses.

Local authority children's homes were only introduced after the 1948 Children's Act required each parish to provide them by 1955. The Act also stipulated the parish had to have a *children's department* headed by a *children's officer*. In 1970 those children's departments became part of *Social Services*.

The late 1970s and 1980s saw the closure of all Barnardo's and Cottage Homes. One reason they closed their doors was the impossibility of replicating home life. The outside world does not resemble an institution, and, when a child is raised in one, it is no easy task shaking free of its vibration.

In an institution it's easy for a child to become a number, an inmate: and subsequently characterless. When a child is not tied in to the wider community the relational threads needed to bring their beauty into the world are impaired. They become *at risk*.

It's interesting to note that Oliver Twist was taken from the workhouse and given work by the parochial undertaker, not for his talents, but for his melancholy demeanour highly valued in the funeral trade.

In the pages of Oliver Twist, Charles Dickens comments – *there is a passion for hunting something deeply implanted in the human breast.* I don't think that's about hunting sports, but points to the more important search of what was deeply implanted in the heart, at birth.

I have felt the limiting grip of an old story, like an iron hand clasping my shoulder, refusing to let go. I know that iron hand is more ancient and universal than my own story. And I know that its grip has an intention to hand me something good - a gift - something that must be remembered, integrated and used. If the gift is carried in the heart, it is also carried in the heart of the story.

The restrictive part of that iron hand I knew well; the gifting part required a slowing down. It required me to keep myself attentive, revealing, listening, and questioning, and to stay dedicated, researching, interpreting, editing and revitalising my memories. It required me to steep my heart in deeper feelings, to fully appreciate just how much loss I had inherited, to rage and mourn, and to forgive.

If some people forget their past in order to survive, then some remember it for the same reason – words I found in the autobiography of African shaman Malidoma Somé. They speak to the heart of it. For a full life we need our roots as well as our wings, and we need a way to see the connective energy between the two.

To acquire more knowledge and feeling of my own root system I began writing my troubled coming-of-age years. I wanted to take a closer look at the river I had travelled down, to wade upstream and explore.

I was fuelled further by a swirling notion that in fathoming more deeply my own journey it would help my children fathom theirs, and be of interest to others whose early circumstances resemble my own. I also hoped to speak to the *orphan* in us all.

How difficult could it be then, to draw lines around events and colour them in. Memories were pressing on me, shifting and hungry for daylight, though few shifted neatly into place. Events are not so easily isolated. While initial writings stirred the soulful elements of my experiences there were wild swathes of obstinate and confusing passages overlaying them. The fertility I was seeking would not come so easily; there was a gardening process to be done. That meant working through the seasons, five years of them.

Help and encouragement came from my children, Kirsty, and Hayley, from my newer family Calum, Clayton, Darren and Marie. My wider family, friends and acquaintances further prompted me.

Impetus especially came from the memory of my much missed brother Dave, who first planted the notion of writing this book. It also came from many people I've contacted who were linked to Barnardo's.

I am also indebted to fellow writers and my professional editors from whom I have learned so much and who have helped shepherd this manuscript out of its hiding place. Special thanks go to my partner Christine for her tireless help with editing and holding this project in esteem over the years.

In appreciation, you have all been invaluable.

PHIL BARBER 2014

Fatherless

"The more you know of your history, the more liberated you are."

Maya Angelou

PART I

Chapter 1

Hallowed Home

My five-year-old eyes locked onto the woman as if I were hypnotised. Though she walked away slowly, she was eager to leave. Bent forward and wearing a faded, green headscarf, she moved up the gentle slope of the lane that led to the old church. The carefree smell of the late summer meadow and the children's laughter was swallowed by silence: the kind of silence that follows a scream.

I watched to see if the woman would glance back. She disappeared, slipping behind the dense trees of the dell.

Something beyond my small life had visited me, like a dark, menacing cloud. My breath tightened. Something felt horribly wrong; as if something was so lost it would never ever find its way back.

It was one of those ripening late summer days in the meadow below the cottages. September 1961, Hallow Park children's home was alive with the sound of youngsters playing and the early afternoon ball game with my friends was in full flow. Unnoticed at first, a woman had walked down the leafy lane that led from the church and stood behind the waist-high, rusty iron fence railings. She called out to my older brother. Dave ran over and spoke to her. Some of the other children followed.

A minute later the group called out to me. "Phil! Phil, come here." I ran to them and the woman spoke to me from behind the fence.

"Hello Philip."

"Hello," I said, smiling politely.

Within minutes, she was walking back up the lane towards the church. As I gazed at that solitary female figure with her head down something stirred in my young self and rooted me to the ground. I should have done something different. I should have spoken more, made her happier somehow. I felt I knew her, or that I should have known who she was.

"Who was that?" I asked the other children.

"That was your mother, stupid!" They laughed.

The moment filled with an awful hurt. I felt a stifling awkwardness and wanted to move away from my playful friends. They must have heard Dave call her "mother," but I didn't know what they meant by *mother*. We all shared house mothers in the children's home, but there was no sense of special belonging to any one of them. Yet, for some reason, I knew I had a connection with this woman; my body told me so.

The day marked a great change in me. Some kind of protective shield was pierced and loneliness surged in. The strife my mother Annie carried wrestled in me, as well, and ensured I and my many siblings would have a crooked story to live out.

Chapter 2

Annie's Prayers

At two years old I had been taken into care with my older brothers Dave and Steve. Local foster parents had been found in Yorkshire, but within weeks they'd asked for us to be returned because of our aggressive behaviour. After months in temporary nurseries in Dewsbury and Huddersfield, we were taken to Hallow Park, a Barnardo's children's home near Worcester.

The Barnardo's intake report of July 1959 describes me and my mother.

He is a vibrant little boy but at times fearful. In September 1958 the mother attempted suicide by gas poisoning, and was removed to hospital, later being put on probation for two years. The three boys were admitted to the care of the Local Authority. Mother – Annie Barber (31) Health – mentally unstable; character – well-meaning but weak and of poor moral character. She has spent several periods in a mental hospital. She has given birth to five children. The putative father of Philip is thought to be a Pole. Recently the mother bore another child. Because of her temperament and poor physical health, the mother was unable to control David, Steven, and Philip. They were brought up in a violent, unstable atmosphere. Her new partner is stated to be a violent man and a bully by nature.

In August of 1956, my twenty-nine-year-old mother, Annie Barber (nee Kelly), struggled to care for us three boys in the cramped one-up, one-down terrace in the bleak Yorkshire mill town of Dewsbury. The terrace was nestled behind a pub called The Shepherd's Boy; the front door of our tiny house faced a high brick wall. Dave was six, Steve one, and I was newly born.

My father was a close neighbour, a friendly but married Polish man called Jan Wondzinski. He was one of many displaced Polish people who'd escaped his invaded homeland during World War II. Jan took Annie dancing in town, something she'd always loved to do. On occasions he took her to the nearby Polish club. Their affair lasted a couple of years and they had two children together, Steve and me.

My mother was investing in a dream of herself and Jan living happily with their two sons. The painful chill of a broken dream bit deep when Jan refused to leave his wife and other son and moved across town. My mother steeled herself to cope with the spurning. But when Jan stopped the child maintenance money my mother turned up on his doorstep in a wrathful state. Despite his wife standing next to him my mother demanded money for us boys, and would not leave without it.

Annie's sober lesson was to expect little from her relationships, especially as things had turned sour in the past. Six years earlier Dave was born from a brief relationship she'd had with Patrick Joseph Patterson, a singer in a local pub when she was twenty three. "He made promises to me, but they turned out not to be true," she explained years later.

A year after Dave was born, my mother married Raymond Barber. Their year-long marriage ended in bitterness and divorce. Worse still, Raymond had taken their five-month-old daughter, Jane, to Leeds and refused to bring her back.

My mother recounted how worn down she'd become by the relentless domination of Raymond and Raymond's mother.

Annie's ailing mental health and commitment to her first-born child, Dave, meant she reluctantly gave up her struggle to reclaim her daughter. My mother returned to work to find money to bring up David.

Annie's was a family of loss. Infant death had taken three of Annie's siblings. Her father, Charles Kelly, was a lonely man and an absent figure even though he lived nearby. Typically, Annie would deliver food to him, or run errands, but he would completely ignore her. Her father's rejections embedded their curses on Annie right from her being a young girl.

The last strands of stability came undone in three days of January, 1955. Annie's mother, Alice, and grandmother, Sarah Ellen Wood, both suddenly died. Days later, her younger sister, Connie, was permanently placed in a mental institution.

Since her late teens, Annie had also seen the inside of a mental institution. The huge Victorian mental hospital, Storthes Hall, was only a few miles away. She endured drugs and padded cells and on five occasions had undergone the controversial electric shock treatment. It took away her memory for a while. "It didn't seem to work at first so they intensified the treatment," she told me.

The stigma surrounding the mental institution bit chunks out of Annie's pride. Because of the way patients were locked in, she privately called the place "the dungeon". But publicly, she referred to her time there as, "hospital visits", because "I'm bad with my nerves".

Alone with three boys, Annie's situation became far worse as her bouts of depression and anxiety increased. For the next two years, she struggled on trying to care for us while undergoing long stays in Storthes Hall.

In the spring of 1958, we moved to a small, back-to-back mill workers' terrace in the Eightlands district near my mother's Aunt Emmy. That summer, Annie fell pregnant again. Shortly afterwards, the local authorities got news of a suicide attempt. My mother told me it was a neighbour she'd feuded with that made the allegation.

In October, Annie left us three boys with Aunt Emmy to seek refuge in yet another week-long "hospital visit".

Aunt Emmy was chair-ridden, and although Annie's younger brother, Tommy, was lodging with Emmy he was illiterate and mentally dependent on Aunt Emmy. But it was the safest place Annie had for us, and coming home she fully expected to find us there.

"Where on earth are they?" she shouted to Emmy.

"They've taken them, Annie," Emmy said in her timid voice.

We had been placed in a nursing home for safety, but the authorities left no word of where we were.

Annie's future battles were not only with male acquaintances; she clashed constantly with the Dewsbury Children's Authority as well. Her attempts to gain ground in either place were futile.

No one in Annie's family had any stature that she could draw from. There was no family member with any harmony to give her an underpinning of mental stability. Alone, unsupported, and under pressure, she would buckle into dependency.

Faced with the realisation that we boys would not be coming home, Annie pleaded with the authorities. "*Please* keep the three of them together."

Dewsbury authorities offered only one solution, a Dr Barnardo's Home in the Midlands, one hundred and forty miles away. It was a six-hour journey involving three trains and a bus ride, and Annie would struggle to make the fare.

In 1958, Dewsbury had around eighty children needing care, but only one 'local authority home', the chaotically run Ash Tree House with just twelve places. Progressive, neighbouring authorities had opened more homes as they developed empathy for the social problems in their communities. At that time, Dewsbury authorities coughed up a boarding fee and transported their *illegitimate* children out of the borough.

Two other provisions for children existed: the Cottage Homes, which had evolved from the infamous Victorian workhouses, and voluntary homes like Dr Barnardo's. The cheapest was always Barnardo's, which made it first choice for the Dewsbury Borough no matter how far children had to go.

The Barnardo's organisation owned and ran over one hundred properties spread over the country, ranging from terraced houses to castles.

In July 1959, I was taken along with my brother, Steve, to one of them: Hallow Park. Dave, who'd been boarded somewhere else, followed later.

I was to become a children's home kid while my mother tried

to make a life with another man with whom she eventually had six more children. Chaos and aggression became her routine, so my younger siblings would also spend many of their early years in institutions.

Chapter 3

Hallow Park

The pastoral surroundings of Hallow Park were a contrast to the blackened Yorkshire stone of Dewsbury, the industrialised West Yorkshire mill town. Hallow was middle England, semi-rural and with the charm and quaintness of village life.

The children's home was a former Georgian manor house which housed the nursery children. School age kids lived in the three modern brick detached cottages in the grounds of the manor. The home was at the end of a quiet lane that ran off the village green. The lane passed through a leafy gateway and opened onto a circular drive around the lawn in front of the main house. Nestled among fields and trees, and watched over by the church spire, it was the kind of surrounding that fed you gentleness and calm. Life there was slow, timeless, conservative, and very English.

In the nursery, I recall the sunlight bursting through the tall windows amid the sound of playing children. The reds, yellows, and blues of the toys attracted me into the playroom. Two uniformed house mothers were encouraging me to play, handing me books and toys. "Your brother is playing in that group," one of them said, pointing. I felt something tug inside me for the boy playing in the other room, who was Steve.

Hallow Park nursery was safe, clean and well-staffed. When left to their own authority, the house mothers were happy and cared for us lovingly. In the early afternoons, we were rounded up and settled in the TV room for children's hour. We watched Andy Pandy, and Bill and Ben, till the static test card reappeared on the screen.

Long summer afternoons of my pre-school years included walks down the meandering path behind the house to the River Severn, or sitting lazily with the house mothers on the front lawn. When the gardener brought a basketful of peapods, I enjoyed helping split them open, counting out the fresh green peas into a steel colander.

The old man who tended the vegetable gardens had a tanned, outdoor face. He wore a rough waistcoat and red neckerchief. He said little, but his deep resonant voice settled me and I followed him dutifully around the growing beds – their tall canes towering over my head. Often, I'd ride in the garden wheelbarrow, with my hands gripping the sides, smiling as he pushed me along.

I'd been distracted and wandered a little one afternoon. Looking up, I couldn't see the old man anywhere. My three-year-old head swivelled. Which way has he gone? Why has he left me?

Suddenly I was alone in a world of plants, trees, and bushes: engulfed and scared. The plants seemed to come alive, tugging on me, pulling me through a boundary between their state and mine. The foliage, trees, and insects buzzed with life and were trying to play with me, inviting me into their lush organic world. At the same time I was being pulled back into my body by my state of agitation.

How long I was there I don't know, but eventually I scurried off to find the old man. It was a relief to see him quietly working behind the potting shed, digging the ground. I knelt next to him where he could see me, then clambered into the wheelbarrow.

The village of Hallow lays two miles north of the cathedral City of Worcester. A majestic oak tree, in the centre of the village green, spread its maternal branches over a wide area. The green was edged by period cottages and picturesque houses. A traditional coaching inn and stone church with sentinel spire completed the community of buildings.

The village held traditional May 1st celebrations. I loved the May Day events and delighted in the spectacular colour and vibrancy of it all. It seemed like everybody in the community was there having fun, their collective dancing hearts welcoming the edge of summer and the new life it brought.

The celebration centred on the maypole. Brightly coloured ribbons were tied to the top of the tall pole, and girls formed a circle around the pole holding the loose end of each ribbon. With great smiles and energy they danced to music in a pattern around the pole, weaving in and out of one another. The dance ended with the ribbons woven around the pole, like woven lives, from the top down in an enchanting pattern.

I saw men inside wooden frames wandering around the green dressed as trees with oak branches fixed to them like a camouflage. When I wasn't alongside an adult, I found those "moving trees" scary. The tree had come alive! I searched for a familiar adult.

Scores of people in imaginative costumes walked round, carrying garlands, offering food, and just wanting to give: apples, pieces of pie, and other homemade goodies. It felt like I belonged to all the people there, as though they were my family. The grown-ups looked down admiringly at me, smiling with delight. The warmth of the festival made me feel alive, loved, and blessed.

Every month, the older children from the three cottages joined us in the main house to watch a film. The man who came with the projector was a popular figure and soon had a gaggle of excited children huddled around him. More often he brought one of the popular westerns, but a different film imprinted itself on me. It was about the French tightrope walker, Blondin, and how he became a worldwide celebrity when he walked a quarter-of-a-mile wire across the Niagara Falls. Captivated by the scene, I felt awe at Blondin's daring and showmanship.

I had the same lasting impression from a visit to a circus. Close to the action, the raw spectacle was hypnotic. The clowns and animals were interesting, but when the high-rope acts appeared I was spellbound. I wanted to be up there with them in the roof of the big top, flying through the air with every muscle of my body stretched full out. I'd tell people, "When I grow up I want to be in the circus - on the flying trapeze!"

Each summer, our home hosted a garden fete. Tombola and skittles stalls were set up on the front and back lawns. Local people sold homemade fare, and majorette dancers performed into the warm evening.

One year, while everyone was enjoying the fete, I felt safe to explore and ventured off to a nearby wood. Wandering back I found myself on a piece of grass about a hundred yards from the house. Dozens of people milled around on the circular lawn, but they were all strangers to me! They were finely dressed, the men in tailored cloth suits and the women in summer hats and smart, pretty dresses. Sounds of gentle laughter and occasional clapping hung in the air.

Who are they? I wondered. I was anxious about approaching these alien people who had invaded the grounds of my home. I crouched on my knees behind some bushes. Where were the children and the house mothers? What had happened to the people who knew me? The longer I stayed the more I sensed I'd get scolded for wandering off. Shall I stay? Shall I run? I tucked in to the bushes, frozen in my hiding place.

A car rolled up the drive behind me. The blue open-top vintage car had a man at the wheel and a woman beside him, again, both finely dressed. The driver saw me and slammed on the brakes. Was he going to tell me off? I ran as fast as I could towards the house.

Sweet relief swept over me as I was recognised by one of the house mothers. "Where have you been Philip?" she scolded mildly. She crouched and looked into my eyes. "Are you okay?" I eased into the reassurance of being back with familiar people, but the experience shook me. I had the feeling I'd been swept into a forgotten world, and left there.

Miss Neale was not a woman to be crossed. Her grey, highly groomed hair and her rigid, spectacled gaze garrisoned her face. Miss Neale was the elderly principal of Hallow Park children's home and, though not seen much, her orderly energy drove itself around the house like a marching soldier.

Much of the time Miss Neale was in a wheelchair, wheeled out like a warrior's chariot. Every month or so she'd conduct a formal review of the children. The staff manoeuvred her into the large hallway with its dark wood panelling. Each child was presented in front of her in turn. Posed in her wheelchair, tartan blanket over her knees, a standing house mother each side, she was every bit the queen. There was something of Miss Havisham in her, elegant but chilling.

"Come and stand here, Philip." The house mother positioned me in front of the three women. Miss Neale looked me over while the house mothers obediently read out progress updates.

"Philip has been helping the gardener."

"Philip can say half of the alphabet."

Miss Neale's piercing eyes had correction in them. I stood rigid, speechless and terrified. Bewildered to know what to do I folded my arms behind my back, and hunched my shoulders. My head dropped as if shielding from a biting snowstorm, but my face flushed hot and I ached to be rescued from her stony glare.

There was huge relief on being freed from the power struggle. I was soft clay, and Miss Neale's reviews left deep humiliating impressions. I had to conform to some image in Miss Neale's head and a piece of me would not rest until I measured up. Though I never knew what to measure up *to*, I knew what pleased her - Obedience.

One afternoon I was playing on the front lawn within sight of one of the house mothers. Three older boys walked past.

"Wave, Philip," said the house mother. "That's your brother, Dave."

The nine-year-old lad narrowed his eyes as he looked in our direction. His school tie, dark blue blazer, and his black hair brushed neatly to the side, gave him a crisp appearance. The other two boys went on their way and Dave came over. The way he looked at me made me feel different, as if we were special to each other.

"I saw you at the film night," Dave said.

"Did you?" I said. "What games do you play?"

"We play football down in the meadow and at school. I live over there in the first cottage. Mr Mayhew looks after us," he said, pointing.

"You like Mr Mayhew, don't you David?" a house mother said.

"Yes," Dave replied.

"Can I come and play over there?" I said.

"You can come with us when you're bigger. Can you play football yet?" he said.

"I can score goals easily."

"See you then," Dave said.

After that I didn't see my brother again for weeks. The older children only came over for special gatherings like films or Christmas. They had their own play area round the back of the cottages so they didn't venture through the gateway into our grounds.

I was on a trike playing with Steve, near that gateway, when Dave rode up to the drive entrance on a two-wheel bike and screeched the brakes. "Watch out!" he shouted playfully.

I looked up and saw him smiling at me. His smiling face pulled a stream of light out of me, and my connection to him tugged. I didn't want to let it go. "Are you our brother?" I said.

"Yes," he said, leaning his bike over for balance.

"Can you come and play with us when you want?" Steve said.

"It's out of bounds," Dave said.

"How fast can you go?" I said.

"Watch!"

Steve and I tried to catch up with him on our three-wheelers. He turned round and came back again. Then, as quick as he came, he was gone.

Chapter 4

Big Cheeses

At five-years-old I moved into one of the three cottages with the older children. It made me feel grown up.

Although Miss Neale was the overall principal, Mr Mayhew ran the cottages, along with three house mothers. Mr Mayhew was a moderate man, firm but kind. He loved his work and was easy to be around. His black hair flopped forward when not set with Brylcreem and he was at his happiest with his white shirt sleeves rolled up and left to direct the cottages on his own.

On Thursday evenings, the banter among the older kids would build as they gathered in my cottage before the weekly trip to the pool. I longed to go with them. Bernard, a new arrival, had just started going.

"I'm going to swim five yards today," Bernard said, rolling up a towel.

"You can come diving with us then," Dave replied. The chatter was incessant as I hovered around them in the kitchen.

"I'm nearly six – can I come next time?" I said to Mr Mayhew.

"As soon as you have your birthday Phil. Right, let's get going!" Mr Mayhew said. With the kids bundled in the minibus, the engine revved and they were off. The cottage went stony silent.

Having never been to a swimming pool I imagined it to be a giant version of the aquarium we had in our cottage. I wondered how people managed to stay under water for so long, like the fish, without coming up for breath. I also worried how they would get out of the water and that they might not make it back.

A year or so later on a trip to Ludlow, I swam in a pool for the first time. It looked enormous, but I loved the way the noise of the children echoed, and the feeling of the blue water on my skin.

As well as ferrying the boys to the pool, Mr Mayhew organised cricket matches on the meadow below the cottages. It was thrilling to take part. "Run, Phil! Run!" he'd holler, in wild encouragement. Sprinting for the ball like an eager puppy, with kids cheering, I was euphoric. I wanted the game to go on forever.

The meadow was our adventure playground. When Mr Mayhew man-handled the beefy petrol mower across it I ran to his side. I marched alongside him, up and down as if in a military band, while I gazed at the shower of green cuttings raining into the front box.

"I'm emptying it this time," I'd say, fighting the others to be the one who took the grass box to the pile for him, yet hardly able to lift it.

Once, Mr Mayhew came across a grass snake. I stood in awe as he fearlessly lifted it onto a rake and lofted it into the air over to the dell. It became the talking point for the day.

Close to Mr Mayhew I felt bigger and brighter, as if he were the very centre of life.

In the meadow, like two alluring islands, were the pavilion and a derelict car. The black car, with its doors missing, was the kind of car you see in 1940s gangster movies. It still had its closed roof, shiny chrome fittings and Bakelite steering wheel. The leather seats spilled their grey matted padding. The orange semaphore indicators that flipped up out of the door jamb still worked, as did the manual choke knob below the dash. We spent hours around that car pretending to be grown-ups. It was great fun to perch high on the driver's seat with the smell of musty leather and cut grass, taking everyone on a journey.

The 'cricket pavilion', was a grand name for a large white wooden shed. Not only was it a trove of children's scooters, bikes and cricket gear but it housed the garden tools and lawnmower. I loved going in there with the smell of bike oil, petrol and wood. I soaked up the smell of maleness like the cricket bats soaked up linseed oil.

At weekends we were allowed a taste of wildness and go beyond the meadow into the dell. Running through the dell was a dry brook with trees on each bank that had vine creepers snaking up the trunks. Under supervision the older boys climbed the trees, unravelled the creepers and swung from bank to bank.

"Come on, Phil. Have a go!" shouted one boy, handing me a creeper.

Spurred on in the fervour, I grabbed it with both hands, bent my knees, pulled up my feet and launched myself across the brook and into the leafy earth of the opposite bank. I was spooked by the rush of wind as I sailed through the air. It was a while before I tried again, but the sight of the older boys was irresistible, flying like Tarzan of the Jungle, screaming with fun. The older boys seemed good at everything, games, tree climbing, knowing lots of interesting things . . . I devoted myself to emulating them.

Each of the three cottages had its own kitchen and dining room but often we'd all gather in ours. At the end of a collective evening meal, a plate full of cheese pieces was passed around. It became a contest of boyish bravado to see who could eat the biggest one! Everyone looked on as the plate hovered.

"Whooooh!" There was great admiration and cheering for the boy warriors who took the bigger lumps, and all would gaze at them as they devoured the thing. Desperate to be elevated into this bold arena, I grabbed a chunk with my little hand as the plate came near. A few sheepish nibbles and it became obvious I couldn't eat the dry lump. The attention backfired as groans of disapproval fell on me, and I was left nursing the cheese until everyone had left the table and I could sneak off.

In the corner of the meadow my six-year-old brother, Steve, and I made a den against the iron fence. An old sheet sloped away from the top rail of the fence and was pegged out to the ground to form a triangle den.

Simon, an eight-year-old, got curious. "Can I come inside?" he said, peering in.

"You know what you need now don't you?" he asked once he'd snuggled inside, "Your own food to survive on! You can eat all kinds of leaves you know, they're really tasty."

The idea of our own food seemed exciting.

"Look I'll show you," Simon said.

Eager to impress we followed his lead and collected leaves from the bushes. Back in the den I timidly pressed them to my lips, but then ate a good supply, ignoring the faint voice in me that said *no*.

"These are really good," Simon enthused.

I felt like he knew lots and we were just learning. Caught up in his words of adventure, and in the fantasy of creating our own world, we didn't challenge Simon on the fact that *he* wasn't eating.

"I feel sick," I said after a while. Clutching my belly, I hurried back to my cottage to look for a grown-up.

"What have you eaten?" Mr Mayhew barked.

"Just some leaves," I said, tears appearing on my red face.

"Well, how many?"

I cried as the yucky feeling in my gut intensified. More grown-ups bustled around Steve and me and fed us medicine to make us vomit. My stomach wrenched. I cried with my head slumped over the toilet bowl as I was violently sick.

"You silly stupid boys!" said one of the duty house mothers. There was no escaping our shame, which was a different but equally painful thing.

Chapter 5

In Search of Words

My mother found her way to Hallow again in the early months of 1962. She travelled from Yorkshire with just enough money for her fare and a cup of tea. Arriving early afternoon gave us less than two hours together.

On this visit I was more conscious of who she was. She brought an orange each for the three of us and we sat on a bench together in the playroom of one of the cottages. Her headscarf was knotted tight to her chin and she clutched the bag on her lap. I did my best to sit still and stay close to her, but before long I fidgeted.

"You stay there and I'll go on the scooter. Watch me through the window," I said.

"Go on then," she said, smiling for the first time. I made a quick circuit of the paving slabs and returned proudly.

"I'm going to school now," I said.

"Oh, very good, do you like it?" my mother said. I nodded.

I scanned her face with curiosity for this person who now belonged to me. She spoke differently.

I listened as she told Dave about a puppy she had brought with her. "I thought it'd be good company," she said. "I was on t' bus in Worcester and it escaped t' lead as we set off. It ran off t' bus before I could catch it," she said, acting bits of the scene with her hands. Somewhere in town she'd completely lost the dog. I worried for the puppy and pictured it wandering around lost and scared. I wondered where it would go when it got dark and who would feed and play with it.

"Where do *you* play?" our mother said, turning to Steve.

"Well, we play outside in the meadow or in here. Shall I show you some games?" Steve said.

We showed her our toys and books and she looked at them for a little while though she seemed more comfortable talking with Dave. The growing silences felt uneasy.

"Will you ask for a cup of tea for me, David?" my mother said. Off he went.

Feeling discomforted and wanting her to be happy I stayed close. I brought out a box of toy cars and played with them near her lap.

"I'll have to go now," she said. Keeping distance between us she waved goodbye. Dave followed her, leaving Steve and me on the floor.

The following summer our mother visited again. Dave, Steve, and I were allowed to walk with her along the lane to the village green where she caught the bus back to Worcester. She'd bought me a red cricket ball and I played with it continually in the sunny afternoon, bouncing it down the lane. I played with it while we waited at the bus stop. "Is it a real one?" I asked, caressing its shiny red surface and holding it against my cheek.

"Yes, course it is," she said, slightly annoyed.

The double-decker bus appeared at the far end of the green. She held out her arm to attract the driver. The bus pulled in. "I'll see you then," she said, reaching for the handle and stepping on. There was no pause for fuss. The bus pulled away and the three of us watched until it disappeared past the church, a strange silence hanging in the air with the diesel fumes.

Walking back along the lane unease came again, churning my insides. I looked down at my shoes, studying them for answers. Was she upset with me for playing with the ball? Had I done something else wrong? Had the three of us done something wrong? Was her house too small for us all?

We slowly passed the fragrant pine trees outside the Hallow

Park cottages, their shade cooling the air. I struggled in the clumsy silence that seemed to embarrass and separate the three of us.

I tried to take my cues from Dave, scanning his face for direction, for a sign of what was right or wrong. I'd follow his reactions. I wanted our mother to stay, but I never found a way to say so.

"When will we see her again?" I finally asked Dave.

"When she has time."

"What shall we do for her?" I asked.

"I don't know!" he fired back. Dave didn't always like me asking. Sometimes he'd look away as if asking the distant fields for help and I knew to stop talking. Dave was eleven then. He'd lived with my mother for seven years before we were taken into care and he had witnessed her turmoil. He despised his helplessness to change anything until he grew up, and my curiosity only aggravated his impotence.

My brother would have been emotionally volcanic, but he'd learned to keep it bottled up. He couldn't wait to leave us and go off to play with his friends. I wanted him to stay close to me and talk things through, but when he ran off I acted like I didn't care.

"Come and meet Aunty Wendy," a house mother told me one Saturday morning. Aunty Wendy was around twenty years old, tender, softly spoken and attentive towards me.

Barnardo's used Aunty and Uncle titles a lot; somehow, it seemed to fit. Aunty Wendy (Wendy Rigg) must have shown an interest in befriending a children's home child, and I was fortunate to be paired up with her. She made me feel like a prince.

She'd take me out in the car for the day with her boyfriend, Mark, and I felt very important knowing she'd come just for me. As Mr Mayhew and a couple of house mothers stood on the drive waving us off one day I bounced in the back seat just as Mark closed the passenger door. In a moment of daring I stuck my fingers in the door-housing. I screamed with all my breath. The adults rushed to the car as I bawled and held my crushed fingertips

"I didn't see his fingers!" Mark said. "I don't know what happened!" The poor fellow felt terrible for causing me such pain, and if he were courting Wendy and wanting to impress her, he was failing miserably.

Aunty Wendy did her best to make the day enjoyable, despite my bruised fingers burning with pain. She hugged me and gave me even more attention, which eased some of my secret guilt. Aunty Wendy knew how to make me feel like 'the one and only'. Coming down to my eye level she held my arms, bringing her face close to mine and locked her eyes onto me. "Are you okay, Phil?" When Aunty Wendy did that a river of belonging flowed inside me. I ached for more of those moments.

One Sunday we arrived at a large church hall decorated with balloons just before some celebratory party games were getting underway. I followed Aunty Wendy around the hall and she introduced me all round. To great cheering, a man sat down at the piano and played *Sidesaddle* and other Russ Conway tunes. His face beamed as his fingers danced over the keys belting out the bright melodies. Whether it was the famed Russ Conway himself, I don't know, but he was being treated like a celebrity and everyone called him Russ.

The music and games were every kid's dream but, for me, the real radiance came from Aunty Wendy. There may have been fewer than six outings with her but, on those days, joy and trust ran through me as naturally as chasing a ball. With Aunty Wendy caring for me I was like the saying of Sri Aurobindo, *an eternal child playing an eternal game in an eternal garden.*

The year played itself out and I enjoyed going to my first school in the village a short walk away. Despite my tranquil surroundings, fires of agitation burned inside me, they showed up in tantrums and bursts of temper. Mr Mayhew would let me yell my heart out and empty my lungs with screams. His only chastisement was the usual one for us boys, to sit alone in the kitchen for hours with a cup of water. An older boy once pointed to the Aga cooker and gave me his advice. "Put your plastic cup on the hotplate and say it was an accident. You won't have punishment in here again." I did as he said and felt lucky to get away with the trick. There was no harsh retribution from Mr Mayhew, just a mild telling off. I still got my small birthday cake and celebration when I turned six in the summer of 1962.

On a fresh November morning I was playing hopscotch on the slabs at the back of the cottage when one of the house mothers shouted out of the back door. "Philip, come here. You're to get ready for the minibus." She put some clothes in a small bag, handed them to me, and told me to go to the front door. "The others are waiting," she said.

I skipped to the front door. My two brothers and three other boys, all looking tense, stood on the drive by the minibus with bags at their feet. "In you get," Mr Mayhew ordered sharply. Mr Mayhew slammed shut the double rear doors, twisting the handle to lock them together. I looked at him through the glass; his mild manner was gone, his jaw was tight and his eyes scowled. He bundled into the driver's seat without a glance at any of us.

The engine raced into life and the minibus slid down the lane and away from Hallow. I looked at Dave but his eyes would not meet mine. Something was wrong. No one was speaking. The boys' faces were clean but there was no life there. Mr Mayhew said nothing, but I could hear his occasional angry outbreaths of air. The icy silence seemed to have its own order and I was to follow it. Time slowed, and slowed, as if it wanted to imprison me.

I fidgeted in the glum atmosphere, gazing away from the boys and out through the window. The November morning sun brightened large swathes of the passing landscape. I wanted to be out there in the freedom of those crisp, open fields. Probably we'll get a chance to play out later, I reasoned. The forty minute journey seemed much longer. I didn't know what it was about, but the tension scared me.

Turning left off the main road the minibus passed through a couple of small stone pillars and entered a long drive with trees lining both sides. We rounded the circular drive in front of a large, white house and Mr Mayhew killed the engine. He slid back the driver's door, jumped out and slammed it shut. Marching round the back he swung open the doors and motioned for us to come out. In my short trousers I felt the cold air rush around my bare legs.

A middle-aged woman with black hair appeared from the front door of the house. "We can't take them here. We don't have room!" she protested, in a shrill voice. Mr Mayhew ignored her.

"I'm sorry, you'll have to take them back," the woman continued, jockeying for authority.

Mr Mayhew lifted out the few bags in angry deliberation. With the last bag on the drive, he gripped the rear doors and slammed them shut. The woman was still protesting but Mr Mayhew stared straight ahead, sat behind the wheel, started up the van, and drove off.

"Stay there!" the irate woman instructed us as she disappeared into the house.

The hum of the minibus faded as it sped away. In the silence we stood as spiritless as six unclaimed parcels in a luggage office. I looked at Dave, the oldest of the group; his strained look told me he was trying to figure out what was going on. He turned his head back down the drive where Mr Mayhew had gone. The other boys looked down in a pained stare avoiding each other.

Wind buffeted the surrounding treetops; the cool air carried the scent of decaying leaves. I looked up at the three-storey house. The vast expanse of white wall looked like a chalk cliff. Who's in charge of us now? We must all have done something very wrong, I thought.

"Right," the dark-haired woman said, reappearing like a snappy sergeant and pulling her cardigan over her shoulders. "Philip Barber and Steven Barber?" she asked, reading from a piece of paper. Steve and I hesitantly raised our hands. "Top hostel with Miss Gillian," she said, pointing to the front door. "David Barber? Bottom hostel," she ordered, pushing Dave by the head. "House group you three," she said to the other boys, motioning them inside.

This was another Barnardo's home in nearby Kidderminster; a place called Spennells. The dark-haired irate woman was Mrs Vaughan (The Matron).

Forty years passed before I discovered that the move to Spennells was instigated by Miss Neale, the principal at Hallow

Park. She was firmly against older boys growing up in the same home as girls. At a certain age she'd move them on. I imagine she feared the scandal of a teenage pregnancy. Dave had reached the age of eleven, so Steve and I were parcelled up and sent with him.

Within weeks of our move, Dave ran away and headed back to Hallow, where for the past three years he'd felt wanted and protected by Mr Mayhew.

Dave recounted to me how he slept rough on the back seat of the old black car in the meadow. Mr Mayhew found him of course, just as Dave would have expected. "I don't want to take you back there, David, but it's out of my hands." Mr Mayhew explained. "I've heard awful reports about the Vaughans from many other boys, I don't agree with the way they run things."

After delivering Dave back to Spennells, we never saw or heard of Mr Mayhew again.

Chapter 6

Spennells

Spennells was home to over thirty boys, from toddlers to seventeen-year-olds. With Mr and Mrs Vaughan in charge the home was split into three groups, each with its own house mother. Miss Ans for 'house group' in the main house, Miss Barbara for 'bottom hostel' and Miss Gillian being in charge of 'top hostel'. Housemaster, Mr Thomas, and Mr Seymour, the cook, made up the permanent staff.

The hostel was a long, single-storey building that had once housed military people. With its salmon red exterior and shallow-pitched roof it still resembled an army barrack. The hostel had a long central corridor, dormitories each side, and washrooms at the lower end. The upper end was the *rec,* a large recreation room with a snooker table, two table-tennis tables, a piano, and a large tea chest full of 'dressing up' clothes.

Connecting the hostel to the main house was a sloping walkway clad in iron sheet and open on one side. It clattered like a thunderstorm when it rained.

Steve and I followed our new house mother up the walkway and into the rec. Miss Gillian was a fresh-faced thirty-year-old with a soft voice. Her long, pleated skirt gave her a traditional but friendly look. "How old are you?" she asked.

"Seven," Steve said.

"I'm six."

The door of the rec slammed behind us and the three of us gathered by the tall, built-in cupboards at the far end. "We'll sort out bedding first," Miss Gillian said, pulling open the cupboard doors. Carrying sheets, a pillow case and a blanket we followed her like ducklings down the corridor to our dormitory.

"This bed is yours, Philip, and that one yours, Steven." Leading us back into the rec she opened another cupboard stuffed with clothes and shoes. "These are *best* clothes, and these are *playing out* ones," she said, matching our sizes from the piles on each shelf. We tried on the horizontal stripe tee-shirts, belt, short trousers, long, grey socks, white shirt and blazer, and regulation, dark blue polyester coat called a *gabardine.*

"Try these *bumpers* on, they're for playing outside," Miss Gillian said, handling the black and white baseball boots tied in pairs with elastic bands. We squatted on the cold floor in a pile of *bumpers* pulling them on for size. We did the same with plimsolls for indoor use. Some items were new but most were clean second-hand. "Leather shoes are for school and for Sundays. We'll take them down to the shoe locker in a minute," she said, putting the remaining items away.

Each child was given a number. Numbers were written on the shoe lockers by the back door and in all clothing. I was number six. Clothes transited the 'sewing room' to have our numbers stitched in. Being number six I often got my clothes mixed up with Ronnie's number nine.

"Are these socks yours or mine?" I'd ask Ronnie, smiling.

At the back of the house on that first day Steve and I made immediate use of the three-wheeler bike, Steve peddling with glee and me riding the platform behind the saddle. An older boy shouted, "You two! You're wanted inside!".

Earlier, Basil, the boxer dog tied up by the back door, had been sleeping. As we ran over, he jumped to his feet and barked at us fiercely. Pulling up quickly, we backed away. "Let's go round the front," Steve said. I ran after him to the front drive where we'd arrived that morning.

"Round to the back door, you boys!" A man in a tie said,

snapping out his command and pointing. We froze. "Boys use the back entrance, understand? Now, off you go!"

It was our first encounter with Mr Vaughan, our first touch of his bleakness. We turned, retraced our steps, and somehow made it past Basil.

The house was positioned among a variety of tall swaying trees, and surrounded by open playing fields. Upper fields were designated out of bounds, and stretched as far as the quiet country lane that separated us from Cadwalader's farm. The tree-lined driveway ran through the middle of the two lower fields. The lower field on one side of the drive included a small football pitch and a hard tennis court. The other side was a field bounded by a stream and woodland. This field had swings, a slide, and a shed for Pickles, the horse.

Below the large back yard were chicken runs, rabbit hutches and several aviaries alive with birds. Behind the main house the caretaker, Mr Kirby, lived in a cottage with his family.

Steve caught sight of the huge pile that was the bonfire at the far edge of the football pitch. "It's bonfire night tomorrow," said Steve. "They're going to light that big fire, and we're allowed to go!"

The next day excitement filled the house, especially early evening, seeing the two life-size Guy Fawkes the boys had made. The heads were fashioned from cloth bags, the bodies from a man's shirt and the legs were trousers, all stuffed with leaves. In the rec a house mother photographed the boys standing alongside the Guys, which were humorously propped on chairs.

After dark that night I followed the crowd over the cold wet grass of the fields, staying as close to Steve as I could. I slid my hands into my gabardine pockets for comfort. Being careful not to stumble in the darkness, we tried our best to keep up with the few torch beams held by the older boys.

A rousing cheer went up as the fire was lit. Flames slowly licked through the huge pile of woven branches, then it crackled and hissed fully into life, the orange glow lighting the unfamiliar faces around us. Mr Vaughan and Mr Kirby lit the fireworks. The sparkle in the night sky had begun. Startled by the loud whoosh of the rockets hurtling into the sky I huddled closer to Steve. The boys marvelled at the spectacle of bangs and fiery patterns, with wood smoke and the smell of spent fireworks wafting through the air.

Every year we Spennells boys built the bonfire. Visitors from Barnardo's or from local charities would receive invites to the well-organised event. The boys devoured home-made toffee apples and trays of delicious hard treacle toffee.

In future Novembers, I'd test my strength, dragging the heaviest branches from the woodlands and laying them against the square wood frame that Mr Kirby, the caretaker, had prepared. The stout frame made a hollow space where the fire could be lit. After each excursion, I rested inside that space. Encased by the compacted branches inhaling the smell of wood bark and dead leaves was like being in a bird's nest. Each time, I dared myself to stay longer in the eerie silence.

That first winter was harsh. Blizzards left Spennells' grounds snow-covered for months and the freezing temperatures broke records. We had great fun building a snowman as tall as an adult, and a second one sitting on a bench reading a newspaper.

The cold didn't penetrate me, but the sound made an impression. With land and buildings cloaked in deep snow the profound stillness wrapped itself around me in a comforting coat. Let loose to play in wellingtons and balaclava I felt I was being gifted something special: that crisp white landscape a message from a bigger playground than my small life. Hope was embedded there and I felt it belonged to me, especially when the sun glistened on the fields.

I had the same wondrous feelings in my school assembly when we sang the hymn *In the Bleak Mid-Winter*. Despite the title, the melody was sweet and I found a refuge in Christina Rossetti's words.

> *In the bleak mid-winter, frosty wind made moan,*
> *Earth stood hard as iron, water like a stone;*
> *Snow had fallen, snow on snow, snow on snow,*
> *In the bleak mid-winter, long ago.*

What can I give Him, poor as I am?
If I were a shepherd, I would bring a lamb;
If I were a Wise Man, I would do my part;
Yet what I can I give Him ... give my heart.

Christmas Eve the air filled with snowflakes and that night the staff organised a snow fight right outside the front door. With the house lights lighting up the drive staff and boys joined one of the two battle lines facing each other.

'Go!' Mr Thomas, the housemaster, shouted. Snowballs filled the gap as each side pelted the other. It was a great sight until, *bang!* I was hit square in the face. The snowball knocked me backwards, stealing my breath. I cried with shock. Everyone carried on throwing! When no rescuer came, it suddenly wasn't fun anymore; I wanted to go inside, but was too scared to move without permission. Holding in my tears I stayed out of range behind the older boys, and pretended to be okay.

Mr Vaughan was a slim man with wavy grey hair that stood up from his head. He mostly wore a jacket and tie, but his right arm always supported a cigarette. Charles Vaughan was a melancholy man, his mood permeating the walls of the house like his tobacco smoke. We boys addressed him solely as "Sir." He always called boys by their surname. With disdain in his voice he referred to me as, "Tiddly Barber."

Sir appeared after breakfast each and every school day. It was toothbrush and toilet time in the washroom for thirty boys before the lineup at the back door. John Gallagher, a fifteen-year-old, stood waiting for one of the circular tins of Gibbs hard toothpaste we all shared. "Hurry up with that toothpaste, I'm late," he said.

Another older boy nudged me as I brushed my teeth. "Get a move on little 'un; you'll be in for it!"

We lined up in school uniforms and gabardines, older boys at the front, little ones farthest back. Mr Vaughan, left hand buried in his trouser pocket and cigarette wedged between the fingers of his right, performed his ritual interrogation. "What homework have you got?" he said to each boy in turn. "Stay in till seven o'clock. Get it done!"

John Gallagher farted in the washroom. It was a pearler! The sound bouncing off each of the bare washroom walls. Hands clutched mouths as muffled sniggers whipped through the lineup. Then, John emerged from the washroom, smiling like a sun god.

Vaughan's tightened eyes locked onto him. You'd think John had just cursed the Queen.

"Gallagher! See me tonight for punishment!" Vaughan's expression sucked up humour like a vacuum cleaner. In deathly silence, Sir sent the boys off two at a time as usual to avoid a group of us walking up the main road. "You and you, off you go."

With Vaughan's glum morning routine, I was always glad to step out that back door and be liberated from his cheerless look. The walk down the long tree-lined driveway was a lush green avenue of welcome fresh air, kindly amplifying my liberation. Often, I'd stop to throw sticks into the field, or collect conkers from the mature horse chestnut tree that sheltered the drive like a caring grandmother.

Coming in from school I hurried to get changed to play outside in the remnants of daylight. I put my school shoes into an empty space in the open fronted shoe locker. "Shoes in the right number locker!" shouted an older boy, "I'm not getting into trouble for you young 'un!" It was an older boy's job, in turn, to clean all the shoes across the yard in the *cobbler's store* that reeked of shoe polish. They faced the wrath of Sir if all shoes weren't clean and put back in the right spaces.

On Saturday mornings, all the boys formed a queue for pocket money outside Vaughan's little office. The scent of wood polish was always strong in that end of the house. One by one we entered. In Vaughan's office, the polish smell was overtaken by tobacco smoke. Vaughan sat in a wooden wheel-back chair with his arm hovering over a ledger. Piles of cigarette coupons sat on the desk, together with a large ashtray and copies of National Geographic. To brave entry into his office I tightened my shoulders, rolled up my liveliness, and put on my blankest face. Taking the pen from his nicotine-stained fingers, I'd write my name quickly, and pick up the sixpence. Out of the door I'd quietly travel as far away from him as possible before my body could unfurl itself again.

Matron, Mrs Vaughan, carried the same energy as her nicotine-charged husband. Active and slim, with thick black hair and pencil-thin eyebrows, she often wore thin, V-neck sweaters. Matron was a first class organiser, but that skill was bridled to an agitated state that oozed tension. All her actions had a nervous haste as though she needed to stay ahead of something that would devour her if she stilled. In her piercing voice, Matron pecked out directives to remind the world not to ignore her. "I'm a trained nurse," she'd say, taking charge on Friday bath nights and wielding the large bristle brush like she was trying to scrub three layers of skin off my back.

Saturday mornings were my favourite. Glowing with cleanliness from the Friday night scrub we frequently went to the ABC cinema club, known as the ABC minors. We walked into Kidderminster in small groups under the care of an older boy. The film shows began with black and white Pathe Newsreels presenting news from around the world. The excited presenter made it all seem very dramatic especially with the matching trumpet soundtrack.

Then the real treat: the short films of adventure heroes like the Lone Ranger, or the masked swordsman, Zorro. The serial films always ended the action on a knife-edge, compelling us to talk about it all week, and faithfully return the following Saturday.

Returning from the ABC one Saturday, I happened to see Martin, a friend from my school. He'd received a new camera for his birthday and for weeks he'd promised me his old one. I'd been excited about the camera and remembered it as he was waving goodbye at the road near to his home. "Martin, how far do you live? I could come for the camera now, if we're quick about it," I shouted.

"I'll catch you up," I said to the other boys, and ran to Martin as fast as I could, mindful of big trouble if I should be late back.

"Wait here on the corner." Martin said. "I'll go and get it."

"Okay," I said, thinking it strange that I just couldn't go with him to his house. But I waited. Please hurry Martin, I said to myself.

I hung on impatiently, rooted by the yearning to have my own camera. Where has he got to? Come on, come on! I looked up and down the road. I ran to where Martin had disappeared. I'd better wait where he told me; I ran back to the spot and sprang up and down on my toes. Come on. Come on!

My nerves took over. I'd only just got off punishment the day before. I sprinted at top speed all the way back to Spennells and, turning into the drive, hoped I'd see the other boys. But the grounds were deserted. They would all be in the dining room. *Oh no! More trouble.* At top pace I put my shoes in my locker and coat on my peg. To enter the dining room I slowed light-footed and innocent. Everyone was eating and Mr Vaughan sat in his usual place to the right of the door. My temperature dropped ten degrees as I passed him. I made two strides to my table.

"Tiddly Barber!"

"Yes, Sir," I turned round.

"Where have you been?"

"Coming back, Sir," I said, dropping my eyes.

Mr Vaughan's dour look felt uncomfortable at any time. Within a sniff of trouble, like now, it was too dreadful to even look in his direction.

"Stand in the passageway."

"He can do without privileges!" Matron shouted from the back of the dining room.

Standing detention in the passageway was a punishment I knew well. I loathed the endless hours and hours, staring at the beige walls trying to pass the weary time. The concrete floor drained the life out of my legs. Within earshot of the other boys, the sound of their play injected another layer of misery. The only mild relief came if another boy had the equal misfortune to be 'on punishment' at the same time.

Mr Vaughan emerged from the dining room. "How many times have you been told Tiddly Barber?" He grabbed the hair by my ear and pulled till I let out a squeal. Marching me up the passageway to his office, he kept the fistful of hair tight so I had to skip alongside him. Outside his office he let go and placed my back to the wall. Bending forward, his face in mine he let loose his wrath, "Tiddly Barber, when will you learn?" Mr Vaughan rhymed off the litany of mealtime rules.

"Yes, Sir," I replied after each directive.

"Yes Sir," he repeated each time I said it. "Everyone but *you* made it back on time. Privileges stopped for two weeks, and you can polish floors this afternoon." Grabbing my hair again, Mr Vaughan marched me down the passageway to the cupboard housing the cleaning tools.

Privileges stopped meant missing TV, film nights, outings, and Saturday morning cinema. The Vaughan's knew how to destroy a boy's spirit. They had no tolerance for dissent, taking it as a personal affront and nurturing an arsenal of measures to meet it.

Half glad to be on a task rather than standing detention, I pulled out the cloths and began polishing the parquet wood floor that was one end of the passageway. The thankless hours of polishing that floor on hands and knees is an enduring image of Spennells, up and down, back and forth till my arms and legs ached. Hemmed in by the beige walls that smelled of punishment, my mind leached colour. Boredom shrivelled me like the small blocks of dead wood under my knees. I'd hear faint chatter from the sewing room that led off that passageway. The house mothers congregated in that room to sew and drink tea. I always thought of it as their private den. Boys walked past me on my hands and knees without a word, but sometimes I'd hear a staff member 'tut', as if to say, 'on punishment *again*'.

Neither of the Vaughans spoke to me till release time. They did, however, if they were going out in the car, have a singular repetitive phrase for the staff. Putting their head round the sewing room door they'd say to Miss Ans, the house mother, "Just popping out Ans. Carry on regardless." That phrase would flow out in their upper-class Home Counties voice, as if accentuating their authority.

In our group on the way to church the next day, having recovered a little of my spirit from the punishment, my mates Jason and Ronnie grabbed me. "Did they say it?"

"Yes!"

"Carry on regardless," they repeated in hysterics, mimicking the Vaughan's accent. I wanted to join in, but the Vaughan's oppressive faces had made a surly imprint. I looked around to make sure not a soul had heard us.

Chapter 7

Whistles and Carbolic Soap

Mr Thomas, Spennells' housemaster, with his black hair and trimmed moustache, had the look of a young Clark Gable. He was in charge of the boys while we played outside. He supervised recreation time, mended bikes, collected eggs from the chicken run, repaired shoes, and organised games in the rec. I loved to hear the boys asking Mr Thomas about his life in the army. "I drove an ambulance for the medical corps, I believe in saving lives not wasting them," he would say.

"Did you drive it fast?" I piped in as I pictured him speeding heroically to save people, with bells clanging and lights flashing. He smiled back at me.

"What did you do after that?" someone asked him.

"I worked in the bank, and then I decided to come and look after you rascals."

Although Mr Thomas adhered to Spennells rules, he shouldered empathy for the plight of the boys. If I weren't playing football I'd run over to him. "Hello, Mr Thomas, what are you doing?"

"Hello, young Phil," he'd reply. After months of me asking, what are you doing? he'd answer, "Hello, young pest." I liked it when he called me pest. My six-year-old self warmed in the endearment.

I loved to watch Mr Thomas fixing the bikes. He was a strong man, at ease in the bike shed among the spanners and levers, removing tyres to fix punctures or taking parts off the old bikes to fix the newer ones.

"What's that for?" I'd ask, crouching near him. Mr Thomas smiled at yet another question while I picked up the tools, just to feel them in my hands.

Mr Thomas took note of my all-too-regular *on punishments*. If he saw me alone on standing detention and the passageway was quiet, he'd breathe out a sigh with hands on his hips, and say, "Oh, Phil, what have you done this time?"

Out on the lower field football pitch I neatly trapped the ball stopping the game and pricked my ears. "Was that two whistles or three?"

"Not sure," said Ronnie. Shall we go and check?"

Mr Thomas had the job of sounding the whistle to call the boys in from the grounds, though I never saw him actually blow it. One whistle was meal time; two whistles meant young boys come in; three whistles older boys, and four whistles everyone in. Too many times I found myself on punishment for not coming in on time. Whistles were not always easy to count, especially over by the stream where I'd often spend time on my own.

I loved to be near the water. A rope swing with a tyre attached hung over the stream and I'd launch myself onto it and across the water. Or I'd throw in a stick and run downstream to watch it float around rocks and branches as if it were a steamer on the Mississippi.

Another world tugged at me, inviting me to defend the small iron bridge from invaders, or become a pirate on the loose. I could build a raft to escape downriver. Then I'd remember about the whistles, and tension would cling to my clothes.

I tried to keep my ears tuned, to stay the right side of the rules. Under constant threat of punishment a hyper-vigilance grew in me. I writhed under the continual notion of being in trouble.

The fantasy of building a raft and riding it far from Spennells – far from punishment – never subsided. And it wasn't my fantasy alone. Steve mentioned it, so did Ronnie . . . come to think of it, who didn't? Our more immediate escape though was playing games.

Returning to the football pitch with Ronnie; in the safety of other boys my defiance would surface, urging me to push back. "Next goal is the winner," I answered. "We'll go in and check the whistles after that."

Age eleven and up were older boys, the rest, little boys. Older boys had a separate sitting room, had their own organised time in the rec, and had separate outings. The older boys' sitting room had bookcases with rows full of National Geographic magazines. On the few occasions we younger ones went in there I loved to thumb through them. The colourful pictures of exotic places drew me in, especially the African tribes people with their colourful costumes and bare-breasted women.

Dave was in with the older boys, which meant we only saw each other in passing. I'd see him in the TV lounge but he'd be bantering with the older boys on the upright chairs at the back. We little boys sat on the floor in front. Walking into the TV room, I'd look to see if Mr Vaughan was sitting in the armchair by the fire. When he was there I'd pale, and sit on the floor wishing I was the invisible man.

It was a real treat to watch the westerns like Rawhide, or comedies like Steptoe and Son. Even though I didn't speak with Dave in the TV room, if I heard him laughing I glowed inside. I couldn't resist turning to see his face. Then I'd quickly look toward Mr Vaughan. Under his spell and acutely aware of him behind me, I was never totally immersed in the drama on the screen.

I had that fresh playtime feel one Saturday morning in late 1963. Coming out of the rec I happened on Miss Gillian sitting on the steps at the top of the walkway talking with house mother Miss Ans and an older boy, John Bromley. They huddled around a small transistor radio. The morning sun was glinting bright but Miss Gillian looked shocked. "The American President has been assassinated!"

"What does assassinate mean?" I said quietly, though I could tell it wasn't good. Miss Gillian explained.

In the rising sun, I was eager to get to the football field, but I had a strong feeling I was supposed to do something with that news. I would have normally galloped out to the field but I slowed and walked. The autumn air was crispy cold and laden with the scent of decaying wood. Everything was quieter than usual. The picture of Miss Gillian's stricken face hovered. What had happened? I passed the tall trees on the drive, they were almost empty of leaves. Time slowed. Then the sound of boys playing broke through from the field and I ran over to join the game.

Morning routines at Spennells were well drilled. In top hostel dormitory we made up our beds, becoming experts at hospital corners and neatly folding back the top sheet, finishing with a smoothing sweep of the palm. Then it was floor sweeping - all before breakfast.

Weekend mornings we spent hours polishing the hallway and rec floors. With folded cloths under our knees and hands we shuffled across the floors like battery powered toy horses.

On the large floors we used the bumper. This was a broom handle with a heavy iron ball at the end that rested in a hole in a wooden plate. The cloth underneath the weighted plate buffed the floor – at least it was supposed to. I could hardly get it moving! With the long handle over my shoulder I tried to tug the ball and plate along behind me like an ox. Over arm, under arm; the awkward contraption only moved in painstaking inches. Determined not to be beaten and seeing older boys master the thing, I struggled till I got the hang of it. Though I could never see much of a difference in the floor's sheen, it was one of those jobs we did till Miss Gillian said it was time to stop.

In the main house dining room five boys and one adult sat at each of the separate tables. On a central plate were eighteen triangular half slices of buttered white bread, three per person, no more and no less. At tea time, another plate sported precisely six cakes, or, six apples.

Mr Seymour, the cook, was a slim bald-headed man in his thirties. He was kept busy on the coal-fired Aga. Food was standard; vegetables, meat and bread. Most was alright but mealtimes could be a miserable experience under the dreaded rule that all food had to be eaten. What was left over from a boy's meal was put again on his plate for the next meal.

My stomach grimaced at the site of bread and butter pudding, macaroni cheese, and any kind of fish paste. Blancmange was a regular desert that tortured me. It was served with a thick skin that felt like chewing a bicycle inner tube.

Hours after certain meals, I'd sit alone picking the food into tiny bits in an attempt to get it into my throat so it didn't appear the next day.

"You silly boy. Stop making such a fuss," a house mother or Matron protested. Lumps of meat gristle were my dining-room nightmare. I couldn't get the gruesome thing anywhere near my mouth. Sitting on my own one time Tony, an older boy, walked past the dining room. "Sssshhh," he said, finger on his lips. He checked the corridor for staff, and then bounded over to me. "Give me that," he said, snatching the hideous lump from my plate. He shoved the gristle into his trouser pocket and made for the door that led to the back yard. As he strolled back along the passageway Tony threw me a wink.

I was so pleased to be rid of it, but worried how to explain my new-found appetite to Matron. I dropped my head on the table, held my stomach, and squirmed as if I'd swallowed the horrible morsel. I got away with it – that time.

We didn't get away with much at Spennells, but most of us harboured an inner compulsion to rebel. Talking after lights out was a regular misdemeanour. It landed us on more standing detention outside the hostel dormitory. There was an absurdity in trading a few minutes of extra play for hours and hours of monotonous standing on aching legs. But it was a common sight down the dimly lit corridor to see a line of jaded boys standing in dressing gowns and slippers. I was often in that line slouching with the rest of them. Keeping one eye on the thin wedge of light from either Miss Gillian or Miss Barbara's bedroom door, we'd pass the time whispering and trying to make each other laugh. We'd risk a quick squat to ease our stiff legs. We soon stood bolt upright if the rec door opened and Mr Vaughan wandered into top hostel. "Why are you on punishment?" he'd say dryly.

It's comical to recall how we deflected attention from our

crime. "Because of Miss Gillian Sir!"

Miss Gillian was the quieter of the two hostel house mothers. Miss Barbara was a stout lady, protective of her group, but fearsome when crossed. "I'll box your ears, my lad!" she'd say, often adding with equal venom, "If it's not one Barber in trouble, it's the other!"

Standing detention when suffered alone felt tortuous. My eyes craved sleep and my body yearned to collapse onto my mattress. I would make elaborate knots with my dressing gown cord, or I'd count out loud in a whispered voice. And then, finally, the sacred words. "Go and get into bed - Quietly!"

Back with the others, I'd hang up my dressing gown and melt into the sheets. I'd soon drop off on my heavenly bed, leaving behind the question, why do the grown-ups hate us so much?

Three times a week our group had a turn in the showers at the lower end of the hostel. Other evenings, it was a strip wash, an all-over clean with a wet flannel in front of the sink. I was seven-years-old the evening a play fight went a bit far. Outside the washroom, in my pyjama bottoms, Robert threw a towel at me and ran off. Miss Gillian appeared. "Pick up that towel, now!"

"I didn't throw it! Robert did."

"Do as you're told!"

Warrior energy soared through me. "That's not fair, Robert threw it."

Despite Miss Gillian's repeated demands, I refused to pick up the towel. Why should I back down? Zorro never did, nor did the Lone Ranger!

Mr Thomas passed us on the way to his room. He paused, but recognising Miss Gillian's jurisdiction, he merely said, "Phil, why don't you just pick up the towel?"

Wanting to please him, I softened a little, but nowhere near enough to respond. I stood solid and stared at the floor. Mr Thomas continued to his room up the corridor and I continued staring, keeping my protest alive. The reformatory scent of carbolic soap and the sound of running showers seemed to spur me.

It was a stalemate. "Pick up that towel or it's Mr Vaughan!"

Miss Gillian had made 'the Vaughan threat' in the past. Sometimes it worked and I backed down. Now the mention of his name raised the stakes and my stomach fluttered wildly. I wanted to give in, but I was corralled by my own bravado.

All the unfairness of my life declared itself in that moment – in that bloody towel.

How desperately I wanted Miss Gillian to say, Phil, you're right. It's not fair asking you to pick the towel up. Now off you go.

"Right, I've had enough!" Miss Gillian shouted. She summoned another boy. "Ronnie, get Mr Vaughan!"

Ronnie set off. *Oh no! I was in for it now.* I wished I could pull him back! - But he disappeared out of sight, and I knew it had all gone too far.

It wasn't long since my last brush with Mr Vaughan and his endless rules. He would surely be settling into a beloved sports programme on television. I knew his fury would boil up as he walked up from the main house. Previously Mr Vaughan had slapped me round the head or grabbed my ear hard, just as I'd seen him regularly do to other boys. Now I stood trembling, waiting for worse.

Striding through the door Vaughan's enraged face said it all. When he'd hit me before he'd knocked my hands down when I raised them to cover my head. To not antagonize him I kept my arms by my side. Vaughan lunged at me hitting the side of the head. *Whack!* Then the other side. *Whack!* With each blow, I jerked my head below my shoulders, my hands thrust over me for protection.

"You again!" *Whack!* Each time he waited for my arms to drop and another set of slaps beat down on my head.

He leaned in. "Why can't you behave Tiddly Barber?" *Whack!* I stiffened my body to each blow as he struck me one way then the other.

"It's always you!" *Whack!* I reeled backwards. My small arms were a feeble defence. Each stinging blow came with stinging words. "Do as you are damn well told!"

Petrified I backed into a corner, my knees pressed together and my back against the wall. My head was stinging and my heart raced. "When will you learn to behave?" *Whack!*

I shrank deeper. I felt I was being struck by a giant. *Whack!* "Get to your dormitory," he spat in disgust, "Out of my sight!"

Sobbing and shamed I scurried along the passageway, a substandard, flawed, irritating and defective child, desperate to hide.

In my dormitory bed I pulled the blanket over my head. Under the covers, I cried the waves of hurt, hot tears sweeping through me. With knees curled to my chest, I pressed the sheet into my face for the small comfort. *Why was this happening?* Nothing felt safe. It felt like they wanted me dead. I hated them all, every single last one of them!

Chapter 8

School Prayers

I tensed in fear whenever the children wandered through the wardrobe and into the land of Narnia. Reading The Lion, The Witch, and The Wardrobe out loud, our school teacher, Miss Hunt, altered her voice to bring the characters alive. Every time Aslan, the lion, came into the story I glowed. "All shall be done," Aslan pronounced. Aslan was the one who held all hope for the unfortunate land of Narnia that was locked in perpetual winter without a Christmas.

But nothing prepared me for the scene where Aslan volunteered himself to be tied to the stone table for sacrifice. I sweated terror as I felt the evil White Witch was tying me up. "Shame him," the Witch said, "Shame him," and they cut off his fur. I turned cold as I felt the Witch plunge that knife into my chest.

My heart fell into a dark pit for what seemed an eternity before the story revealed "the deeper magic from before the dawn of time" that brought that wondrous animal back to life. Relief was sweet to be told Aslan's heart was beating again, and so were the children's.

Lower Comberton Junior School was mostly an enjoyable place, especially playing for our school football team where I shone along with a couple of other keen players. Our deputy head was a tall sturdy man who carried the flag for sports, but otherwise, I saw all too little of him.

The worst moments occurred in assembly. I could never

understand why they continually forced us to pray. I knew there was a heaven, and during our dusty prayers my mind would wander there. It was just outside the door in the playground playing games with my friends. All the references to Lord and God and Jesus made me feel cold. It seemed they were names made up by people who didn't really care for the people standing next to them.

I'd squint open my eyes during prayers and look at my school mates. I longed to know everything about them, I longed to hold them close and have fun with them.

Mrs Hudson, the headmistress, had a golden Labrador called Ben that followed her everywhere – like the Queen with her corgis. Mrs Hudson was not a sporty type, but interested in literary things. I recall sitting on the floor listening to the musical composition *Peter and the Wolf*. Mrs Hudson narrated the story. "Now children, each character in this story is represented by a different instrument." The first time was enjoyable but *Peter and the Wolf* seemed to get brought out regularly, especially if a lesson was cancelled. Mrs Hudson had to fill the time and she was obviously more taken with the story than we were.

On those occasions, I did pray. *Please, please, please, tell our headmistress to stop bludgeoning us to death with this damn story and let us loose outside with a football!*

I also wondered what possessed Mrs Hudson to force dreary hymns upon us in assembly. They droned on like funeral dirges. Even the teachers looked as bored as concrete posts. There were exceptions of course. *In the Bleak Mid-Winter*, which I've mentioned, and another that stood out for its melody and imagery of renewal.

> *Morning has broken, like the first morning.*
> *Blackbird has spoken, like the first bird ...*
>
> *Mine is the sunlight, mine is the morning ...*

I wanted to sing *Morning has Broken* among my friends every single day. It brought a glimpse of the divine, especially if I were standing next to Heather Groves. Heather was a young dark-haired beauty, much admired among us boys. Wandering to the far side of the field at lunch times she would let me kiss her if she were in a happy mood. Kissing Heather was a magical thing, like escaping into another world. The magic ended abruptly one day when she announced, "My mother says I can't kiss anymore, because it causes cold sores on my mouth."

I could swear a comet landed on the town of Kidderminster, plunging the world into darkness.

Anthony became a good friend at school; he was a talker and easy to be with. He was going my way one day, so he joined me for the twenty minute walk back to Spennells. Usually I'd wave goodbye to my school friends on the housing estate outside the school. Then I'd feel a sickness walking home to Spennells, especially if I were 'on punishment' that night.

But today I was having fun walking with my new friend, and I allowed a new brightness in my step. Anthony chatted on and on, and asked, out of the blue, "Can you come to my birthday party next week?" A glow of excitement rushed into me. I'd never been asked that before.

"Come down the drive with me now. I'll ask while you're here!" I told him to wait outside the house while I got the okay from Miss Gillian. I got a yes after she cleared it with Matron.

Oh man! I ran back to Anthony bouncing like a seal. My very own friend asking me to go to his house! We stood a little way down the drive joking and bantering about things we would do. "I'll ask my mum if you can sleep overnight," Anthony said. Wow, now I'm plugged into a 500-volt generator.

"I'll see you tomorrow then!" he said, turning to go.

Just then, Matron burst out of the back door and screamed at the top of her voice. "Tell him you're not coming! If that's the way you treat us! Fooling around there, knowing its tea time! You can forget his party!"

I was stunned. Anthony looked at me and I caught the fear on his face. Matron was still in her rant. "It's your own fault," she said, "Tell him you can't come."

"I can't come," I mumbled, glancing at Anthony before dropping my eyes. Nothing else would come out. Anthony turned and started back up the drive. I watched him till he was out of sight. The treasures of my life left with him.

Defiance rushed in. Fear would normally have me scurry to the dining room but I stood upright and looked at that huge white building. I despised it – every damn piece of it! I had never liked or felt safe around Matron. Now I hated her.

After tea, I went outside, past Pickles' shed and the swings over to the stream. I wanted my own company, as far from the house as possible. Sitting on the iron footbridge in the fading light, I dangled my legs over the stream and stared into the flowing water. I wonder when my mother will visit again. I'll tell her I hate it here and she'll change things.

Even the setting sun looked sorrowful. Things were stirring inside. I felt a huge piece of me had been stolen, leaving me so lonely. It opened up a huge craving and the feeling there was something I was fated to chase.

I heard the whistles to signal young boys to bedtime. Walking up to top hostel, I realised I should have known it was close to tea time when Anthony was there. Why didn't I think? *Can't I get anything right?*

During that time a nightmare would recur. A female wolf with a ferocious appetite chased me. Try as I might to get away from the growling animal, my legs and arms moved as if in treacle. I'd wake up gripped in panic and sweating. Then, after a few moments came the enormous relief of seeing the other boys in their beds alongside me.

My life inside the home became one world and my school life became another. A sick and haunting pain was growing, ashamed of where I lived and everything about my home life. Trying to live in two worlds was tormenting. It wasn't long before the split was clean, as if an axe had done the job.

Each day I went through a mutation on my way to school and on my way back. I was afraid my school friends would disown me if they knew where and how I lived. My friends had normal coats;

Spennells boys had gabardines. I hid my orphanage-issue coat in a bush along the route, retrieving it on the way back. Other boys did the same. I'd brave the cold to not wear it, but if it was too cold or raining I'd put it on. Then I'd take it off, turning it inside out before I went through the school gates.

Outside Spennells grounds I was on guard, keeping secret the polluted home life for which I had no explanations. I lived with thirty or more boys that had no father. *Dad* and *Mum* were foreign words. I could not speak them. They were jammed fast somewhere deep inside refusing to come out. And if my school friends used those words I moved away, feeling ashamed of my own presence.

Living among a large group of boys did serve up luminous moments, they had their way of piercing through.

On a small patch of ground outside the back door, we played marbles. All the Spennells boys were crowded around a game when one lad brought his radio outside. As *The Animals* began their anthem, he cranked the volume full.

We got to get out of this place,
If it's the last thing we ever do,
We got to get out of this place,
Girl, there's a better life for me and you!

Everyone joined in and picked up the chorus. There were grinning faces all around. No one cared if the Vaughans could hear; they couldn't throw us all on punishment!

There had been rumours that an ex-Spennells lad was coming back to give Mr Vaughan a taste of his own medicine. Whether it happened I don't know, but just *hearing* about it offered a strand of justice. And I clung to it, realising I was not alone in my feelings.

I felt the injustice even deeper when I saw my brother Dave, head in his arms, crying his eyes out. "What happened?" I asked. Dave's friend Stuart was standing loyally by.

"Vaughan!" Stuart said, in a sickened voice. I knew it then. We boys were totally alone and powerless against the injustices of the Vaughans. Seeing Dave broken like that killed any childish notion in me that someone would come along and improve things. It plucked out the few threads of innocence I had left, and bitterness fired its way in. A compulsion to do something burned inside.

I began to hatch a plan to get us out of the wretched place. I would put my newly learned writing skills to good use.

"Let's write a secret letter to our mother," I said to Dave.

"I've been thinking about that," Dave replied. Writing secret letters was a hot topic among the boys when things got rough, though I doubt many got written. My writing experience was limited. I'd replied to cards from Aunty Wendy (Hallow Park) at birthdays and Christmas even though she had moved to London. The only other letters I wrote were to Santa Claus.

Ripping a page from a school book, I struggled after, "Dear Mother." I went looking for Dave and found him up in the rec, sitting waiting for a game of table tennis with a bat in his hand. "What do I put next?" I whispered.

"We'll talk about it tomorrow," he said. Impatient to get a game, Dave's eyes never left the little white ball being whipped across the table. Table tennis was a favourite pastime for most of us, and not much got in the way of it.

The next day, again I mentioned the letter to Dave. "I'll think about it," he said, not even stopping to talk.

I felt myself a nuisance. Maybe writing a letter sounded stupid to Dave, or maybe he knew nothing would happen anyway. I still thought it a good idea, even though the only address I had was - Yorkshire.

Steve and I were given a message from Miss Gillian. "Go to Mr Vaughan's sitting room. There's someone to see you."

"Maybe it's our mother," Steve said. I skipped along the passageway and, meeting up with Dave on the way, the three of us were ushered into the Vaughan's sitting room at the front of the house. Mr Vaughan and Matron were sitting with another woman. Ah, I thought, this accounted for the deserted passageways. There was a noticeable absence of boys polishing floors or on standing detention when an outside visitor came around.

"This is Mrs Greenwood from Dewsbury," Matron said.

Mrs Greenwood was the children's officer from our home town. She was dressed like the headmistress of an all-girls school, with spectacles to match. Poised on the edge of her armchair she held a cup of tea, her little finger stretched itself out like an aircraft wing. Her other hand held the saucer like a landing pad. "Hello boys, how are you getting on?" she said, smiling with all the conformity of a librarian.

"Alright," Dave said, in a discomforted voice. It was a little like being back in front of Miss Neale and her reviews, the same creepy cocktail of fear and embarrassment.

"Which part of the house are you in?" Mrs Greenwood asked Steve and me.

"We sleep up in the shed," I replied, pointing out of the window.

"We call it a hostel, Philip, not a shed!" Matron said curtly.

The three of us sat still while the Vaughans and Mrs Greenwood continued their conversation across us. Mrs Greenwood asked us more questions, smiling as if she were enquiring about a garden fete. Feeling progressively awkward, we gazed out the window. As we were ushered out, Mrs Greenwood smiled again, "I'll speak to your mother and tell her you're in good hands."

Emerging from one of Mrs Greenwood's subsequent visits, Steve and I scurried after Dave. We wanted Dave to tell Mrs Greenwood how much we hated the Vaughans and their rules. "I'll tell her next time," Dave said, annoyed at the two of us.

Getting past the Vaughans was too big a task for Dave. Added to that, Dave had a well-formed cynicism about telling anyone anything. As the yearly visits passed and I witnessed the remoteness and timidity of Mrs Greenwood I understood his reticence. Even so, at the time of her ineffectual visits, the mere idea of telling her the truth brought some comfort. Then Mrs Greenwood would take tea again, her little finger aloft, and with each lost opportunity, another shovel of coal was flung on the scornful fire burning inside me.

Chapter 9

Sweet Games

It lay just below the surface of my thoughts, but it was there – a perpetual dream to break free. Occasionally, the dream was pulled into wakefulness by film and television heroes. My favourite heroes rode horses and I'd imagine myself arriving at school on a fine chestnut horse with the whole school crowding round us.

Lower Comberton Junior School was a mile away from Spennells. Walking out of the drive, on my way there, I'd look for Pickles, Spennells' black horse. Shouting over the fence, Pickles' head would turn, and his deep eyes gazed right at me. He looked powerful and wild. The Vaughan's son, Owen, and an older boy named Randall were the only people I ever saw riding Pickles.

Sometime later Pickles left. Like so many things it just happened with no explanation. But Pickles' corrugated iron shed remained and still contained something of his spirit. I'd go in there whenever I ventured into that field.

To ride a wild horse, that is something. To ride *the spirit* of a wild horse, now that is something else. Faster and faster, faster still, until we are moving faster than the speed of thoughts. That is freedom. No burden is fast enough to attach itself. That was the state I reached during games of football on the scrub grass next to the tennis court that was our small pitch. A zest for life ran through me, melting away trouble like magic.

Football came as natural to me as breathing. In a game I'd claim the ball at every opportunity and run with it on that swift, wild horse. Hungry joy quivered inside me when the ball – with my name on it – was lofted high in flight towards me. A slight chance at goal and I'd take it.

I'd always regarded a ball as beautiful, especially a football, which is the perfect sized ball. It's responsive and begs to be played with. It's electrifying to weave a path through opponents towards goal, elbows flayed for balance, body and football in a dance. It's a heavenly thing to shape its flight by striking it with a sweet touch.

To quote the gifted footballer, Platini, it's *The Beautiful Game.* To misquote Benjamin Franklin, *Football is proof God loves us and wants us to be happy.*

When the evenings became light and we boys were immersed in a game, the whistle would sound. That whistle marked a return to the profane grey world the adults inhabited. It was always too soon for me. I wanted to play until we dropped or until it got too dark to see the ball. I wanted that game with my friends to never, ever end.

With so many distant and ineffectual adults around us it's no wonder we boys loved to make a life-size Guy and send it up in flames every November 5th. But there were times when all that heat morphed into exuberance. Despite their daily treatment towards us, the Vaughans really knew how to organise events and everyone was touched by the enchantment. We were given glimpses of that at Spennells. They came at Christmas with well-planned parties, brightly wrapped presents, games, and pillow fights. There were summer fortnights by the sea, and Easter celebrations.

The morning of Easter Sunday saw us hunting for small chocolate eggs among patches of long grass, shrubs, and nesting boxes in the tall pines at the front of the house. We younger boys were set loose first. "One, two, three go!" It was a gold-rush scramble to get to the shiny red, blue and green eggs before the other boys. Then suddenly - there it was – that strange statement, "you've had enough fun now!" It left little room for debate.

The older boys had their turn next. Some of the eggs were hidden higher up in the trees and tucked behind bird boxes. "Getting closer!" the house mothers shouted at an older boy until he scaled the right tree and clutched the egg, the rest of us cheering him on.

Every year, a charity delivered a huge chocolate Easter egg two-and-a-half feet high. As a table centre-piece it looked impressive surrounded by sandwiches and fancy cakes for the evening party. I could not take my eyes off it. In the following days, the chunky chocolate pieces were handed out on a plate. "I'll have that one!" Ronnie said, his eyes widening while the rest of us scanned for the biggest piece to grab before someone else did.

The one event that gave me the most fun and was the most surreal was the Easter football match. It was such a reassuring feeling to watch the adults put on their play clothes. I mean literally! Staff, plus invited grown-ups, raided the clothes box in the rec and dressed in costumes to challenge the boys to a match. A full-size pitch was marked out in top field and everyone played, or cheered from the touchline. It was as much a pantomime spectacle as a match.

"Come on then, let's kick off!" Matron shouted, dressed like a pirate with black eye-patch and plastic sword. Mr Vaughan dressed like a granny, with a dress and headscarf, placed the ball on the centre spot. Another man had a long stick and a metal dustbin lid resembling a jousting knight. Most of the adults had the ball skills of a kangaroo so it was fairly easy to weave among them, turning the ball past their clumsy feet. I ran my legs off in the hunger for that ball, fuelled by the rush of power that came from knowing I could outplay them.

"Pass the ball, Phil!" Dave shouted. I fed it to him and watched him sweep it past Matron and Mr Seymour. Ronnie! Dave! Norman! Everyone was shouting for the ball.

Mr Thomas wore boxing gloves, knee-length breeches and a black and red striped schoolboy jacket. He looked as ridiculous as his football skills. He'd kick the ball in the direction he was running regardless of which way the goal was. I nearly wet myself watching him turning. Instead of sidestepping and leaning his body, he followed the contour of a large arc, like a wheel in a groove.

Miss Barbara, in outrageous leggings and woolly gloves, dived into the game like she was back in her schooldays. Going in for a tackle, she ended up kicking thin air as the ball was whisked away by one of the boys.

I loved that high play. It was a circus of a time, and in the middle of it, I shook with joy.

The enormous chocolate Easter egg pieces had been put in a store cupboard at the end of the passageway in the main house. One Saturday morning, Steve and I had been put on floor polishing punishment by Matron. Everyone was outside enjoying the welcome spring sunshine. Steve and I shuffled on hands and knees, buffing the same old section of wooden floor. Mr Vaughan drifted past me. I heard him deliver his infamous line, "Just popping out Ans, carry on regardless." I thought about our joke, but couldn't summon any humour.

I had polished that oak parquet floor so many times I knew every inch of it. Some of the small wooden rectangles were worn and some had loosened. The surface was uneven in places and the folded pieces of cloth under my knees often snagged. The floor's slight slope meant shuffling down was a little easier than shuffling up. Steve was working on the section of floor that extended into the cupboard containing the chocolate; the cupboard having been unlocked for him.

"Put that polish away. You can write your lines now," Matron snapped at me, ferrying pencil and paper. She placed them on the food serving hatch farther down the passageway. The hatch between kitchen and passageway had a flat surface that extended into the passageway to transfer items into the dining room opposite. Standing up by the hatch I began writing one hundred times; *I must learn to do as I am told.*

"Pssssst, Phil." I looked up. Steve pointed inside the cupboard and mouthed, "The chocolate Easter egg is in here."

"How much?" I whispered.

"Loads." Steve poked his head around the door for another look. "I'll grab some and go to the bogs; I'll hide some in there and give you some."

"Not yet!" I said. I was in enough trouble.

Before I had time to ready myself, Steve marched down the passageway loaded with chocolate. He dumped two huge pieces on the serving hatch and carried on to the toilets. I bit one straight away to make it smaller to hold; the other I clutched in the warmth of my left hand. No one was around so I finished off the first piece just as Steve returned from the washroom and made it back to the cupboard. Then I heard Matron's voice coming from her sitting room just beyond Steve. *She was coming this way.*

Matron's voice got louder, as she appeared I felt as if an African drummer were pounding on my heart. I closed my hand as best I could around the stolen chunk, but my hand was too small to cover the melting chocolate. I dipped my head to fixate on my writing. The pounding in my chest got louder. I felt Matron pass behind me. I held my breath for several more seconds, and then my body eased as she went out the back door.

As I wrote my lines, I could still hear Matron humming in the background. And then it grew louder. *She was coming back!* The African drummer in me was going mental! Again, Matron passed behind me. Then, she grabbed my hand and the stolen goods dropped on the hatchway. "Where did you get that?"

Before I could speak, Matron grabbed my ear, yanked it upwards and pulled it along the passageway, my feet scampering behind to stop it being torn off. With my ear burning as hot as her temper she shrieked at me. "You'll learn, my lad!" Matron positioned me outside her sitting room. "Stand there for the rest of the afternoon." I caught the smell of the polished wood and tobacco smoke that I'd come to associate with the dreaded Vaughans and their end of the house. Matron went off to deal with Steve and I smarted in a cloud of shame. I clutched my ear to ease the blinding pain. Blinking fast I tried to hold back my tears.

"Never let them see you cry," an older boy had once instructed me. He'd said it like a holy mantra. Now, outside Matron's room, I tried to follow it.

My legs wanted to buckle after several hours of standing detention, broken only by a visit to the toilet. It was an unwritten rule that no one spoke to boys on punishment. Later Matron eventually broke the banishment. "Go and have your tea!" Then, in an attempt to extinguish any fire left inside me she added, "After that, wash and straight to bed."

It was a relief to sit down at my table but I ate in miserable silence. Even among the other boys I felt myself locked in a naughty boy's prison.

I crept up the walkway to the hostel, the bustle of the main house fading behind me. I looked across at the swathes of daffodils in the rockery garden. Only last week they had been a riot of yellow; now they were all brown and wilting as if they had also been given a dose of Matron's nursing.

The hostel was empty and in the silence of the washroom I immersed my hands, palms down, in a sink of warm water. I fixed my gaze on them, wondering why I always end up on punishment.

I turned down the counterpane and lay in bed, staring at the wall. Blighted and cursed, I listened intently for the sound of Ronnie, or Robert, or Steve. I ached for their bedtime so they'd join me and ease my scornfulness.

Colour came back into the world with the promise of a special day ahead. In late June Matron was in queenly heaven as the yearly fete was approaching. It was her creation, and the whole of lower field football pitch was covered in stalls. There was tombola, cake stalls, a coconut shy, treasure hunt games, raffles, hoopla games, darts games, and my favourite, kicking a football at a board that had holes in it for goals. Our back yard became a car park and people teamed out of a coach that pulled into the drive. Accompanied by his wife, the local Mayor, wearing his gold chain, gave a speech from a raised platform outside the front of the house. Also on the platform were a suited Charlie Vaughan and a glowing Matron, in hat, best dress and shoes, being presented with a bouquet of flowers.

My win in that first year came on the stall where the aim was to pick a whole egg out of a sea of eggs in a sand tray. As only half of each egg was showing it was a guess as to which egg was whole, among the half empty shells of the decoy eggs. I picked up a full egg which had the number six written on it. I shone with delight. The number six prize on the table was a bottle of Heinz salad cream. That bottle stayed on my table in the dining room for months as I added salad cream to everything I could, while sharing it with all on my table.

In the six-week summer holiday a trip was arranged to Colwyn Bay in North Wales. We camped in a church hall in rows of fold-up beds. On a gusty afternoon we made a trip over to the Island of Anglesey and crossed the small swing bridge to South Stack lighthouse. On the way we stopped off at the Welsh railway station, Llanfairpwllgwyngyllgogerychwyrndrobwllllantysiliogogogoch, counting out the fifty-eight letter name.

In the autumn we might have an organised day trip. Often it was to Ludlow just thirty miles away, where all thirty boys were let loose in the indoor pool with its high diving board. A visit to Ludlow Castle and the rowing boats on the River Teme completed the day.

In the run up to Christmas, we wrote the customary letter to Santa Claus stating our requests. Christmas morning we all gathered in the big boys' sitting room where presents had appeared under the tree. "There's Father Christmas!" a younger boy shouted, pointing through the window. Sure enough there he was walking around the circular drive with white beard and a red sack. We younger ones ran out to meet him. Sitting by the tree Father Christmas called out names as he handed out presents. In my letter I'd eagerly asked for a Beatle record and to my amazement there it was. *Rubber Soul*, their latest long-play vinyl! "Crikey, look what he's got!" Stuart, an older boy, shouted across the room in obvious envy. Other kids received board games, model cars, trains, reading books and sets of Meccano.

For Christmas dinner, the tables were dressed and set out in a U-shape. Bright, coloured streamers decorated the ceiling and windows. All wore party hats and pulled crackers. It was a marvellous atmosphere, as if an amnesty had been called and a warm breeze of joy blew into the house. We had party games like skittles and shove-halfpenny in the rec in the evening, and one year we even had a local pop group set up a stage in there.

My Beatle album felt very special and I cherished that lovely smelling vinyl. The thick record felt solid and unbreakable, much more robust than the smaller 45 rpm singles. I loved the cover photograph, the four Beatles staring down at the camera all moody and confident. I liked all the songs and soon knew the words to *Norwegian Wood* and *In My Life*. They captured my head with imagery and sound, and I escaped into the world they were singing about.

Owning the record also afforded me some power as I saw the gratitude on the older lads' faces when I would loan it to them. Someone, however, must have let his envy get the better of him. It was returned to me a week later with the words *piss off* scratched on the cover.

The older boy in top hostel, John Bromley, frequently poked his head into our dormitory at lights out. "Phil," he whispered, "can I borrow your *Rubber Soul*?" I always said yes, gratified to know we shared a love for the songs.

These Christmas gifts came from *Rubery Owen, The Round Table*, and other charitable organisations. We often had things donated to the home: boxes of toys, bikes, and back copies of National Geographic. The strangest thing that arrived was dozens of boxes containing wrapped tubes of Horlicks sweets. The sweets were given out liberally one Saturday.

"Have a packet of sweets," Ronnie said generously, after he'd tasted them.

"Those are disgusting," I said after trying one. We kept opening the new packets to see if they tasted any better. I guess it was a failed idea from the Horlicks manufacturers; instead of ditching them they found their way to us.

Chapter 10

Out of Touch

"Your mother's here. Go to the big boys' sitting room," Miss Gillian told Steve and me.

My body tingled, and my lungs sucked in the breath of a new world. *My mother's here!* With my head full of sunshine, I beamed like a torch as I ran down into the main house with Steve.

My mother was sitting alone in an upright chair wearing a brown woollen coat and a headscarf. She was gazing out of the tall windows at the front lawn. Dave came in and the three of us pulled up chairs next to her. Pride washed over me; *I have my own mother.*

I knew nothing of her life or what kind of person she was. I didn't care, not while I was bathing in the special feeling that she had come to see *me.* I had a thread to a bigger and brighter world and a person I belonged to. It was a promise that fed me like a king.

Sitting with my brothers stirred up more waves of belonging. This was the only time we sat together and my internal heating system turned itself full on.

"What have you been up to, then?" my mother said.

"We play football, on the field over there," I said, smiling and pointing through the window.

"Oh, that's good," she said in her broad Yorkshire tone. She looked at Dave. "Uncle Tommy was asking about you."

"That's great. Thanks for your letter," my brother said. "I'm going to Sea Cadets now."

"We had a party at Christmas," Steve piped up. "Santa came and I got a cowboy hat!"

"And I got a bow and arrow," I said.

"Oh," she said, turning back towards the window. Her gaze remained there till the defensive pinch in her face eased and allowed a return. Her shoulders pulled into a hunch. Her sad hands clasped each other.

"What did you do to your knee?" she asked me.

"I fell out of a tree over by the stream," I said, inspecting the scab.

My mother lit a cigarette and Dave got her an ashtray. It wasn't long before a struggle to find conversation threw us into awkwardness.

I remembered a trip to the cinema. "We went to see the Dr Who film," I said, not mentioning that the full technicolour battle with the Daleks had scared me witless.

A house mother brought in a cup of tea. "Oh, thank you," mother said, clearly grateful. Its arrival helping to break the tension and her body eased around the cup and saucer.

Dave took an Elvis record out of its sleeve and put it on the gramophone by the window. The music rubbed a little soothing oil on the dry search for things to say. But still I was thirsting inside. I wanted a headful of her stories. *Where was the news of a new house and the day when we'd get to live with her? Where was the news of her meeting someone with power and goodness? A person we could trust.*

My lustre was dulling quickly. I wanted a bellyful of her fun, rolling me around on the floor. I craved my share of lightness and play. It hurt to see my mother so empty of words when I wanted to worship her.

Dave began gazing toward the window, again and again. Outside, George Tinney walked past. George was Dave's closest friend at Spennells. Together they'd tamed a grey squirrel enough to feed and house it in a box secreted among the trees on the other side of the stream.

"You two stay here, I've just got to tell George something," Dave said, slipping off. *Dave didn't want to be with us!* Sorrow stabbed me.

As Dave passed through the doorway more fragile strands of life were pulled from our little group. Dull and struggling our lowliness riddled me with hurt. But I could not afford to view my mother as anything less than radiant. I needed my dream intact. My mother was a woman who would soon find her power and come and claim me. My dream put her right where she belonged: on a pedestal. I liked her broad Yorkshire way of speaking; her longer vowel sounds had colour and were different to our crisp Midland accent.

Our visit lasted a couple of hours and before she left we all congregated in the Vaughan's sitting room. "Phil is very often late for things," Matron reported to my mother lightly.

"Oh, he'd better pull his socks up then," my mother said, injecting a little humour in the absence of any stature.

Matron took charge of the conversation and added other comments about Dave and Steve. Then Mr Vaughan asked my mother about train times.

The gulf between my mother and the high-status Vaughans bedevilled me. It wasn't the Vaughan's fault, but something in their clinical conversation accentuated it. Anyone could see my mother felt overpowered; it made me wince. In that huge house, next to those pillars of authority, she looked almost childlike. Just like us, my mother sat waiting for her next orders. I wanted to battle to protect her, to stand up tall for her. But the proudness in my heart could not form words, and even if it could I was too fearful to say them.

Matron stood and raised her arm to motion us towards the door. "Now, boys, off you go and play."

This was one of two or three visits my mother made to Spennells. Dave never spoke to us about the private revelation of the bruises she wore, and her off-hand comments about her partner's violence.

I never saw my mother arrive, or leave, and her visits all had the same initial hopefulness followed by a grey choking flavour.

Mysteriously my mother went on her way, and we returned to

the four walls of the institution, the three of us going our separate ways, each of us dealing with our confused thoughts in our own way.

On one of her visits my mother stayed overnight and slept in the main house. Meanwhile, in our hostel dormitory, four of us boys went to bed sharing a boisterous mood. We had a student house mother that night. After lights out, Ronnie threw a small teddy bear, sending it flying across the room at me. I hurled it back, giggling wildly as it spun through the air and hit him clean on the head. All four joined in the fun. After each throw we dived under the covers in case we'd made too much noise. We listened out for a minute, but no one came. "Throw the teddy back," I whispered hoarsely.

With our spirits high, Tony, one of the new boys, jumped into bed with Ronnie. Muffled laughter came from under the blankets. Tony popped his head outside the covers. "Come on! Let's all get in." Caught up in the fun, I tip-toed over in a run and dived under the sheets. "Take your pyjamas off!" Tony said. "It's fun!"

It felt good touching our bare skin together, the warmth of our bodies soothing as well as playful. Steve joined us. We four were in one bed, half-dressed, bundling onto each other like a family of monkeys. "Who's got hold of my leg?" Ronnie said, quaking with giggles.

Then the dormitory light snapped on! "Right! Get dressed, the lot of you!" The student house mother stood in the doorway. "Dressing gowns and slippers on!"

She marched us out of the hostel and down the walkway into the main house, our faces white with shock. "Stand there," she barked. We lined up, backs against the cloakroom wall like prisoners of war, while the house mother headed down the passageway. I knew where she'd gone and I sweated fear. *We've bloody had it now!* My eyes closed wishing we were somewhere else. The next voice I heard was the one I most dreaded.

"You dirty little boys," snarled Mr Vaughan. "Which one of you started this?"

"Don't know Sir," each of us said, in turn.

"Don't know Sir. Don't know Sir. You disgusting little urchins!"

He pointed at Steve and me. "I've a good mind to tell your mother what you've been doing." His threat made me want to vomit. What if she sided with Sir and joined in the scolding?

Smack! Smack! Smack! Smack! Down the line Mr Vaughan went, clouting each boy's head. "Standing detention now and see me for punishment tomorrow." Sir glared. "Now get out of my sight!"

Scarlet with shame, we filed out of the cloakroom and hurried up the walkway, our dressing gowns catching the breeze from the gardens. For the next two hours we stood along the hostel passageway, our spirits flattened and our legs throbbing. There was no banter that night; our humiliation deadened it all.

The following morning, still in fear of my mother being told of the previous night, I washed, dressed and did my jobs in fragile obedience, making myself invisible so as not to create the slightest wave.

Vaughan's many scoldings haunted me, and not only in waking hours. I dreamed incessantly, the same episode over and over. I am balancing on the crest of a gigantic tidal wave. The rushing water is deafening and the power in the wave is colossal. I am trembling and have to fight with all my energy to stay on the crest and not drown. The wave transports me for hours across an entire ocean. Then, overwhelmed I sink under the water. Finally I am washed up on a beach, the wave having receded. After the thunder of the massive wave, the silence is serene and blissful. I awake in my dormitory feeling fortunate to have survived, but, also, wondering how I had.

It was always a relief to be away from the oppressive ordering of the home. It was even more heavenly when two Barnardo befrienders, Mr and Mrs Clarke, were paired with Steve and me.

We were in high spirits when their white Skoda turned out of Spennells drive with the two of us in the back seat. It was a lovely feeling to arrive at 'Aunty Vera' and 'Uncle Tom's' bungalow, a haven of normality. Several times Steve and I visited them all day long on a Sunday, which had the added bonus of us missing church. They took us to visit their friends or allowed us to help in their garden. That's when the neediness of Steve and me really started to surface. If Steve was commended for something, I'd rush in to show myself as if my survival depended on it, and he'd do the same if he felt I was getting more praise or attention.

On our first overnight stay at the Clarkes', I felt a softness surrounding me, like the embracing wings of an angel. The rooms in their bungalow were lushly carpeted; even the bathroom had a soft-pile mat and matching cover for the toilet seat. We stayed up late watching television, then Steve and I slept like mice in our soft, warm beds. On waking, a bright new feeling claimed me as I realised where we were. After washing I buried my face in the thick towels Aunty Vera had put out for us.

I'd brought along a chemistry set that I was struggling to use. Uncle Tom sat with me, diligently read the instructions, and carried out an experiment. I huddled next to him in anticipation of a display of fireworks. Uncle Tom mixed the powders and liquid and finally held up a test tube. "Now Philip, are you watching?"

"Yes!" I said, eyes transfixed. Uncle Tom poured liquid from one test tube into the waiting display test tube. "Oh!" I witnessed the tame sight of liquid change colour in a test tube. I tried to disguise my disappointment.

"Can we do it again?" I said, quickly dropping my let-down and basking in his attention.

Aunty Vera doted on me. "Can I call you Pip?" she asked. How could I say no? Secretly I hated the sound of 'Pip'. I thought it made me sound like a girl. Aunty Vera's Sunday dinners were also a strain. She'd spend hours in an apron labouring to produce a roast that filled enormous plates. With homemade apple sauce and chipolatas wrapped in bacon, it was a work of art. Uncle Tom encouraged us to eat it all, but Steve and I struggled, which seemed to disappoint Aunty Vera. I couldn't care less about the dinner and was frustrated when she'd be hours peeling vegetables and handling trays in and out of the oven wearing thick gloves. It consumed her loving attention which I craved, and my time with her was short.

They'd taken us one Sunday to an elaborate christening party hosted by a friend. Coming back in the car, Aunty Vera asked, "What would you like to eat, boys?"

"Can we have beans on toast?" we said eagerly. There was a noticeable silence in the car, though Aunty Vera later indulged us.

Back at Spennells that Sunday evening, Aunty Vera mentioned our food request to the staff. As soon as Aunty Vera and Uncle Tom left, Matron pulled the two of us up short. "How dare you show us up like that in front of those kind people?"

It was the kind of scolding that left me scratching my head. Maybe Matron would have been pleased if we'd requested pheasant or roast duck. Spennells meals were hardly high cuisine, and anyway, I'd never ever been asked what I wanted to eat in my whole life.

Aunty and Uncle owned a drapery shop close to my school. I saw Aunty Vera coming out of the shop one day. She opened her arms to greet me. "Pip!" I ran straight to her and buried my head into the soft fur collar of her coat until she released her arms. Feeling awkward I nervously looked around to make sure I'd not been seen. The spontaneity of our moment together punctuates those years. I hadn't hugged anyone since Aunty Wendy.

Chapter 11

Mr Thomas

I smiled whenever I saw Mr Thomas, the housemaster. He smiled back and our bond seemed to grow naturally. Out on group walks I'd be first to hold his hand and the last to let go. He'd venture into the chicken run with a wicker basket to collect eggs, and we boys would shout, "Can I come in, Mr Thomas?" More times than most, he chose me. "Come on then, little pest."

If a group of us were returning from an outing in his white Ford van, Mr Thomas would stop just inside the Spennells stone pillars, then, one-by-one, he let us steer. Somehow it became an unspoken rule that I always had the longest go. I gloried in the extra attention, but it triggered squabbles between me and some of the other boys who were just as needy for a father figure.

I sensed Mr Thomas and I were on dangerous ground, and though I couldn't form a reason, I felt I had to limit my connection with him. I wasn't aware of the Barnardo rule forbidding any bonding between staff and children, but I had an awareness of being watched. Inside the chicken run Mr Thomas showed me how to feed the chickens as well as collect the eggs. Among the clucking chickens a sense of rightness surged through me as we did the tasks together. I followed him around wanting to stand close to him. Coming out, I felt myself wrong for staying with him longer than I should and it was a relief to be on my own again.

The staff must have covertly had their favourite boys, but my growing connection to Mr Thomas scared me. I yearned for his attention, but when it came, an awful awkwardness would wreck my natural play. The pull and push of it was wearing. I felt more at ease if a small group of us were playing with Mr Thomas. Then I could clamber on his back, as naturally as any of the others.

Some weekends the house mothers rounded up the younger boys for an afternoon walk. We'd take nets and jars to fish for sticklebacks and tadpoles in the small lake known as *Spennells Pool*. Most times we took the well-worn circular route through the tiny hamlet of *Stone* and into *Chestnut Wood*. Like all old woods, Chestnut Wood held its magic. The trees with low branches were ideal for climbing, and swathes of bracken gave ideal cover for games of hide-and-seek. Way above the path there was even a cave. There we could be out of sight of the grown-ups, if only for a while.

Walking through Chestnut Wood was the first time I saw people fox-hunting. Dressed in red tunics atop their powerful horses, we had to stand aside while they galloped through. I admired the smart looking riders. Moments later, I caught the red copper-coloured flash of a fox and was glad to see it escape at the far end of the wood. Another time I saw a fox in the centre of scores of snapping hounds. Fighting for its life, with little chance of defence, the hounds sank their teeth into its back. I felt crushed at the merciless sight.

The circular route back brought us through the muddy farmland opposite the entrance to Spennells. Running on ahead we challenged each other to jump the biggest puddles. At times, a sugar beet crop was piled high on that farm. The story among the boys was that, should you run away, you could survive by eating those sugar beets. Many times we stole one beet each, tucked it under our coat, and hid them behind a tree in our drive when the staff weren't looking. I never put it to the test but, like a prisoner-of-war with a tunnel in the planning, it was a rousing thought.

A line of fir trees bound a long flat strip of land in front of the hostel. The strip was divided into small patches by edgings of old red brick. Each boy was allocated a patch of the weed laden ground to try his hand at gardening.

The morning air had spring warmth one Saturday when John Bromley handed out seed packets. "You have these radish ones," he said, throwing them for me to catch.

"What do I do with them?"

"Dig over the ground, rake it, and spread them in."

Excited to follow the bigger lads and get planting, I gathered some tools on my plot. Struggling with the big rusty spade I barely made a dent in the hardened ground. To keep myself heartened, I copied the older boys and neatly re-arranged the brick edgings around my plot. Then – as it so often did – football beckoned, and I abandoned my tools to join the game. That same weekend, I wandered back to my weedy patch and wondered how I would ever get it dug.

"Will you come and help me?" I shouted to Stuart, who was busy down the far end of the strip.

"I might do, when I've finished mine," he said. But Stuart never got round to it. I gave up the idea of gardening and abandoned the packet of seeds among the contents of my bedside drawer.

Later that week after school, I skipped along the concrete path by the garden plots. I spied a good-looking, freshly dug section and leapt over to it. The scent of newly turned soil filled the air as I looked for my own patch. Where's it gone? And then I recognised the brick edgings I'd worked so hard to rearrange. *This one is mine!* Exhilaration pulsed though me. I looked around, wishing for someone to tell. Look at my lovely turned soil; it's the best patch here! I studied the ground in wonder and felt myself in a magical story, as if I'd made a wish for this, and it had come true!

Eager to plant the radish seeds, I ran off to get the packet. The seeds were soon in the ground and I watered them diligently each time I passed. "Mr Thomas," I called out one afternoon, "My garden has been dug over and I'm growing radishes. Shall I show you?" He smiled at me as if to say, *I know.*

To my delight, the green shoots soon appeared and it wasn't long before I was on my knees, digging up the little red bulbs, like I'd gained some mystical power. I pulled up six at a time, proudly washed them and presented one for each of us on our dinner table.

It was such a joy to share them, but the second time I felt some of the boys looking at me suspiciously. I couldn't help thinking they'd discovered who had dug my garden. The thought made me feel like I'd been found out living a lie, so I toned down my excitement. If only he'd dug all their gardens too, instead of singling me out.

Mr Thomas was making plans. He was treating me like I belonged to him, which I liked, but in among all those other boys it came with a price. A dream of fostering me and my two brothers had taken hold of him. Through the winter and spring of 1964 he became more deliberate about spending private time with me. When the evenings became lighter I would be given instructions: *meet me the other side of the chicken run*. The two of us would wander into the woods at the edge of the grounds. I felt excited to have his attention, then awkward about our secret behaviour. To stave off that feeling I acted out. "Look at me, Mr Thomas, watch me climb this tree." I shimmied up the trunk and into the lower branches.

"Be careful, Phil. You could fall."

"I won't fall, Mr Thomas, I won't. Watch me!" No sooner had my words found air when I lost my grip. I fell into the bracken and caught my leg on the way down. My vision went fuzzy. On my back and looking up at the sky, I could feel stinging in my grazed knee. My hand touched it for comfort and I felt blood seeping from the scratches. "I'm alright," I said bravely.

Mr Thomas gathered me up, trying not to laugh, and I hobbled around till the pain wore off. It was then he told me of his plan to leave Spennells and buy a house in Old Colwyn, where he grew up. "When I've got the house, I'll come back for you, and Dave and Steve," he promised. "I want to be your dad, Phil. Foster you."

I didn't really know what he meant, but it sounded good. I remembered Old Colwyn from a two-week Spennells summer camp in North Wales. The picture in my head gave me a warm glow. Mr Thomas would leave and become like the 'Uncles and Aunties' who came to the homes to visit and take us out. I would get to stay with him for holidays, by the seaside.

Mr Thomas lived in the lower section of the hostel. If the others weren't around, I would spend ten minutes or so alone with him there. He was a watch and clock enthusiast, and had all the equipment to clean and repair them; it supplemented his Barnardo's wage. I gazed at the dozens of ticking clocks, each one with its own distinctive sound. "Are these all yours?"

"Well, this clock I'm mending for the church warden. This one, I'm cleaning for Mr Townsend," he continued, putting the owner's name to each timepiece on the shelf.

"Whose is this?" I said, picking up a big, silver pocket watch and holding it to my ear.

"It's mine," said Mr Thomas. I loved the loud tick. It was a reassuring sound and I picked it up whenever I had the chance.

I was mindful of the rule that boys should be only where they were told. I knew if I were found in Mr Thomas's room there'd be trouble. Or worse, Mr Thomas would be in trouble with the Vaughans, and that was a terrifying thought.

In the early hours of the morning, in the months before he left Spennells, Mr Thomas came to my dormitory. Picking me up, he carried me down to his room in my dressing gown. Rubbing my tired eyes, I ached to lie down. But I was wakened enough to talk. The attentiveness felt good yet the secretiveness riddled me with guilt. At the same time, I couldn't tell him I would rather have been in my bed.

On three or four occasions Mr Thomas asked me to stand in front of him and he opened my dressing gown. He inspected my penis, as though he were a doctor. "This won't take a minute," he said quietly. In silence, with a damp flannel cloth, he painstakingly removed the small white particles from my penis.[1] It seemed to take ages. I felt ugly and embarrassed and was relieved to cover myself when the strange process ended. I was left struck with fear that someone would discover us and terrible things would happen.

I trusted Mr Thomas but I wanted to say, *I don't want you to do this.* No words came out. And each time I buried the memory in the place where children bury such things.

---

[1] *Prior to this time The Lancet had published an article that put forward the view that the smegma on a boy's penis could cause cancer.*

Chapter 12

Secret Saviours

John Bromley, a mild-mannered fifteen-year-old, was tall for his age. His Buddy Holly spectacles covered his face, and his thick black hair put inches on his height. He often got gentle ribbing from the more active boys for his soft voice and pastimes like reading and stamp collecting. Safe from harm, I'd tease him as well. "Have you polished your glasses today?" I'd say, with a wide, cheeky grin.

"Little squirt!" he'd fire back. Sometimes I'd push him and race away, knowing he didn't run as fast as I could, or wouldn't even bother trying. If I saw John later in the day, he would never react with maliciousness. "Watch it squirt," he'd say, grabbing my arm in mild irritation.

Once Steve and I had dug a wide hole in the woods over by the stream; we covered it with small branches and leaves and lured John towards it. Shock misshaped his face as the ground collapsed under him. We split our sides. Luckily, John saw the funny side.

I bumped into John one evening as I came out of the TV lounge. Watching the black and white set, I'd been astounded to see Cassius Clay (Muhammad Ali), the new World Boxing Champion, shouting at reporters. "I am the *greatest!* I'm the prettiest fighter you ever saw! I shook up the *wooorld!* I shook up the *wooorld!* I shook up the *wooorld!*" *Wow!* I'd never seen anyone so spirited, so alive! I'd never seen anyone attract so much attention! There was something totally infectious about the man, I couldn't take my eyes off him. He was lighting up the whole world with his confidence.

I skipped out of the TV lounge and headed out to play, buoyed by what I'd just witnessed. Looking ahead, I saw John leaning forward, elbows on the counter of the serving hatch where the boys on punishment stood to write out their lines. Immersed in writing, John's head was bowed and his backside faced me. Beyond him, the back door was wide open and I could see the last rays of sunlight lighting up the play area.

In a flash, the hilarious scene unfolded in my mind. Running fast, I'd slap John on the backside then leap through the open door like a gazelle. I'd gallop all the way to the playing field, laughing my little head off before John Bromley could raise his shaggy head.

I started my run. *He hasn't twigged!* My excitement built! The grin on my face grew wide! As I approached at full speed, my hand rose to deliver the slap! - Just as I came alongside, time slowed, and slowed . . . I looked on as if I had left my body. My raised hand seemed to speak: *I wouldn't do that if I were you!*

I caught a glimpse of John's face from the side. But it wasn't John Bromley at all! It was Mr Vaughan!

Keep moving! Please Phil, keep moving! Please!

Somehow this gazelle kept running. I floated on a cushion of air and glided through the back door.

Mr Vaughan was oblivious! And yet, I felt like I'd actually hit him! I imagined my fate – my death – right by the back door.

Run Phil, run. I sprinted across the backyard and threw myself into the lower field. I ran past Pickles' old shed, scanning for a hiding place. I tucked in behind a tree, and sat against the trunk, looking towards the stream.

My heart thumped hard with a sound that pulsed through my head, and my body tingled under my sweaty clothes. I had morphed from a gazelle into a fox that just escaped the baying hounds.

In my heightened state, the stream and the trees looked more vibrant than I had ever seen them. Light bounced off the thick intertwining branches. Birds flew playfully into the soft undergrowth. The running water in the stream bubbled with sound and I caught sweet snatches of breeze scented with wood bark and grass.

The panic gradually diminished, the heat in me slowly subsided and my breath grew even. The security of my hiding spot seemed to infuse my whole being. *Relief, sweet relief!* It was the same relief I felt upon waking from the wolf nightmare and the roaring tidal wave dream. I felt an outpouring of gratitude to whatever invisible guardian had saved me from an awful fate.

I couldn't speak about what happened to anyone; I was terrified that the story might be relayed back to *Sir.* That would surely bring the hiding of my life.

Mr Thomas owned a Royal Enfield motorbike that he stored in the pavilion shed in top field. Top field was deemed out of bounds, so I rarely ventured up there.

In July 1964, shortly before my eighth birthday, Mr Thomas walked me to the shed and fired up the motorbike. "You know I'm leaving very soon, Phil. I want to take lots of photos of you smiling." Perched on the huge bike, I grinned widely at his Brownie box camera. "Fire your bow and arrow for the last photos," he said.

Within days, Mr Thomas left Spennells for good. I don't remember his final leaving. There was no organised send-off; he just seemed to slip away. I didn't feel upset, but was left looking forward to joining him for the seaside holidays I had pictured.

In the year that followed, Mr Thomas made several clandestine visits to Spennells under cover of the woods beyond the chicken run. Mr Kirby, the caretaker, helped Mr Thomas relay a message to us through the older boys playing outside. "Phil, quietly go behind the chicken run. Mr Thomas is there." I rushed over to join Dave and Steve.

"I can't stay long lads. I don't want you to get into trouble," Mr Thomas said. "How are you all?" There was power and excitement meeting in secret, especially knowing the Vaughans were unaware of it. One time Mrs Thomas also came along. "This is Jean," Mr Thomas said. "She's keen to have you come and stay." I could see how gentle and mild she was, happy to listen and not say much. As well as being quiet, Mrs Thomas had a cleft palate, which made her speech quite difficult to get used to.

Mr Thomas told us how much he missed Spennells and how much he missed all his friends in Kidderminster. "I'm going to visit some of the Spennells old boys," he said. He mentioned their names and what jobs they were doing locally.

"I've bought a motor caravan for holidays," Mr Thomas said. "If we're quick, I can show you." We followed him through the wood to the cream and red Bedford van that was parked on a nearby road. It had fitted curtains, cooker and lift-up roof. It was a beauty, and filled my thoughts with freedom.

After those visits I felt high, like we'd got one over our oppressive guardians.

"I'll sleep in the top of the caravan!" I said to Steve later, "Where will you choose?"

"Me too. There's two bunks up there." I felt closer to Steve when we talked about Mr Thomas's secret visits, but Dave was soon dashing off to join the older boys in their games. I think Dave thought Mr Thomas was more for Steve and me, but I was sad that we couldn't share the adventure with him.

Once when Mr Thomas came, I was on standing detention in the passageway. "Mr Thomas was here," an older boy whispered.

"Which way did he go?" I said, fired up at the injustice of missing him. An impulse to run after him bolted through me, but I was too scared to leave my punishment spot.

I knew it would be ages before Mr Thomas would return. I settled down to sleep that night, annoyed with myself for being on punishment again.

Mr Thomas must have camped nearby because in the early hours he climbed into top hostel rec through a loose window. Waking me up, he carried me into the rec in the dark. He sat on a chair, with me in his lap half asleep. "I've been decorating your room," he whispered, handing me a chocolate lime sweet. "We've got a young boy called Nigel staying with us. You two would play well together," he said. He also told me he would call next time he had a holiday. I worried again that we'd be found and was relieved when he left.

The next morning, I was fearful thinking of the huge risk that Mr Thomas had taken. I pictured him being caught and locked up.

Amongst my anxieties, I was also heartened to know he still wanted me for a holiday at his house.

I couldn't tell anyone for fear of the Vaughans getting wind of it. I couldn't even share it with Steve, as I sensed he'd be jealous that I was receiving that attention. The secretiveness of it all weighed heavy on my small shoulders.

Chapter 13

Special Treatment

There seemed to be no escaping them: the web of rules. I tangled myself in them, no matter the penalty. Where there was not total compliance, the Vaughans dreamed up more punitive corrections.

Michael, who'd only arrived a week before, was soon marked out as a bed wetter. I had wet my own bed on several occasions and, as I received little sympathy from the staff, would scurry to deal with the sheets. Michael's mattress, though, had become so drenched the staff had to find a new one.

The morning after one of Michael's accidents, all thirty boys and staff were seated for breakfast in the dining room. Matron got wind that Michael's bed was wet, yet again. As he walked to his table, Matron, at full volume, opened her attack. "Is that the way you repay us, wetting the bed again?"

The room silenced. All eyes fell on Michael. Rooted, his body tightened with fear. He flushed shades of red as he took Matron's arrows. To see Michael's pitiful face was to stare at the full torment of all our helplessness. I had to turn away; it was like witnessing a murder.

With arm outstretched, Matron fired again. "After all we've done for you! Go stand in the passageway! Go on!"

Thankfully, my own bed wetting ceased, though on some mornings - especially when the weather drew cool – I would cling to my warm bed for comfort. Those soft soothing minutes would slip by, and in the wink of an eye, I was late. The prescription for lateness was writing lines or *bed practice* after the evening meal. This required a boy to strip his bed and make it, over and over again, till bed time. *Dressing practice* was another dreamed-up punishment, hours of stripping naked then getting dressed again. At first, dressing practice was carried out on my own, in my dormitory.

On one of those mornings when my bed cocooned me so warmly, I arrived late for breakfast once again. Matron's eyes widened as she looked down at me. Her voice could have pierced granite, "You can do your dressing practice in the passageway from now on!" Everyone looked up from their plates. The passageway was a conduit to the kitchen, the dining room, the sewing room, the sitting rooms and a back door. It was in constant use. Solitary standing detention in the passageway had its shame, but the thought of dressing practice there stapled my breath. My eyes showed no tears but I could taste and smell them.

That evening, Matron kept to her threat. "Stand there, undress, and fold your clothes properly until you learn," she said, and marched away. With my eyes lowered I stood quiet for a moment. Slowly, I pulled my tee-shirt over my head. A familiar self-loathing gushed in, but with a soaring intensity. I folded my shirt neatly, as if folding up my dignity. *I am a misfit that can't follow simple rules.* I placed the shirt on the floor. *I am lazy.*

Unbuckling my belt as slowly as I could, I curled it into a circle and lay it down. I studied my plimsolls like never before. Slipping my finger inside the elastic, I prised them off. My socks slid off easily, and I caught sight of the sewn-in number 6. My feet cooled on the concrete tiles. I looked up and down the passageway, listening acutely for movement.

Down to my underpants I waited till the passageway was clear. I hesitated. I could not go the last step. I pulled my socks back over my feet, my skin warming in their reassuring touch. Slipping my tee-shirt back on I felt its protection.

A sudden draft brought the smell of wood polish up the passageway. Fear swept in. *I must do as I am told, I must do it right, I have to learn.*

My tee-shirt came off again, my plimsolls, socks, and short trousers, all in a pile. *I will try to be obedient, try to please Matron, try to be a good child.* My heart chilled. I took off my underpants and folded them onto my other clothes like a religious offering. I closed my eyes to hide myself, my body heaving with loneliness.

And then I dressed again. Clothes on and off, over and over. When anyone walked past, my eyes hit the floor and I grabbed at my pants to pull them over me. My mouth dried. *I can't get anything right. I am not like the other boys. I have to be constantly told what to do. I have to be punished.*

Stuart, an older boy, came in through the back door. He stopped in front of me. "Who told you to take your clothes off?"

"Matron," I said, in a whimper, scanning his face for support. He looked up the passageway towards the Vaughan's sitting room. He looked at my pile of clothes. Stuart didn't say anything, he just walked on. I was afraid he would speak to Matron and make things worse, and although desperate for an ally, I was glad when he turned left into the big boys' sitting room, not right into the Vaughan's quarters.

The passageway went quiet. A couple of boys walked past, then a grown-up. I continued the dressing practice. *I must be bad. I don't deserve anything. I am dirty. I am a disgrace.*

Images of my school friends flooded in. Heather, Phil, Linda, Anthony . . . I was bonding close with them – had called for them on my way to school that very morning. I desperately wanted to be like them, and I longed for them to like me. *How can I show my face when they know all these things about me?* Someone would surely tell them. Half undressed more humiliation crashed in as I pictured their faces. *They are so special! They are the normal world! They loathe me, they can see how flawed I am. I can't look at them now.*

My face burned hot. *I hate myself for not being good. I hate my mischief. I hate my stupid body for not getting dressed quickly. I hate myself for always being in trouble. I hate myself for being different. I hate my face.*

I was like a tree, felled in anger, and left to rot in the snow. Matron had her way. With the public stripping, shame swallowed me whole.

Chapter 14

Glimpsing the North

In the summer of 1965, it was arranged, by the Yorkshire authorities, that we three boys should visit our mother. An official was sent to collect us. We had no warning till Matron briefed us on the doorstep. "Behave yourselves in the car; you're going to stay with your mother for a little while."

Dave sat in the front and talked with the driver. The three-hour drive to Yorkshire was monotonous and, lying in the back seat, I fell asleep for much of the journey. Eventually the engine strained as the car climbed a steep cobbled slope through rows of identical back-to-back terraces. There were no gardens and no trees and the stone houses had turned black with years of pollution. People were packed together in this poverty area, known as Eightlands, originally built for the influx of Victorian mill workers.

The official dropped us at our mother's door, 17, Back Barber Street. "I'll pick you up in a week," he said.

I could not believe the freedom in what I'd heard! "Are we really staying all week?" I asked Dave.

I relished being away for a week, and also having Dave to hang around with. Dave led us into the house and he was glad to see our mother. She wore a pleated skirt and blouse and looked younger without a headscarf. Her thick head of frizzy dark hair was nearly down to her shoulders. She was living with her partner Stan. The newer children weren't around, so I guessed someone was looking after them for the week. My mother told us the names of the six younger children, but nothing more about them was mentioned.

These terraces didn't have bathrooms; the toilet was allocated in a block at the end of the street. That first evening, Steve and I clambered onto the roofs of the stone toilet blocks. From up there we could see into the area in front of the next row of terraces where children were playing. Some kids looked rough and ready. About eight of them came over to find out who we were. "Where's thou from?" one lad called out in his broad Yorkshire tongue.

"Kidderminster," Steve said.

"Say something then, Kidderminster," he shouted up to us.

Steve, more confident than I was, started talking. "We live in the Midlands. But we come from Dewsbury."

"Where did tha learn to talk posh like that?" one boy said, smiling. I was excited to talk with them but I felt edgy as well. I was going to jump down from the roof but stayed by Steve as one or two of the lads looked unpredictable.

"What's thou doing here?" one girl said to me.

"I've come to stay with my mother for a week. She lives over there," I said pointing, and liking the attention she was giving me.

"I'll come throu't ginnel tomorra and call f'ya," she said.

Steve and I looked at each other. What was a *ginnel*? "A ginnel," our mother said later with a mocking laugh. "It's the alleyway. You'll have to get to know Yorkshire ways."

We slept three to a bed in one of the rooms upstairs, my mother in the other. The floorboards in the bedrooms and stairs were bare. Downstairs, the single room, smelling of cigarettes and coal dust, struggled for daylight from the dismal window that faced the grey cobbled street. A washing line spanned from corner to corner and over the enamel sink. Two fusty and worn armchairs were pushed near the open fire grate of the black cast-iron Yorkshire range built into the wall. Stan was often dozing in one of the chairs when we came down in the morning.

In the row behind our terrace, my mother's brother, Tommy, lived with my great Aunt Emmy. Aunt Emmy had been chair-bound for years. She was a tiny woman, quite overweight, with straw-like hair and a screwed-up wrinkled face. Emmy would sit staring at the fire with her elbow on the chair arm, cheek cupped in her open palm, mulling over that day's gossip. At regular intervals she retrieved a tin from down the side of her armchair. Pinching the snuff powder from the tin between thumb and forefinger, she'd inhale it sharply up each nostril. I thought it comical.

Aunt Emmy showed little interest in me, so I never felt any closeness to her. Uncle Tommy was friendlier. He was a gentle character, tall with dark, straight hair brushed back. My mother told us that he'd left school at twelve-years-old when they labelled him 'backwards'.

When my mother's mother and grandmother died, Tommy moved in with Emmy – who instructed his every move. They were a good match as she needed someone, too, if only to fetch and carry. Tommy spilled his wages to Emmy and she allowed him small amounts, for beer and his favourite Woodbine cigarettes. He led a simple life, working shifts at the Woollen Mill, running errands for neighbours, or doing odd jobs like moving furniture or collecting firewood in an old pram he'd been given.

People seemed to care for Tommy because of his slow nature, though others would use him for cheap labour. I liked my Uncle Tommy and he liked us. In fact, he seemed to worship us. He smiled wide every time we saw him; he made you want to smile back. "Ay-up our Philip, how ya goin on?" he'd say, beaming. There was little conversation after that. "You're a grand lad," he'd maybe add. He'd soon light up another Woodbine, which he kept behind his ear, or he'd ask my mother for one if he was short. His appreciation of us was genuine and at times overwhelming, almost childlike.

A couple of days into our week we three boys and my mother got food poisoning from eating a tin of Spam. We all became violently sick and suffered with diarrhoea. My mother didn't seem to know what to do. Dave and Steve were suffering badly, and as darkness drew in we all worsened, and I became very scared. I sat on the top step of the staircase huddled against the wall and clutching my belly. I wailed continually. My mother lost patience and shouted at me to stop crying, which made me more frightened. A doctor visited in the night, but he seemed irritated and wanted to leave as quickly as he could. After endless trips up the street to the toilet my mother gave us a bucket to take turns on. We argued as we all needed to use it. She also gave us sheets of old newspaper for emergency, to toilet and be sick on. We had to use them and it made the place stink awful.

There wasn't much food in the house but for a loaf of bread, an odd tin of soup and a packet of tea. There was no mention of going to a swimming pool or an outing to a park or a fairground. Money and my mother never kept company for long. She was a hard worker when she worked at the mill or the laundry, but she never had anything to show for it. What little money she earned seemed to evaporate by the middle of the week. We boys had to find our own way of amusing ourselves.

Sadly we didn't see much of Dave that week. Derek, a cousin of ours, called round for him in the mornings and they went off together. Steve and I kicked a tennis ball in the street, or explored the maze of ginnells through the terraces. Some days were scorching hot and the tar on the road melted in places. A local lad showed us how to pull up lumps of it to play with. I liked the spirit smell, but the tar put black stains on our clothes and hands, for which we got scolded.

"Why don't you go up to Dewsbury Park?" my mother said. Steve and I wandered up the hill into the old Victorian park. The green open spaces were a relief from the grey of Eightlands, but walking near the old stone buildings in the park I felt strangely disturbed. My body felt lonely and cold. The stone had blackened, and the damp winters had weathered them, leaving random patches of subtle mossy green. Though I felt alien there, something old was grabbing me. It was as if there were men soaked into the stone, men laden with grief - lots of it.

Seeing there were plenty of places to hide and eager to run off some energy I played hide-and-seek with Steve for a while. It lightened my mind. But walking near the buildings again I became inquisitive, and a part of me felt I should know more about the place my mother had sent us to.

We sauntered back down the hill, wiping sweat from our faces in the lazy afternoon heat. We had picked up the message to stay out for a good while, to give my mother some space. I felt she was struggling with something and the last thing we wanted was to be a cause of irritation for her.

Later that day my mother sent me on an errand. I was glad to do tasks, both to stay occupied and to feel I was helping her. "Get me two tins of baked beans from the shop at the top of the road," she said, slipping the exact money into my hand.

The shopkeeper seemed friendly. "Buy this large tin; it's much better value."

"Thank you," I said, pleased I had done something good and getting some change to boot. Skipping back home, I smiled up at my mother. "The man gave me this tin. It's better value!"

My mother's face turned ugly. "Do what I tell you, not what he tells you!" she screamed. "I sent you for two tins. Get back to that shop!" Her viciousness tore through me. Trembling I spun back out the door.

I returned to the shop. "My mother says I have to have the two tins, please," I said sheepishly. Mumbling under his breath the shopkeeper took back the single tin, and I took two tins home. I desperately wanted to please my mother. *Surely she has to be right?* I was dazed and couldn't figure anything out. *I must have made a mistake.*

If my mother's Stan were home, he'd usually sit in the dark corner of the room, his shirt sleeves rolled up and his cigarette glowing red as he drew on it. Towards the end of the week he tired of us, and we saw his vicious temper. He'd often be sleeping in the chair and we'd be too boisterous. "Cut out that bloody noise!" he shouted.

"You're not in charge of us!" Steve told him.

I was shocked to see Stan lift Steve clean off his feet and pin him to the door. "I'll bloody show you!" he said. My turn came later after a challenge, too. My mother had been pressurising Stan about going out window-cleaning, and he'd shouted at her to leave him alone. I told him he didn't need to shout. He picked me up and hung my head over the washing line that was strung wall-to-wall in the house. "I'll teach you!" he shouted. I stayed clear after that, glad to be away from him.

Most of the time, though, Stan made himself scarce, no doubt hoping the end of our week would come as soon as possible.

My mother's two newest babies came home one day from wherever they'd been staying. "We can take them in the pram if you want us to," Steve said. The heavy, coach-built pram was easy to coast down the steep Eightlands' terrace, but coming back up we struggled, and on a steep section, we stalled.

"Push together and it'll move," said Steve. With all our strength it wouldn't budge.

"Let me help you," a woman offered. She got us moving, but we stalled again a little farther along. We were gone much longer than expected, and I felt anxious. Worry began to rise in my stomach. Moments later I saw my mother running towards us. "You stupid kids!" she screamed. "What are you doing down here?" Her aggression made me tremble again, but at least, this time, I could see a reason.

Despite our mother's behaviour, Steve and I nurtured a picture of her as a marvellous mum. It was far easier to just blame Stan for all our frustrations.

On our last night in Yorkshire, mother had promised us money for the cinema, but when the evening came, she was nowhere to be seen. I asked Stan, "Can we have the money for the cinema?"

"Nowt to do wi me," he said, shaking his head and drawing hard on a cigarette stub.

We had looked forward to the treat of the cinema all week. "We can stand outside and ask people for the money," Steve said. I loved the idea. I'd overheard it said that Yorkshire people were generous. It also seemed a fun and edgy thing to do, and as a take-home story for the boys back at Spennells, we wanted the rumour to be true.

"Excuse me," I asked the first passing woman, "can you give us some money for the cinema?" She looked a little shocked, but gave us a couple of sympathetic pennies. "Can you give us some money to see a film?" I asked a man.

"Don't you know that's begging!" he scowled and walked on.

"It's your turn now," I said to Steve. He tried, but people just walked on. We got strange looks, odd comments and sympathetic words, but no more money. We sauntered back to the house in the fading light, weighed down with embarrassment and rejection.

It was still baking hot on the afternoon the stolid official drove us back to Spennells. The boys were playing wildly in the stream and we grabbed our trunks and ran to join them. "Hey, what did you get up to?" everyone wanted to know.

"We had a great time with our mother in Yorkshire and we went to loads of places on our own!"

"We might be going to live with her soon!" I said, enjoying the wave of importance the trip had given me. My brothers and I basked in that buoyancy for days. Dewsbury was so different from Spennells that it took on a lusty sheen. The trip jumped around our hearts like a wild adventure. Any ailments we felt were projected onto Stan.

"When I grow up I'm going to get a gun and shoot him," Dave said.

"Yeh, we'll help you," Steve and I agreed. I felt light hearing the two of them express my own feeling. It gave hope that my mother could be defended.

One more thing happened during that week in Yorkshire. The three of us were in Dewsbury town centre with my mother. She stopped and touched my shoulder. She pointed to a man across the street walking with a boy in a Sea Cadet uniform. "You see that man over there? That's your father. That boy is his son, Alan," she said, as if pointing out a local landmark.

It was the first time anybody had mentioned I had a father. Nothing in her tone made it anything out of the ordinary. We continued walking but my head swivelled back till the man and boy disappeared under the railway arches towards Bradford Road. I felt a tug in my chest. "What's his name?"

"Janek Wondzinski." my mother said. "He's Polish."

I liked the fact that his name sounded unusual, and I realised that he was from some other country. No more was said. Dave didn't react, as it was not his father. We walked on into town. Janek Wondzinski was a ship passing in the night.

Chapter 15

Carry on Regardless

We can work it out. The Beatles new song played full volume. The bright melody and positive lyrics boosted my spirit, and the music seemed to wash my head clean. While a group of us gardened in front of the hostel, John Bromley had brought a record player to the open window and played the song over and over. We gathered under the window and soon learned it, singing along like a choir.

Church on Sundays never matched that. At the morning services at St Georges in Kidderminster, my spirit would sink. Under orders to attend, the only saving grace was the thundering sound of the organ as we huddled onto the wooden pews. But I fidgeted through the colourless service and prayed to be let back in the fresh air. I'd have sworn Sunday worship was another Vaughan punishment, as I never saw them in church.

Strangely then, the Vaughans expressed profound dismay at the revelation we three brothers hadn't been baptised. A ceremony was hastily arranged at St Georges with one of the house mothers attending as a witness. A day off school was always welcome, and I relished any extra time I could spend with Dave. During the ceremony at the font embarrassment crept all over me. I felt it all done in haste, and that everyone knew that and were putting up a cheerful front. We boys just had to be obedient so the adults could be happy. We then waited for what seemed like ages in the windy entranceway for the vicar to come and hand us a certificate.

I slipped my certificate into my pocket, just as Dave did. I was glad to be told that the three of us were allowed to walk back to Spennells on our own. Knowing everyone else was at school added to the freedom of the walk, and we knew we'd have some free time to play out when we got back.

Dave never passed up a chance to play football, so later we took a ball out to the field. But whatever had just happened at the church gave me that 'change is coming' feeling, like an invisible hand was paving the way for change. Just as we were whisked away to our mother's, we were never told of any plan that concerned us; change just happened.

It was a couple of weeks after the baptism when I ran over to the football field to join the older boys' game that was in full swing. They'd let me join in as I'd become able to hold my own against many of them, and I was soon immersed in the play. But five minutes in, I felt something missing. "Where's Dave?" I said to one of the boys.

"He left last week," he replied.

"What do you mean? Where did he go?"

"He went to Anglesey, to a sea school. Didn't you know?"

I tried to stay in the game but all desire for it drained out of me. Dropping out I looked vacantly at the stark white-painted house. I wandered into the next field and sat on the bridge by the stream, brooding. Some while later I heard the whistle for bed time.

Dave had gone to a sea training school on the Island of Anglesey in North Wales, a place called *Indefatigable.* Mr Brookes, a Barnardo's official, was an ex-navy man. He had fixed it for Dave to finish his school years there. He had seen Dave's eagerness to get away from Spennells and go in the navy. Maybe Dave's leaving prompted the haste for our baptism. Nothing was explained. No fuss or big scenes. As the Vaughans always said, *carry on regardless.*

A surge of renewal swept through the home as our yearly adventure by the sea approached. Every summer, we all bundled into a coach for a fortnight's holiday; most times to the Welsh coast. There was always fierce competition to be the first to shout, "I can see the sea!" A big cheer went up knowing we were close.

Our hotel, as usual, would be a church hall where dozens of wooden folding beds were lined up like railway sleepers. The hall took on an enchanted atmosphere as all the boys occupied the same room and we were allowed to stay up late playing games. With so much activity, and the excitement of another beach visit the next day, sleep eluded us.

The summer holiday of 1966 marked a change in that we stayed in caravans on a park in Morfa Bychan, North Wales. We could hang around with other children on the site and have a little freedom to roam just as they did. A large hill overlooked the park and I was eager to scramble to its top.

My little group made particular friends of Sally and Robert in the next caravan. We'd see them every day and their friendly parents fed us toast and squash. I watched the way Sally and Robert skipped to their mum and dad when their names were called. A sickening feeling rose in me, as if I had a hole in my chest that ached for something; it made my eyes well and my breath stick in my throat. I yearned to be close to Sally and Robert. My last thoughts at night and my first thoughts upon waking were of dashing to their caravan to call for them.

I could hardly believe it when they said, "We're going to climb that hill this week, do you want to come with us?" Each time they mentioned it I quivered with excitement.

"Can we go with them?" we asked the house mothers.

"No, sorry, you can't." Despite that answer, we kept asking. The hill wasn't that far away and we'd be with their parents. I was nine years old and couldn't see any reason for not being able to go. Climbing with our friends and their parents would have been such a joy.

"When are you coming with us?" Sally asked again.

On the day of their hike, we asked one last time. "No, you can't," said our house mother. "We're going for a walk ourselves and you're coming with us. And that's it!" I was livid.

On the group walk I could not get Sally and Robert out of my mind and seethed about the ban from the hill. In rebellious mood I listened as Michael, a fourteen-year-old, talked about how he'd run away on several occasions. He was sounding off about going again, and the chatter picked up pace.

"I'm coming with you," I told Michael.

"So am I," said Steve and then another boy declared he'd join us.

Early that evening, the four of us slipped out of the caravan park. Under Michael's instruction, we had grabbed jumpers, pocket money, and a few biscuits. We galloped away down a lane and set off for Porthmadog. There was an exquisite energy in our break for freedom, and from picturing the stony faces of the staff when they realised we'd gone. "We need to avoid the roads," Michael said, enjoying his leadership role.

We eased up to a fast walk, still panting from our burst of legwork. The path skirted around the hill high above the caravans. We looked down and smiled. "There's our caravan," Steve said, and we all waved at it in defiance.

Our adventure fused us together, and a stream of companionship rushed through me. The fresh coastal air and the scent of evening grass made my chest expand. I felt immortal. The yellow light of the late sun spread over our path and out over the hills, and the sea's horizon in the distance beckoned.

The shadows from the stone walls lengthened as the sun dipped. We were almost in darkness when we got to the town. The temperature dropped, too, and we pulled our jumpers over our heads. "I'm still cold," Steve said, after we'd walked around a little.

"So am I." In my short trousers, the chill nipped at my legs. "Let's go and sit in that café," I said, relishing warmth and light.

"Don't be stupid," Michael said. "We'll be seen. We need to stay where it's dark. Let's find the railway station," he said, trying to keep our spirits up. We had no money for train tickets, but it gave us a boost to go off and look for it. After locating the station, we wandered by the harbour. The sound of the halyards clicking on the masts of the empty yachts echoed in the night air. It was dawning on us that we didn't have a plan. For myself I had considered no further ahead than the hill path and a vague image of some new life where someone would be helpful to us.

"I'm hungry. Please let's go to that café."

"Come with me. I'll get you something." Michael wasn't joking.

A sweet shop stood just back from the harbour. Michael picked up a large stone, wrapped his jumper over it to muffle the sound, and flung it through a glass window panel. Releasing a window catch like an expert, he climbed in and grabbed handfuls of sweets. "Do you want more?" he whispered from inside the shop.

"Some chocolate," I said – uneasy, but caught in the thrill and danger of it.

"Hold the window," Michael ordered, and climbed out. We stuffed our pockets full of goodies and ran, sticking close to Michael. He wanted to get clear quickly, but he also needed to stop for a pee. We settled a while, sitting propped up behind a wall eating the chocolate. Then it got really cold, and the darkness weighed heavier. We three young ones became more edgy and Michael was having a hard time keeping us calm. Creeping fear and cold was denting our ambitions.

A couple of hours later huddling in a bus shelter, we were still talking about what to do when a police car drove past. The car reversed. The window slid down. "What you up to, lads?" We mumbled some incoherent replies.

We had been reported missing. "Okay," said the officer. "Jump in the back." Minutes later, we once-brazen boys were speeding back to the caravan park. There was huge relief from the house mothers. Amazingly there was little punishment – just a mild telling off and instruction to get into bed. Thank goodness, the Vaughans were back at Spennells.

Michael was annoyed, though, that we hadn't backed him. Being the eldest, the house mothers blamed him almost entirely, and he took the punishment for all of us. Now I was embarrassed that we'd got so scared. Michael wasn't to blame; we all wanted to run. How we all wanted to be free of the expressionless face of Spennells.

Later that year, Michael and Steve received more of the Vaughan's creative punishments. The two of them made another run for it. Charlie Vaughan chased after them in the car and caught them on the road into Kidderminster. He persuaded Steve to get in the car, but Michael wouldn't hear of it. Michael had no intention of coming back.

Returning to school after the summer break our new teacher captured our attention with the news of Francis Chichester and his solo circumnavigation in his yacht Gypsy Moth IV. Over the next months the teacher pinned up newspaper cuttings of his voyage, and we marked his progress on a world map.

Our headmistress had insisted we had daily writing practice by tracing over large letters of the alphabet laid out in a book. The hours of practice bored me senseless. The adventurer in me kept looking up and thirsting on those photos of Gypsy Moth IV beating through the waves, and one of Francis bent over the chart table in his famous gimbaled chair.

Changes kept coming that year. Not only was a brand new building being constructed for Spennells home, but girls started to arrive. Three sisters joined us: the Drummond girls of West Indian origin. Their arrival somehow ushered in a gentler atmosphere. I certainly didn't do more dressing practices in the passageway again. There was also an absence of boys being punished with whacks on the head or standing detentions, as Mr Vaughan became less visible.

It must have been so hard for those girls to land at Spennells; the eldest girl in particular looked completely lost. She hardly spoke, and many times I saw her standing alone, nervously picking at her fingers by the back door of the house.

There had been plans to demolish Spennells house and hostel for years because of its high maintenance costs, and its high land value if sold for development. Back in 1964, work had started on a new building in the top field. Although the area was declared *out of bounds,* we occasionally had sneaked over there and played in the piles of building sand. The new building was designed in the shape of a cross, which gave it four wings. The ultra-modern design was made up of white painted concrete and lots of glass. In late 1966, the new Spennells was finished. On a chilly December day we all moved in.

The change was radical. The top hostel group was now like a separate home with its own kitchen and dining room on the upper floor of one of the wings. Gone was the numbering of children, the system of whistles and communal dining. In place of the cold linoleum floor in the hostel dormitory, our bedrooms now had comforting carpet. It felt gentle and forgiving to my bare feet; its new broadloom smell mixed with that of the fresh paint. Large windows looked onto treetops and flooded the rooms with light. The warmth and newness felt so unreal; so soft and so homely that I couldn't settle. I was waiting to be told, *this is not for you.*

Another feeling also overcame me; a jittery sensation in my belly told me something was afoot. Things went unnaturally quiet. I stayed occupied by reading or carefully rearranging a few belongings in my cupboard space. Two days after the move into the new building, I got the news from Miss Gillian. *"You're leaving this morning, Philip."*

My face creased. I tried to speak, but my questions stuck. I turned away from Miss Gillian and the twisted silence between us. I was being discarded. That's all I could feel, as if it were another punishment. My world drew away, opening a void between me and everything I was familiar with: the other boys, the fields and stream, my school life, Miss Gillian. Despite my treatment at Spennells, it was the life I knew and I wanted to clutch hold of it. I had yearned for change, but I was scared of what was coming. The only consolation lay in knowing that – whatever was coming – Steve and I were facing it together.

"Where are we going?" I asked him.

"To Yorkshire, near our mother." My emotions were swinging. *Was this good or bad?* I craved normality, but I had no idea where that might be. I gathered the things from my cupboard: a few clothes, some school pens and pencils, and some games. My prized possession, The Beatles' *Rubber Soul* album, I tucked between the soft shirts in my bag.

There were no goodbyes. No show of affection. No, "I will miss you, Phil." It was a clinical break, and I felt an insignificant child passing through a boarding house. Maybe Miss Gillian was putting up her defences. She had looked after Steve and me during four eventful years, through birthdays, Christmases, and Easter Sundays. We had shared holidays, day trips, and walks in the country. How many times had we top hostel boys sat in Miss Gillian's bedroom in our dressing gowns – playing games, looking at her photographs, listening to her favourite records by The Seekers and the Irish singer, Val Doonican. But in what seemed like seconds, Spennells was a vanishing picture from the rear windscreen of Mr Vaughan's car.

Mr Vaughan's nineteen-year-old son, Owen, sat next to him in the front seat of the Vauxhall. Owen was going back to his Air Force base after taking leave. The two of them chatted on the journey, talking in clipped sentences about his life in the Air Force. In the back seat, Steve and I stayed silent, gazing at the passing scenery and waiting instruction. Cold air rushed in as Mr Vaughan lowered his window to tip the ash from his cigarette.

I was used to feeling small around Mr Vaughan, but that day leaving Spennells in his car, I touched a new level of insignificance. Mr Vaughan's indifference filled the air with toxin more corrosive than his tobacco smoke. Steve and I were just another two boys being swept out like cigarette butts.

The car pulled up to the railway station and we tumbled out. "Go with Owen and do as you're told," Vaughan said, climbing back into the car. We followed Owen dutifully onto the platform.

Many years on, more than a glint of irony swept through me as I saw my Barnardo's 'leaving report'. The Vaughans had written a comment: *He seems to be becoming a bully.*

PART II

Chapter 16

Ash Tree

My mood switched to excitement when I saw the yellow-fronted engine snake its way towards us for my first train journey. "Look, there's the driver!" I said to Steve. The heavy wheels clicked and clunked and, with a metal grinding sound, the engine came to a stop. The smell of oil and warm diesel fumes added to the feeling of a brand new adventure.

Owen boarded with us and we travelled together to Birmingham New Street railway station. Joining the bustle of that huge central station I suddenly felt important. "Look at that, you lads! A steam locomotive still in service," Owen said. I studied the weighty beast, leaking steam from its undersides as if it couldn't wait to release its pent-up power. I felt dwarfed by it.

"Come on!" Owen shouted. We followed him to the platform for the Leeds train where he found the uniformed train guard. He handed us over. "Get off at Leeds. Mrs Greenwood will meet you there." Owen repeated the instruction, and waited for our nodding heads.

The guard took us to the carriage at the back of the train just forward of the guard van, so he could keep an eye on us. "Would you like a mug of tea?"

"Yes, please," we replied, liking the attention. The gentle old chap reappeared with tea in two mugs the size of plant pots. I could tell by the way he handled our small bags in the rack above the seats that he wanted to look out for us. "I'll get those down for you when we get to Leeds."

In 1966, carriages were closed compartments, with the gangway running along one side. We had the carriage to ourselves, so we perched on the worn, musty smelling seats near the window. Gazing out in wonder, the large window made it feel like we were watching a movie. The guard put his head in the door occasionally as he passed. "Everything okay, boys?"

The landscape slowly changed from the green and brown patchwork farmland of the Midlands countryside to the smoky, grey buildings of the North. We sited the strange, giant, concrete cooling towers with steam belching from their insides. I was mystified. "I wonder what they're for," I said.

"They burn dead bodies in there," said my brother.

"Really?" I marvelled. Steve's fourteen months on me seemed a massive gap. He seemed to know everything I wanted to know. But I was anxious being alone with him. He was old enough to dominate me, but not old enough to be any comfort like Dave had been.

I felt safer when some grown-ups came into the carriage. The lack of conversation allowed me to sink back in the seat. My mind filled with the flighty impression I had entertained at Spennells – that I would adventurously run away, and eventually tell my story to a wise and kind person like the man who helped Oliver Twist. Now I was actually on the move maybe I was one step nearer to finding my own rescuer.

Steve and I had a sense we were nearing the end of our journey when the train pulled into a station. We thought this may be our stop, but there was no sign of the guard so we asked another passenger if this were Leeds. "Yes," she said. "It's part of Leeds." The train was about to pull away when Steve and I looked at each other. Was that a yes? Neither of us wanted to get in trouble for missing our stop, so we grabbed our things and jumped off.

The train went on its way, and the few people who got off with us went on their way. The platform fell quiet. We looked up and down the station looking for a solitary woman, the Mrs Greenwood who was to meet us. "Maybe she hasn't got here, yet," Steve said. I half believed him, but it was obvious he didn't know what to do any more than I did. A familiar 'in trouble' feeling washed over me.

Steve and I amused ourselves by walking on the benches and running up the platform, hoping someone would turn up and claim us. "We should have stayed on!" Steve said.

"It was your idea to get off. Don't blame me." With that Steve ran over the bridge to the other platform; I scurried after him.

We waited for what seemed like hours, each minute increasing our worry. Eventually a station master appeared. "Are you Steven and Philip?" he said in a gruff Northern accent. "I've to put you on the next train to Leeds."

Mrs Greenwood had rung through to Normanton, a smaller station just before Leeds, to see if we were there. Relieved I was glad to be shepherded onto the next train.

Mrs Greenwood stood on the platform looking like a tetchy headmistress. In matching hat and coat, her hands gripped a small bag in front of her thin body. "Hello, boys," she said, trying to hide a look of panic. "I thought I'd lost you."

Darkness closed in as we put our bags in her car. Steve and I peered out of the car windows wondering what our new house might look like. There were lots of tightly packed houses, brightly lit shop windows, and the streets were flooded with light. "We share the same birthday, you and I, Philip. August 22nd," Mrs Greenwood said. "All the best people are born in August," she joked. It was something she'd point out on numerous occasions. It gave her something to say.

Half an hour later we arrived at Ash Tree House children's home in the Saville Town area of Dewsbury. The dark stone building stood proud in its own garden surrounded by a stone wall. It was one of several detached houses on one side of Orchard Street; on the opposite side stretched a long row of terraced houses.

Aunt Yvonne, the head of the home, met us at the door. She was a fresh-faced, rotund figure standing in a full, bosomy dress pinched at the waist. "Better late than never," she smiled. Her assistant, Aunty Gaynor, was thin, with long hair and an air of timidity that, we came to find, was not difficult to exploit.

Arriving twelve days before Christmas, I was comforted to find the house colourfully decorated with tree and trimmings. Inside it was noticeably warm. We followed Aunt Yvonne upstairs. "This is the boys' bedroom," she said. I looked at the six beds. "You take that bed Philip, and Steven, that one next to it. Come down to the lounge when you are ready." I'd rather she had put me at the far side of the room, to avoid any clashes with Steve.

In the small lounge, a gas fire blazed where the other ten boys and girls were watching *Daktari* on television. I knelt on a rug by one of the two arm chairs kept for the aunties. Aunty Gaynor was knitting and smiling with the children.

Both aunties allowed the children to huddle close to them, and they did not expect the children to stay quiet. I sat silent though, unsure of how to behave in my new homely surroundings where youngsters mixed with the older children. An older girl wearing make-up and fashionably styled, jet black hair walked in. "Pat," Aunt Yvonne said, "these are our new boys, Steven and Philip."

"We don't want them!" Pat teased. Everyone laughed. I laughed too, but Pat scared me. How could children speak so self-assuredly in front of adults? I was not used to girls, especially one with a voice. Pat really doesn't like me, I thought.

Despite Pat's comment I gradually warmed to the milder Yorkshire accents and, in turn, the other kids seemed to like our posh Midland way of talking. Not that I said very much over the next few hours. At bedtime, we younger ones gathered in the kitchen in our dressing gowns to collect hot water bottles and drink mugs of hot chocolate. I felt I didn't deserve this cosiness. It seemed unreal, like I'd landed in a strange land.

Stuart Tranter, the eldest boy, was the first of the kids I got to know. Stuart had become an apprentice painter and decorator and would move out soon. Stuart was more distant than the others, likely because of his age, but also – I would come to realise in later years – in the way that some men have less emotional ease.

The reality was I felt safe and was drawn to Stuart, as he wasn't aggressive. One evening he left a packet of cigarettes near his bed. For a joke, I hid them under his pillow. He saw me smiling and soon found them. Secure in his friendliness and thinking this a jolly game, I hid even more of Stuart's belongings. "Will you tell him to leave my things alone?" he complained to Aunt Yvonne. I'd pushed too far and I felt bad for upsetting him. The last thing I wanted was to lose his friendship.

Harry Jacques, stocky and more vibrant, was the other older boy and in his last year at school. I took over Harry's task of lugging up the coal from the cellar to feed the Aga cooker. "Don't use the shovel like Aunt Yvonne tells you," Harry said. "It will take ages, here's the easy way." He rammed the scuttle along the floor into the coal pile. It gave a satisfying crunching sound and the scuttle was filled in no time. I liked Harry instantly from that moment.

Violet Crawshaw was my age. With long blonde hair and a pretty face I had a crush on her straight away; so did Steve, and we soon learned, so did most boys in the neighbourhood. Violet was regularly caught stealing make-up from the local chemist shop. She was mature for her age – and wild, which made her even more attractive. After bedtime, we younger boys and girls would call to one other across the landing. Violet would lead the other girls acting out a fake striptease just outside their bedroom.

Violet was vibrant and fun to be around, but her confidence swelled into a bullying of the other girls. In Violet's company, a new and painful shyness had me running scared of her. At the same time, I was envious of local lad Andy Dawson, whose mother owned the confectionery shop two streets away. He often called round to play football with us in the garden. Andy had a natural ease with Violet, and I'd see him kiss her for ages before he finally went home. The jealousy that surged through me could have powered a steam-roller. On top of that he had his own mum - and a mum who owned a sweet shop!

Andy's mother had sent packs of liquorice allsorts for us all at Christmas. Christmas day was more casual, with kids playing their own games rather than the organised kind of fun we had enjoyed at Spennells. Kids found their own space and did things more in their own time.

The smaller home forced Steven and me to spend more time together. As the weeks went on, we began to clash over almost everything. I was beginning to miss the open fields of Spennells where we could go our own ways. I missed the stream, the field with the swings, separate friends, and the endless football games.

One afternoon, I was in the dining room setting up cutlery for the evening meal. Steven was in the children's sitting room with all the other kids. I overheard him talking about his new friend at school. "You should see Greg fight! He showed me how to grab someone by the head and knee them in the face." I heard Harry Jacques laugh. Something told me I had that coming the next time Steve and I argued.

It came sooner than I thought. After setting the table, I went into the sitting room where Steve had blatantly opened my cupboard and taken my favourite board game. He knew I'd try to claim it back. "That's mine!" I said, grabbing the game. The inevitable battle broke out and I found myself in a headlock, Steve's knee banging into my face while he mocked my hopeless defence. Violet Crawshaw laughed in excitement. As I lifted my head, I saw her sickening, gleeful look, as if she were cheer-leading the whole thing.

"Your mother's coming to take you out this Saturday. You need to be ready at ten," Aunt Yvonne told Steve and me some weeks later. Eager to see our mother we were both ready and waiting.

From the children's sitting room we heard the doorbell. Aunt Yvonne opened the door and my mother's voice filled the hall. "Oh, it's windy walking up that hill," she said, retying the knot on her head scarf. "I've been working part time down at the bus station café," she continued loudly, hardly letting Aunt Yvonne speak.

In our best clothes, we joined our mother by the front door. She kept her hands buried in her coat pockets and hardly looked at us. "I'll bring them back for five, then," she sang, ending the flow of words to Aunt Yvonne as she stepped away from the front door with us in tow. "I might take them to the pictures next time," she called over her shoulder.

The walk down the hill into Dewsbury town centre was quieter. My mother kept her head bowed, her face pinched with impatience. "We'll get the bus to Emmy's," she said.

Twenty minutes later, after a bus ride, we were climbing a

steep hill of terraced houses in Batley. Emmy and my Uncle Tommy had moved there. Aunt Emmy was cooking up a rabbit in a large black pot on the Yorkshire range. The dark room smelled of poverty: a mixture of old and damp fusty clothing, Tommy's Woodbine cigarette smoke, burning coal and boiled rabbit.

Tommy smiled as soon as he saw us. "How yer goin on, our Steven and Philip?" he said. We smiled back and replied with something friendly. Tommy looked at us and smiled some more. "Fine lads," he said. Whenever we saw Tommy after that, it was the same routine, the same words. The welcome, from his depths, came right through his eyes. Seldom has someone been so pleased to see me that used so few words.

Tommy was always pleased to see my mother. I could see how protective of him she was, giving cigarettes and a little beer money. Tommy was happiest keeping himself useful running errands. He loved to please people, especially Emmy.

"Now, do you know what to get?" Emmy was saying impatiently to him.

"Bread, bacon . . . um, eggs," Tommy said, struggling and looking at a list she'd given him. Little did I realise he couldn't read or write. The list was to show the shopkeeper if he got stuck. But Tommy still had his pride, and he'd stand gazing towards the window drawing on a cigarette, studying out his coming tasks like a battle plan. Finally setting out on his errand, he'd turn for a last smiling look at Steve and me. "You Tatie Ash." (Tatie rhyming with Katy) It was a local endearing phrase Tommy always used.

Aunt Emmy's son, Laurie, called in. He was a small, thick-set man of few words, and only stayed briefly. When he left, Emmy recounted how Laurie had beaten up the rent man for asking about arrears. "Don't you dare come round here and ask my mother for money," Emmy said, repeating Laurie's words, and laughing. I couldn't understand why she thought it funny.

Hour by hour, the thrill of being with my mother began to wear off. When she talked with Emmy, her voice boomed; her conversation full of aggressive squabbles with the neighbours. And she was scathing about the children's authority and "that bloody Mrs Greenwood." She mimicked Mrs Greenwood's upper-class voice, telling us the story of how Mrs Greenwood visited to tell her that Dave had run away from Spennells years ago. "David's absconded," she said mockingly.

After listening to my mother's stories for what seemed like ages we were glad to be on the move again.

We took another bus to see my mother's elder sister, Eileen. It was the one and only time I met her, and it was a short visit. Aunty Eileen didn't come near Steve and me, and as we left the house, my mother was in a foul mood. It appeared my mother and Eileen didn't see much of each other. My mother recounted, years after, how Eileen had once visited her in the mental institution. "They'd locked the door behind her; she got frightened by that and never visited again."

My mother's unpredictability scared me and the shock of poverty and constant talk of family troubles seeped into my bones. There was no mention of our many younger siblings; I think some were in other local homes. I was glad when the day ended and we went back to Ash Tree House. I could tell Steve felt the same way, but we never talked things over together. In the absence of any discussion we were distancing ourselves from our family, though we did not realise it. It left me confused and sad. In my musings I'd felt that things would be better now we were living near our mother.

Speaking of our return to Dewsbury many years on, my mother said, "You lads talked different, like strangers, and I didn't even know if you took sugar in your tea."

Chapter 17

Anchors and Storms

Dave had completed his sea training on Anglesey and had joined a ship. He would visit Ash Tree House briefly on leave. I loved it when Dave was home; my heart grew bigger when he was around. He was awash with stories of travelling and friendships, and he spun them out with gusto. "Copacabana Beach in Rio de Janeiro, the most famous beach in the world, it's amazing, pretty girls everywhere and teenagers playing football all day."

Dave had already been to interesting places like Texas, Venezuela and Brazil. My ten-year-old imagination leaped into wherever he'd been. Dave was yet to turn seventeen, but I felt my brother was a grown-up as he didn't seem to fear authority. As well, Dave had his own money and he would buy Steve and me extra sweets or, our favourite drink, Dandelion and Burdock, from the shop at the end of Orchard Street.

"I'm going to take you two into town for a special meal," Dave announced during one of his visits. He had arranged with Aunt Yvonne for us to miss the evening meal. On the twenty minute walk into town, Dave revelled in his resourcefulness. "When we were in Galveston, Texas, we had an enormous great steaks, my mate couldn't eat it all. And it was so cheap." With every description Dave uttered I walked taller, and by the time we walked into the Royal York restaurant I felt like a king.

Surveying the expanse of smartly dressed tables, the town

centre restaurant looked grand. It was still early and no one else had arrived. From behind the kitchen door, I could hear the muffled sound of pans and plates. A waiter appeared in white shirt, waistcoat and tie and pulled out our chairs. "I'll leave you for a minute to choose," he said, placing a jug of water and some menus before us. The white linen tablecloth smelled fresh as I scanned the menu. "What can we have?" I whispered, leaning into my big brother.

"Anything you like," Dave said.

"What are you having?" I asked, clueless. And then I spotted something I recognised. I looked around to see if the waiter were near. He was arranging other tables and well out of earshot. "What about beans on toast?"

With our mutual taste for plain food, we settled on beans on toast for three! Our plates overflowed with three slices of toast and a large piping-hot helping of beans. We tucked in with joy!

Choosing a meal in a proper restaurant for the first time was a leap into a big world for me. With Dave in the lead, our hearts swelled with hope. It was our first venture together, and one of the few times the three of us were alone with a degree of harmony. In those moments we were free from life's weight.

Over forty years on, I can feel the harmony, but also an undertow of sadness for the three orphan boys huddled together surrounded by empty tables. But that day my brother gave us something rare and precious – a simple treat, a beautiful one, and I loved it.

Dave was more than a year older than Harry Jacques, and Aunt Yvonne could see Harry's admiration for him. She was wary of Harry being led astray. Many times they bought bottles of Pale Ale or cider from the corner shop to take back to the house and drink together. Aunt Yvonne wasn't keen but she allowed it.

"Don't you be going into any pubs, Harry," Aunt Yvonne warned, as the two young men set off one evening. She must have known what was coming, because about a mile away they sneaked into the Anchor Pub. Harry was new to drinking and tried to keep up with Dave. Two hours later, Dave needed a plan to keep a drunken Harry away from Aunt Yvonne. "Walk in quietly through the back door," Dave told him. "Shout goodnight into the living room, then go straight upstairs to bed. They won't notice anything."

"Okay, Dave," Harry slurred.

Back at Ash Tree House, Harry flung the living room door open, strode in, and announced, "I'm blind drunk and I don't give a damn!"

Dave was blamed for the whole thing and wasn't popular with Aunt Yvonne after that. Harry loved the brush with wildness that Dave provided, but the two spinsters at Ash Tree struggled to accept the attraction.

Harry loved the middle-of-the-road singer Harry Secombe. "He doesn't need a microphone he has such a powerful voice." But Harry soon dropped that idol when Dave played Beatle records.

As soon as The Beatles *Sergeant Pepper's Lonely Hearts* album was released, Dave bought it. We played it endlessly on the small, portable record player in the corner of the children's lounge. We all sat round trying to identify the characters on the cover. Harry was right at the centre of our group.

For a short while, Dave dated Harry's sister Pamela. She was besotted, as Dave was worldlier than the local lads, especially when he walked around in the brightest flowered trousers that were available at the time. I often saw Pamela crying over Dave, though I couldn't make out if they were tears of affection, or tears of desperation. Likely, it was both.

I never knew the situation with Harry and Pamela's parents. I don't ever recall any of the kids talking about their parents, although I felt a kinship from knowing their stories were similar to mine. Decades later that feeling of kinship swept through me when I heard the awful news that Harry's life had been cut short. Memories rushed back . . . the times he'd taken us to Tom's barber shop for a trendy *square neck* haircut; the times he'd played with us in the half-demolished houses down the street, showing us how easily the pieces of old linoleum could be set on fire.

Harry was a gentle soul, fun to be with, and much-liked. His death made me think of the many popular characters I have encountered that harbour so much self-doubt underneath a cheerful facade. I also heard that Stuart Tranter took his life after a relationship ended; another fatherless child falling into a gaping hole.

Dave had discovered his boxing talent at sea training school and often recounted stories of his fights. I listened more in support than interest as I was only inspired by his travelling stories. One of Dave's sea school teachers was an ex-navy title holder and had coached Dave to school champion. Eager to show us two younger brothers how to spar, Dave found two sets of boxing gloves and marked out a ring in the garden. "Come on," he said to Steve and me. "Let's see what you can do. Show me some moves." I agreed just to please him, trusting he'd not see me hurt. "Have one round sparring together and I'll watch," he said.

Steve was delighted when Dave didn't pull us apart while he let loose punches. With each punch came the same mocking laughs. I could not believe Dave left me unprotected. I became despondent and lost trust in him. Dave went back to sea again, and I felt even lonelier as my enchantment for him fell away.

I was much happier playing football. I played for my new junior school, a short walk through the *ginnels* between the terraces across the road. Many Asian families had moved into the area during the migrations of the 1960s, and their children attended the Saville Town Junior School as well. I befriended two Indian boys, and remember their placid and friendly nature. They were slight in build and loved cricket, always having a bat between them. We played endlessly, with stumps marked in white chalk on the stone school wall. Ajay and Deepak must have felt themselves outsiders in England. Moving back to Yorkshire had accentuated my own painful feelings of separateness. I felt at home with these Indian boys, and found it easy to join with them. Mr Ely, our schoolmaster, took good care of them, as well as taking good care of me.

I could tell Mr Ely loved being a teacher, and he liked nothing better than to get us talking about everyday topics. One day he held up the front page of the daily newspaper. It showed a large power boat skimming across a lake. "This is Donald Campbell attempting the world water speed record on Lake Coniston in the Lake District. Yesterday, January 4th 1967, is a sad day because, tragically, he died, but I want you to know about it," he said.

During a 300mph speed run Campbell's boat, *Bluebird K7*, flipped over backwards. He was killed instantly in front of crowds of people and the world's press and television.

The world had been fascinated by speed, with barriers for flight, over ground, and on water being continually broken. Something in the story about Donald Campbell moved me. It was the first time I became aware of someone dedicating their life to something unachieved, and pursuing it with a passion. The story expanded me; it lifted my mind above the smallness of everyday life. I couldn't help but admire Donald. I didn't feel the urge to cry at his death – it was all too abstract – but he embodied the saying, *better to live one day as a lion, than a thousand years as a sheep.*

Donald's Campbell's father was Sir Malcolm Campbell, the celebrated speed champion and holder of thirteen world records in cars and boats. Having such a powerful father can be a blessing and give a son direction, but can also burden him. Donald attended the same public school as his father and named his cars and boats *Bluebird*, the same as his father's. But his father had been a distant man and the heyday for those speed records belonged to the 1920s and 1930s, Donald's father's era. The world had turned its attention to space travel and the more complex challenges of human rights. It meant Donald had to struggle much harder to gain sponsorship for his own adventures in speed.

There is a fragile and haunting feeling watching the last movie reel of Donald rocketing across that lake with water clouds in his wake. Seconds after the crash, the boat and driver sank, leaving only debris on the water's surface.

Mr Ely asked us to write about Donald Campbell. He spurred us with sentiments like, *man and machine, carrying the nation's dreams, going faster and faster.* Although I admired Donald Campbell's desire for thrilling adventure, it left me in a reflective mood. Even at ten years old, I knew that impulse to seek new levels of life, and to prove oneself. I tried to put the fullness of my thoughts into words. I didn't think of it as just an accident; I felt something had gone horribly wrong with him, like it had with me. Moving my pen across the page I only managed to write the facts I could get from the newspapers; mainly, that he wanted to keep the speed record safe in British hands.

Mr Ely kept trying his best to make lessons interesting but something made him keep his distance and I could have used more personal help. Approaching eleven, I sat the *Eleven Plus* junior school end-of-year exams. I did well, but didn't make the grammar school and was disappointed that others had fared better. I was graded for technical school, a level down from grammar, and was pleased to find a couple of friends, Martin and Mario, were going there as well. "It's an achievement to get into the Dewsbury Technical School," Mr Ely said to me sincerely.

I was more preoccupied with my trousers though, as all my school friends were changing from our boyish shorts to adult trousers.

"Please, can I have some long trousers for upper school?" I begged Aunt Yvonne.

"No," she said. "Harry had to wear short trousers until he was fifteen." I began the year in short trousers and endured the laughs and jibes from the other kids. The 1960s was a time of fast-changing attitudes, and Aunt Yvonne hadn't quite caught up.

Ash Tree House was barely two miles from where our mother lived, about a half-hour walk. She likely thought we could find her if we wanted, as she didn't come to see us again on an official visit. In the following months, however, there were two unarranged visits that showed her despairing condition.

Early one morning Steve and I walked down the driveway together. Our mother was waiting just outside the gate. Pleased to see her, we both smiled, but she burst into a fiery rage! "Don't you laugh at me. I'm your mother. You don't laugh at me!"

I couldn't understand what was wrong and I wanted to explain. But hate stormed from my mother's eyes. As I tried to speak, she shut me down. "Don't answer me back, you little bastard. I'm your mother; I don't care what they teach you in there!" Her face looked ugly. She looked ready to kill. "You listen to your mother, not them in there!"

I was terrified, scared to speak and scared to move away. We set off down the hill towards town, Steve and I pacing alongside my mother receiving more lashes from her tongue while feeling embarrassed that someone might hear.

"I'm your mother!" she shouted. "I'm your mother! – I'm your bloody mother!"

At a road junction just before town, we parted company. Shell-shocked Steve and I walked on. My mother walked off into the uncaring Dewsbury morning, a little less burdened.

Annie's mood swings were extreme. Years later, I found out my mother had been diagnosed with Manic Depression, or Bi-Polar Disorder, and had been *sectioned* on many occasions. She had been taken to the mental institution, Storthes Hall. Unable to cope with her hopeless situation, some incident would tip our mother over the edge. A violent and hyperactive episode would follow the mental collapse, with all her hurt and loss gushing in like a tidal wave.

I was told how she bundled her younger children in the pram while she let off steam in Dewsbury town centre. She would break windows and then try to avoid the police and social workers who would be looking for her to take the children to safety.

It was during one such episode that my mother came again to Ash Tree House. Aunt Yvonne recounted the scene in a letter to me in my adult years. "You little Polish bastard!" my mother screamed at me. Aunt Yvonne and Aunty Gaynor tried to shield me, but felt a huge damage had been done. Amazingly, I have little recollection of this second incident.

At Hallow Park my mother had given me a red cricket ball. It was a little piece of her fire that I had played with. Now she was hurling a thousand fiery red cricket balls – at me, and anyone in her path. If she could have articulated why, I imagine my mother's words.

I'm angry with my own helplessness.
I'm angry with the Dewsbury Authorities for stealing my

children.
I'm angry with myself for giving them up.
I'm angry with the children's home for keeping them.
I'm angry with my children for building a life without me.
I'm angry with men for being violent.
I'm angry with your father for abandoning me.
I'm angry with myself for trusting him.
I'm angry at the world for letting me down.
I'm angry at my mother and grandmother for dying so suddenly.
I'm angry with my father for being so cold and resentful.
I'm angry with my family for their lack of understanding.
I'm angry with everything being so bloody unfair and not allowing me the basic right of being a mother to my own children.

Although these words did not come out of her, they were a part of my mother's daily life and I felt them in her presence. I heard them in her voice, saw them in her face, and in the following years read them in her letters. Her silences were dark and bewildering; hurt and despair choked her. The sweet little girl that had loved tap dancing and writing was exiled long ago.

My mother was a descendant of too many unresolved wars. She was a fighter but it would be difficult to find her wins. There was no trace of a homely mother left, no softness to rest in. She was my mother, but a stranger looked out from her eyes. She could not erase the fact that all of her ten children had spent most of their childhood in children's homes.

One thing she would say, in later years, cut through all the turbulence of her life. "All I ever wanted was a cottage at the edge of town so I could raise my children all together, in peace."

Chapter 18

Feeding the Longing

Several months after arriving at Ash Tree House, Steve and I were running back from the local playing fields, coats over our heads to keep off the heavy spring rain. Turning into the drive, I glimpsed a van parked opposite. Inside we hung up our coats. "Steve, that looked just like Mr Thomas's van across the road." I ran out to take another look and my brother followed. Mr Thomas was walking up the drive. His smile was filled with tenderness and longing.

"I just saw you run past," he said, overwhelmed. My face opened like a daffodil in the morning sun. The three of us stood on the drive, memories of Spennells years flooding in, hardly minding the soaking from the rain. Mr Thomas put a hand on my shoulder, as if anchoring himself.

Mr Thomas introduced himself to Aunt Yvonne and she welcomed him inside. I heard them discussing the restriction Dewsbury authorities had put on his contact with us; his yearly allowance was one visit plus two letters. Seeing Mr Thomas's caring nature and my reaction, Aunt Yvonne said she was happy to relax the ruling. That very day, she allowed us to go with Mr Thomas for a few hours' drive in the camper van. Mrs Thomas had come along with him, together with Julie, a young girl they'd fostered. When Mr Thomas left, he made a private arrangement with Aunt Yvonne to come and see us again.

His limited holiday time, plus the three hours' drive time from

Wales to Dewsbury, kept our visits at least six months apart, but we began writing regularly back and forth. Our birthdays were due soon, and Mr Thomas promised to buy Steve and me a bike on his next visit.

It was a sacred day when Mr Thomas arrived, on his own, and took us both to Bill Hargreaves' bike shop on Bradford Road. The shop owner was a real enthusiast. "You need to try lots of bikes," he said. Steve and I grinned with delight as we mounted one trusty steed after another. "Now put both feet on the ground and let me look," Mr Hargreaves said, in a fatherly way. I felt reassured to have him guide us patiently. We settled on two shining, drop-handlebar racing bikes. My bike was deep blue with light-blue mud guards. Mr Thomas paid extra for saddlebags and water bottles. I gleamed at the bike; it was the best birthday present I ever had.

Back at Ash Tree House, Steve and I posed for photographs with our bikes on the front lawn. After the picture-taking, I walked alone with Mr Thomas for a few minutes. On his previous visit he had mentioned that he had met my mother, so she would know him when news of his attempt to foster us reached her. He spoke very highly of her. That comment had sparked in me the most marvellous brainwave to sort out our problems. "Why don't you marry my mother?" I said as we walked. "We can all live together!" It seemed a simple and perfect solution. Mr Thomas stopped and smiled at me with affection, not knowing quite what to say.

The gift of the bike tied Mr Thomas and me closer, and we wrote more frequently. The letters were about ordinary everyday things, but they carried great spoonfuls of hope. I knew Mr Thomas would come to see me as soon as he could, and I longed to see his house, 250, Abergele Road, in Old Colwyn. Each letter added more colour to a precious picture building in my head.

Mr and Mrs Thomas were fostering children, in keeping with his dearest wish, but he had taken a job in a factory to maintain the house. It hurt me to think of him toiling in a factory after the outdoor life of Spennells. Prior to one holiday, he wrote *it will be lovely to be away from the factory for a fortnight, for one gets sick of it.* I longed to be of help to Mr Thomas and build a sunny life together.

The bike had already given *me* a better life. I was wedded to it and rode around the streets on my own, delighting in the freedom. I loved the look and feel of the drop handle bars, and I replaced the coloured grip tape at frequent intervals. I wrote to tell Mr Thomas I was saving my pocket money for a bright yellow cape. *Then I will be able to go out cycling in all weathers.*

In August, the home had a two-week holiday in Scarborough. A local coach company, *Stanley Gath*, did the run each year and knew our destination well – a draughty church hall near the south shore. Folding wooden beds lined each wall, just like on the Barnardo's holidays. This, too, was a super adventure, a release from the shackles of ordinariness.

I loved being near the sea; it expanded me. I was allowed to go off on my own and explore. The Scarborough seafront was alight with slot-machine arcades. The flashing colours, shiny metal cabinets, and music made for an attractive atmosphere, and Steve and I gravitated there. Our extra pocket money amounted to a couple of shillings a day. Converting our silver coins into pennies made the gaming last longer, but soon the entire day's money was gone. The desire to beat the machines was so compelling, and the odds so slight, that it always left me feeling cheated. But the addictive quality was overwhelming for us needy kids.

Most of our time was spent at the salt-water pool, where Aunt Yvonne had arranged a beach hut. The pool had a high board that fascinated Steve and me. We had stood on the lower level boards and watched the divers and jumpers leap into the air, but the high board was three times the height. "Let's climb up, just to have a look," I said.

Steve considered for a split second. "Come on, then." Climbing up was exciting, but stepping onto that top platform, I suddenly felt exposed. I could see for miles. That huge oval pool and the beach beyond looked incredibly small. Gusts of wind blew over us and I wished I hadn't been so hasty. My heart raced and a woozy feeling stole my stability. I laid myself down flat. I was shaking, overwhelmed by the view and the sensation of being suspended in mid-air.

"I'm going back down," Steve said.

"I daren't!" I said, my face hugging the platform. I wanted someone to come and get me. Steve climbed down but I couldn't move, too scared to edge myself onto the step ladder.

"Just crawl over and hang on to the rail," Steve shouted. Eventually I calmed enough to get my feet on the ladder. Aunt Yvonne was waiting at the bottom, distressed and furious. "Don't you dare go near that board again, you silly boys." I didn't need telling; I never went near that diving board again.

The remainder of the holiday we spent swimming and wandering around the seafront. I enjoyed a relaxing time, as change loomed again. On our return, I would be moving to Dewsbury Technical School where I knew I'd be a singular boy in shorts among a sea of long trousers.

Despite carrying an embarrassment about my trousers, I put great hope in going to Dewsbury Technical upper school. I felt something new and good would happen to me there. I also liked the feeling that I had merited a place.

On the first day, I'd arranged to meet up with my junior school friends at the bus station. Just as I arrived, the bus pulled out, and my heart descended when I saw Martin and Mario waving from the upper deck. I followed a crowd wearing the same school blazer as I was, boarded the next bus, and arrived at school in a hyper-vigilant state.

I mingled as best I could, but my clear-cut Midland accent stood out. "What nationality are you lad?" a tall and much older boy asked me in the washroom.

"I'm British," I said shyly, wondering why he'd asked.

"No you're not. You're Australian," he said.

"Cobber! We'll call you Cobber from now on," said Tony from my class. The name stuck through my time at the Tech. Cobber is an Australian term meaning close friend, which is ironic as I didn't feel close to anyone and would do almost anything to fit in and be liked. In the playground, there was frequent joking about being from a place called *Storthes Hall,* the mental institution. At the time, I didn't know about Storthes Hall, but gathered it was a home for lunatics. I laughed along with the rest of them.

Our school was one of many so-called technical schools, geared towards practical and science skills. The technical drawing, metalwork and woodwork departments were all well-equipped. I found I was naturally adept in the practical departments and felt myself equal to the other boys in those lessons. All my anxieties melted away when I was heating metal in the forge, or pouring bubbling hot aluminium into the sand moulds to make castings. The metalwork teacher, Mr Bradford, singled me out in praise for my efforts.

Working in wood was my favourite and I was to become very skilled at it, though the woodwork teacher, Mr Blackall, could be vicious and my start was shaky. Well over six-feet tall with short brown hair he always wore a brown carpenter's overall. His thick glasses meant I was never quite sure which way his eyes were looking. Frequently referring to himself as an 'expert', Mr Blackall showed his complete mastery of the tools as he demonstrated how to cut and shape the wood.

I had just made my first attempt at fashioning a mortise-and-tenon joint. It had not gone well. "Barber, what the hell is this?" he bawled from behind me, knocking me on the head with the wood. The whole class stopped. Warm blood gushed to my face as I rubbed my head. "Start again, laddie," Mr Blackall said, as he threw my work into the rubbish bin.

There had been a lesson on identifying wood, which I had missed, so when Mr Blackall sent me to the wood store to find a piece of mahogany for a new project I was fraught with anxiety. Too scared to ask for help I made a guess and cautiously returned from the wood store carrying my wood. I'd got it completely wrong. I nearly dropped where I stood seeing the look of disgust on Mr Blackall's face. "Come with me laddie," he said, snatching the wood off me. He marched back to the wood store with me scurrying behind feeling a complete imbecile.

At lunchtimes, fights were breaking out among some of the new arrivals as they jostled to sort out their pecking order. After two days at school, a classmate, Gary Addison, challenged me. "I'll fight you Cobber." His self-assuredness shocked me. I knew he was capable and I didn't want to fight him, but I also wasn't going to back down. "Friday afternoon after school," Gary said.

My mind grappled for reasons to get out of the fight, but nothing came. As the week progressed it seemed everyone knew about the pending showdown, even the staff. Maybe one of my teachers will stop it, I thought optimistically. But Friday took on a momentum of its own.

When the day came, I considered walking home as normal. It was my only plan to get free. I saw a crowd of kids gathered outside the gates. I walked through it and the crowd followed me. "C'mon there's a fight in the park," someone shouted. The crowd got larger! My bravado took control, overriding a desperate wish to call it off. *Where were all the adults?* My last hope was that someone might say, "Phil, I can see you don't want to fight. Go on home."

I crossed the road through the small gate in the wall and into the park, still desperately hoping for an intervention. On the field, Gary was standing like a prize-fighter with a group of older friends at his side.

The brutality of fist-fighting disturbed me, and I had no desire to hit anyone in the face. At junior school, I had tried to protect a friend and come off really hurt when I wrestled with his attacker. That boy had no intention of wrestling. Punches had rained into my face and covered me in blood, sending me into shock. Apart from scrapping with Steve, I'd not been in a fight since.

Gary took off his jacket. "Take your coat off," a boy bellowed at me.

I ignored him. Gary came straight in with his fists up. I grabbed his arms so he couldn't swing and I wrestled him to the floor. "Get on with it!" a boy shouted, annoyed at the lack of blood. Gary struggled free. I grabbed the sleeves of his school jumper. He let the jumper slip over his head and I was left holding it. *Oh, bloody hell. He's free now.* Gary came back in, fists flying. He caught me hard above the eye. Again, I grabbed his arms to stop the punches.

The crowd was suddenly distracted. I saw a policeman on the other side of the wall. He stopped to look at us. Gary put his coat back on. *He'll come over and it will all be over.* But the policeman just stood and looked. Then he carried on walking. I felt sick.

What's the matter with him? Can't he see I need help?

"Go on, Gary. Carry on!" a boy said eagerly. Gary's coat came off again and I tried my best to wrestle him down. Each time, he broke free and landed blows to my face. I took a terrible beating in front of sixty baying kids, including girls, which seemed to make it worse. It ended when I stayed down not wanting any more. I hadn't thrown a single punch.

"You could have done better than that," someone mocked.

"Not much of a scrapper, are you?" said one girl. I was glad it was over, but I felt a complete fool. With blood on my face and clothes, I walked the couple of miles back home with Martin and Mario. I didn't know what to say to them, or them to me. Embarrassed and ashamed, I was baffled as to what I could have done differently.

Back at Ash Tree, I swung open the kitchen door, knowing the two aunties would be milling around the Aga cooker preparing the tea. I purposely had not cleaned the blood off my face. I was yearning for an adult to explain what just happened so I could reclaim some dignity to shape myself with. Neither aunty said a word. I finally spoke to Aunt Yvonne. "I've been in a fight."

"Right, go on upstairs and get washed. Tea is nearly ready." I couldn't believe her response. The apathy first from the teachers and then from the policeman had astounded me, but Aunt Yvonne's indifference felt like I'd been hurtled into the dark sea. I climbed the stairs silently, my heart flattened and my mind totally confused as to how to be with myself.

The blood had dried, so maybe it was less noticeable. Aunt Yvonne had no idea what I'd been through, and I was too sensitive to express it. I never did tell her.

I often wondered why I didn't fight Gary properly. Gary was no bigger than I was. If I had traded punches, I'd have had equal chance to come out on top. Gary was not a nasty character, nor a bullying type, but he certainly wasn't afraid to use his fists to see me covered in blood. Gary had some inbuilt security, while I was peering out of a bunker, afraid to make a move. I was petrified if I hurt Gary in case his family would be out to get me. I imagined his older brother or his parents lying in wait after school. No one would defend me and I had no way to cope with anything like that.

Also, I had no meaningful reason to fight Gary; he wasn't bullying my family or attacking anything dear to me. I had no anger towards him at all. If I had wanted to quarrel with anyone it was adults, not people my own age. If I had hurt Gary, I'd have felt sick. It was fighting for fighting's sake, something I felt was pointless. Nonetheless, I longed for protection and for someone to show me how to handle the conflicts that so often seemed to come my way.

When I met Tom I would have loved him to teach me such things. Tom Ellis was a Royal Navy man. Well into his thirties, he was stout with thick, black wavy hair, a broad forehead, and a good flush of red in his smiling face. When he was on leave every six months he would visit Ash Tree House and stay for a couple of days.

Tom was considering a career in charge of a children's home, like Aunt Yvonne. He liked children and was testing the waters to see if he were cut out for a vocation a world away from his life at sea.

When Tom visited, I'd find a seat next to him even if he were deep in conversation with someone else. I liked to watch the expressions on his stubbly, bright face while he was telling stories. He sometimes helped me with jigsaws for a while, and then I followed him from room to room.

I liked jigsaw puzzles; the more difficult the better. Aunt Yvonne borrowed many a puzzle to keep me occupied. "I don't know how you've got the patience," Aunty Gaynor would say. But I found them comforting. I loved to strategise ways to complete them quicker and get to see the whole picture. Once, when Tom came, I set up the biggest jigsaw I had on the dining room table, in full view of the hall, knowing that he would come in and help me. It was a strategy that worked!

It was my first birthday at Ash Tree. I was eleven and a card came from Tom, with an enclosure.

"Ten shillings!" I said, waving the crisp, new banknote for Aunt Yvonne to see. A tingling of specialness rippled through me, knowing Tom had taken the time to write a card and send it for my day. I sniffed the note and rubbed it to feel the texture on my fingers.

"He never forgets birthdays," Aunt Yvonne said, smiling.

Each of the kids received a birthday card and ten shilling note from Tom on their day, but that didn't matter to me. I felt loved. It wasn't the money, it was a symbol of something much more: a bigger, brighter world – a world where I would be validated.

Chapter 19

Bridges and Fences

Tom Ellis' birthday card spun my thoughts back to Hallow Park, and Aunty Wendy. She had once sent me roller skates for my birthday; I sent her some bookmarks and cards that I'd made at school. I was so happy to receive Aunty Wendy's letters that I kept them all, but they became more difficult to read as they stirred up my feelings of being abandoned. Every time she wrote, I longed for Aunt Wendy to come and see me like she used to.

Aunty Wendy had given birth to her own son, Timothy, not long after I'd left Hallow Park. She wrote about all the things she was doing with him. *I've taken Timothy to the beach, crabbing. I've taken Timothy horse riding.* Her letters painted a picture of their exciting life together, their adventure holidays, and later, Timothy's good times at school. I would have given anything to be doing those things with Aunty Wendy, and feeling the sweetness and devotion she'd imbued into me years ago.

I could have screamed when I read, I've *taken Timothy sailing.* Sailing was the thing I most wanted to do. Envy ripped through me. I felt cheated. I longed to be Timothy. I knew Aunty Wendy cared about me, she always began her letters with *My darling Philip*, but with each mention of Timothy I felt her drifting farther away.

I was feeling the loss of Aunty Wendy in the run up to our second Christmas at Ash Tree House; how our closeness and her natural mothering had poured sunshine into me. I saved and bought her two crystal glasses. I spent hours wrapping and boxing the fragile pieces before presenting them at the post office. Sending Aunty Wendy's gift on its way my chest lifted higher and I dreamed that someday soon, I would see her again.

I always asked Dave to write to me from sea, and while he intended to, he never seemed to manage it. He came home in the late autumn and for a little while the world seemed right. He'd been to South America again, Brazil and the Venezuelan island of Curacao. Steve and I had him to ourselves for the first day, after that Dave was out with his mates. He took us both to the shop again to treat us. He bought the largest bottle of Dandelion and Burdock on the shelf and told us to share it. On the way home, Steve and I marked lines on the bottle to make sure we weren't cheated out of our share.

As soon as Dave came home, he bought the latest Beatles album. This time it was *Magical Mystery Tour,* the double EP. I was pleased because it gave me chance to spend time with Dave as we played the tracks over and over, singing the songs together. We laughed over the wild lyrics of, "I Am the Walrus": *Crabalocker fishwife, pornographic priestess, boy, you've been a naughty girl; you let your knickers down.* And I heard the beauty of the song, "The Fool on the Hill." I imagined myself as the fool on the hill, lost in my own world, not caring what others thought.

As Christmas was coming round, Dave asked Steve and me what we wanted. "A Scalextric," we said, without hesitation, hardly believing we'd get the electric car racing set. The lifelike track and the bright coloured sports cars with the speed controllers was the must-have game that year.

Aunt Yvonne was against us having one but Dave said, "If I just buy it anyway, it will be hard for her to say 'no'." Aunt Yvonne knew best in the end, though, as Dave bought the Scalextric for Steve and me to share. Neither of us liked giving ground, and we fought over the gift like starving waifs. The delight of the Scalextric quickly became grief and argument. Dave, meanwhile, within a couple of weeks was gone again.

My relentless battles with Steve were extremely painful, as I always came away the worst. I was so glad we went to different schools. But I dreaded coming home, always on high alert knowing I could be seconds away from a fight. When no adults were around to referee, the tension was worse as I had to fend off my brother by myself.

One Saturday morning in the yard, I could smell more trouble coming. I was enjoying the warmth of the early sun, bouncing my tennis ball against the wall. Steve appeared. "Throw me the ball, then."

"I'm playing with it," I said.

Steve pounced and grabbed it. "Have your fucking ball, then!" he said, as he flung it at my face.

"Fuck off, will you!" I screamed. I was too scared to retaliate, but I refused to run from him. Steve picked the ball up again, came in closer, and threw it as hard as he could at my head. Still, I didn't move. Repeatedly, Steve retrieved the ball and threw it at my head, laughing each time the ball stung into me. I could only just stand the pain.

The tantalising Violet Crawshaw appeared. I knew he'd keep torturing me to impress her, so I picked up the ball and threw it at him as hard as I could. "Go fuck yourself!" I shouted, as I ran for cover.

I could never understand why my brother hated me so much. It seemed all his frustrations ended up in my lap. I was especially puzzled because I always felt Steve was the favoured and more talented of the two of us. He certainly appeared to do everything better than I did.

Conflict was our norm, but occasionally Steve and I played well together. In March of 1968, we were eager to join a sponsored twenty-mile night walk. Harry and Pam Jacques were going, and the walk seemed well-organised, so Aunt Yvonne stretched her trust and allowed us to go. There was a jubilant atmosphere as tens of hundreds of walkers gathered in Dewsbury Town Hall for the live music pre-walk entertainment. At the stroke of midnight, a cheer went up and we set off. Marshalls along the route served hot drinks and crisps at community halls and other strategic points. We basked in the attention from the grown-ups and we journeyed along in beautiful camaraderie. Our feet swelled and our legs ached, but Steve and I stuck at it together and made it to the town centre finish line just as dawn broke. I prayed for no trouble to come between us, and it didn't.

Some things we really enjoyed together, like the trip to the cinema to watch *The Alamo*. One of the fighters defending the famous fort was Jim Bowie, renowned for his knife skills. Steve and I excitedly saved up our pocket money and bought *Bowie knives* from the Army and Navy store in town. The knives had carved wood handles and came with a sweet-smelling, polished leather sheath that fitted onto a belt. Together, we practised being Jim Bowie, throwing the knives into a tree in the back garden.

We also stole a coil of rope from a nearby lorry depot and rigged it between the two large trees in the garden. The rope stretched from the top of one tree to the lower trunk of the other to make a zip-wire. Fashioning a handle to hold, we were pleased how well we abseiled the ten metres or so down the rope. "Let's go down together," Steve said.

"Okay!" I said, invincible. With both of us clutching the handle, we leapt out of the tree! But we each lost our grip! Crashing to the ground, we knocked ourselves unconscious.

My next memory was lying on the grass beside Steve, who was out cold. I tried to get up, but couldn't balance. Through my blurred vision, I saw Aunt Yvonne approaching. "What's happened?"

I stumbled to my feet, but couldn't focus and fell down. I got up again, but wobbled around on the lawn like a drunk. I was laughing as if the whole thing were a funny dream. I felt no pain, just light headed. As the effect gradually wore off, Aunt Yvonne took us both inside. "Just lie there quietly for a while with that blanket over you."

When Steve and I tried to get along we could be really creative together. Then, something would occur to send us crashing down into chaos, just like the zip-wire.

After yet another fight it was clear we could not live together. Steve was moved on to Moorcroft Drive, another home several miles away. I heard from my mother that the move was good for him, as the husband and wife team there gave Steve freedoms he lacked at Ash Tree House. And he could continue attending his school.

The move gave me some relief. Ever since we'd moved to Ash Tree, fiery tension headaches had frequently left me debilitated. Also, inflamed boils sprouted on my back, shoulders, waist, and neck – some over two inches across. My neck and waist were the worst, as my clothes rubbed the boils and they bled on my shirt. Following the doctor's advice, I constantly applied hot poultices. Then I had to go through the grimacing ritual of squeezing out the green pus from the head that had formed, which left a cavity like a mini volcanic crater. The boils mirrored my internal state, seething anger boiling just below the surface of my life.

I craved the settled routine Aunt Yvonne had given some of the others kids. I was also jealous seeing some of the girls fall into a hug from Aunty Gaynor when life overpowered them. But that kind of intimacy and openness was alien - *and scary*. The only time I felt Aunt Yvonne's concern for me was when I got knocked off my bike. I had turned off the main road without signalling, and a van sent me sprawling along the tarmac. The driver was in shock and so was I. Luckily, I came away with only bruises and grazes, and the bike only needed a new wheel. Aunt Yvonne went over some road safety rules with me.

Aunt Yvonne struggled to build a bridge to Dave, Steve, and me. She remarked that the three of us disliked women, though she never explained why. She knew of the regime at Spennells, and sympathised with our difficulty to adjust to a more homely way of life. When Steve left Ash Tree House she said to me, "You need a man to take an interest in your life – in your football, and in the things you like."

I hated her for saying that. I thought she wanted to have me moved on, and she was preparing me for it. I retreated into a moody silence. Clinging to the shallow roots I had, I lived in fear of being moved. At the same time, my sensitive state made me defiant and argumentative. One time, for a punishment, Aunt Yvonne locked up my bike in an outbuilding. In a surge of uncontrollable rage I kicked down the heavy wooden door to retrieve it.

The idea of me needing a male influence was building. The talk made me feel inadequate, and triggered my deep feelings of rejection, which made me even angrier.

Without my knowledge, it was arranged that I would visit another children's home thirty miles away in Ripon, North Yorkshire. A male children's officer drove me there. We parked on a pretty tree-lined avenue as the sun lit up the yellow autumn leaves. The Victorian red-brick building looked attractive, and so did the weathered oak gate that spanned the short driveway. A house mother let us in and showed us to a lounge.

"Sit there for a while. I'll go and talk to Mr Hughes," the children's officer said, setting off to see the principal. I had said little on the journey, and now I sat on my own in a room with magazines and books. It felt like a doctor's waiting room, and had the fingerprints of a dry institution all over it. It was a mini Spennells. I couldn't stop a familiar collapsing sensation in my chest.

I wanted to cry and I wanted to cry out. I could have screamed obscenities. But I just sat: jaw tight, eyes sinking, shoulders hunched. *Why don't they stop pretending and just call it an open prison for boys nobody wants?*

After their private conversation, the children's officer returned with the principal, who showed us around. I met some of the kids, mostly boys. Both men knew I had a passion for boats, and they made a big fuss about having one. "You'll get a chance to sail with us. I'll teach you," said Mr Hughes enthusiastically. The boat looked a beauty and I would have loved a day out in it; but just a day.

I was not interested one bit in moving to that place. My silence and my face said it all. Neither adult asked me about my life, my family, or about Mr Thomas. Maybe I gave them little chance, but caring people don't hold conversations behind your back. In their plan all the adapting had to be done by me. I was sick of not having a home, someone to trust, or belong to.

I had no trust in those men; they'd not earned it. I just wanted to get back in that car and return to Ash Tree, where there was at least of glint of homeliness.

Some years ago I had a dream about that children's home with the boat. I saw my eleven-year-old self arriving in the car. I saw the pretty house with the oak gate in a leafy suburb. The emotion in the dream was definite; despair, misery, and a smell like death.

Aunt Yvonne was right about a male figure. In the summer, Tom joined all of us kids for a couple of days during the Scarborough seaside fortnight. I attached myself to his every move. I stood in awe as he swam right out to sea before he joined us in the salt-water pool. "Go on then. Dive off the top board!" I said, pointing up at the spectacular high board I'd climbed the year before.

He laughed and to my huge dismay he said, "I can't go up there." I expected my hero to swan-dive stylishly from the top board with everyone watching. Then I could stand alongside him, grinning with pride. I pointed insistently to the lower boards where teenagers were launching themselves fearlessly into the air. "Look! Those kids are doing it!"

"Okay, I'll have one go, then." Tom climbed to one of the lower boards and, after what seemed like an endless wait, launched himself into the water. Olympic diver he was not! To my disappointment, Tom landed with a wild splash, and nearly hurt himself. "I'll leave the diving to the youngsters," he said, climbing the pool steps clearly annoyed with me. I felt bad for pestering him, and I realised he'd only gone up there to please me. It's a wonder I didn't ask him to swim over to Holland to fetch me an ice cream!

When a warship arrived off the coast, I wondered about life at sea, and how the men found their way when out of sight of land. I fired questions at Tom, and sat attentive.

"She's at anchor just now. She's pointing that way because of the wind and the tide. She'll swing round soon." Sure enough, the ship did just as he said!

Later that day, Tom was diving from the sea wall into the crest of the sweeping waves. Perched on the edge, he waited to time his dive for maximum depth. I stood near Tom when another lad came up from behind and pushed him. Tom was not ready and dived clumsily. Coming up for air, he yelled at me, "I'll clip your damn ears if you do that again boy!" I sank with hurt. The anger in Tom's voice scared me. Twice that day I'd riled him, and I felt sick with panic, thinking I'd messed up my closeness with him. Tom calmed down after I managed to explain, and when he said he was sorry, I felt so relieved.

Tom had a warm heart. He was worldly and had a love for the sea. I didn't just want to be around Tom, I wanted to be Tom! He stayed with us barely two days. And in that short time, he tried his best to share his companionship with all the kids.

The morning Tom left, I sat by myself on the sea wall, nursing a twisted and wrenching hunger deep in my gut.

Chapter 20

Something Really Hurts

My dear Phil. That was how Mr Thomas began his letters. It gave me a spark of brightness. I'd go upstairs in the bedroom where it was quiet, read the letter and fill myself with the promise it held. But Mr Thomas' letters also triggered weighty and sullen feelings of loss. The promise of forward steps seemed to amplify the disturbing thoughts I was having. *Nothing about me is okay. My problems are my entire fault. I must work harder to be accepted and make friends.* I was twelve, but I felt old. My trust in life was drowning in disappointment.

Without realising it, I'd swing between *melancholy* and rage. I'd begun to have the irritation of hay-fever, and the tension headaches I'd always suffered became more severe and happened more frequently. Aunt Yvonne had me visit the doctor to be checked over to eliminate the possibility of a brain tumour.

The next time Mr Thomas travelled from Wales to visit me, my neediness had become a gaping wound. I don't remember much about where Mr Thomas took me; I just know it was good. Anywhere we went together would have felt vibrant and right.

I smiled like a son when he joked about the time at Spennells when I fell out of a tree. "I won't fall, Mr Thomas, don't worry," he said, imitating my seven-year-old voice and making me laugh. I loved everything about Mr Thomas: the smell and roughness of the brown, tweed jacket he always wore with the familiar blood donor's badge on the lapel. I loved the Bedford camper van that he nicknamed Betsy. I loved the warm politeness he showed people, and I loved the gentleness and caring in his voice.

I was clinging tighter to him these days. There was so much I wanted to tell him. But any thoughts I tried to put together faltered like wings clipped short. Mr Thomas was the only authority who held any promise. He was the holder of everything that was right with the world. Mr Thomas was driving back to Wales that night - and it was time for him to go.

Inside the front door, I stood beside him like a puppy while he exchanged friendly talk with Aunt Yvonne and Aunty Gaynor. I held his hand. "*Please,* stay five more minutes," I said, looking up at him. Mr Thomas smiled and squeezed my hand. All the ills of my life suddenly made themselves felt. I wanted to heave sorrow from my mouth. "Just stay five more minutes, *please.*"

I kept saying it over and over, each time with more pleading. It was all I had. The two aunties chuckled at my reaction and I felt myself boil over at them. I didn't really *mean* five more minutes. Five more minutes were the only words that came to match those dying moments. I was trying to say, I don't know if I can cope without you, now.

I don't remember seeing Mr Thomas go; I must have blocked that out. I wandered the house for a place to put my loneliness. What I really wanted was to go home, and I didn't have one.

I sat near the window in the dining room, looking at the dull green lawn. My breath collapsed. I gulped down despair. My eyes watered but no tears came. If I had cried someone might have seen the depth of my sorrow. I had not one reason for my life to carry on. I was like the person in Antonio Machado's poem, *I have no roses; all the flowers in my garden are dead.*

I began stealing. For over a year, I'd been venturing into town on a Saturday to go shoplifting. Woolworths was an easy target as it was crowded and stacked with low-priced goods. At first it had been with Steve. He and I had some success, keeping lookout for each other like a couple of military raiders.

With my brother Steve gone Leonard took the vacancy at Ash

Tree House. Leonard was the same age as I was and roughly the same build. His face was round and freckly and his fine, brown hair hung down in a fringe. When it came to stealing, Leonard was a veteran! Once, he brought home a large cardboard wallet of coins with about eight pounds sterling. They were mint samples of the old currency; half-crowns, florins, shillings, sixpences, pennies and three-penny bits.

"Where did you get that?" I asked.

"I swiped it off my mate. He'd been given it as a birthday present and brought it to school to show us."

"Bloody hell! How did you steal it?"

"When he went to the toilet, I slipped it in my bag while no one was looking. He went home crying," Leonard smiled. I was speechless. I couldn't help admire his audacity. In the North they call it brass. Though I never told him, I was sickened at how easily Leonard did that to a friend. Pilfering from big shops felt okay but I didn't want to steal from friends.

Leonard and I became pals and together we began shoplifting in a small and sporadic way. But with each success we grew cockier. We'd steal batteries, toys, watches, torches, penknives, and packs of cards. There was enormous daring and fun in pitting our wits against the store owners, testing the boundaries of what we could get away with. We devised tactics to cover each other while stuffing things into duffle bags and coats. It was exciting to get clean away with goods our pocket money could never buy.

One time, in a town shop, I was on my own and feeling frustrated without Leonard and the efficiency of our joint tactics. I didn't want to go home empty handed, so, in a burst of frustration, I grabbed a handful of torch batteries from a cabinet near the entrance and bolted through the doors. Darting through the crowds into the back streets, my heart pounded till I was far and away. I took a different route home, keeping myself on the move. I sensed I had gone too far that time and stayed clear of town for weeks.

Leonard and I thought we were smart, but our pride was short-lived. Aunt Yvonne had noticed the little extras we brought home. One morning she called me into her sitting room. Sitting with her was a barrel-shaped man wearing a dark grey, double-breasted jacket. He stood up. The man had dark slightly greying hair and a deep, crisp voice. "Hello, Philip. Do you know who I am?"

"Er, no," I said, frowning, but recognising trouble when it stood in front of me.

"I'm Detective Inspector Dawson, West Yorkshire Police." The officer made it clear he knew what I was up to. "This has got to stop, Philip!" he said smartly, looking me straight in the eye. "Yes, these are large company shops, and you may in many ways feel deprived, but this is *still* stealing."

I had immediate respect for Detective Dawson. Some instinct told me he had my best interest at heart. There was fatherliness in him. There was no shaming – no moralising beliefs that would make me fearful. I didn't feel guilt; I just saw what I'd been doing from a more adult viewpoint. I never went shoplifting again.

Leonard and I remained friends. We both owned good bikes and would go off cycling much farther than I would ever venture on my own. "Let's see how far we can go in one day," I said.

"Great! Where shall we go?"

We borrowed a road atlas from Aunt Yvonne so we could make up our own maps. It felt marvellous to have an adventure to look forward to. I picked a route through Denby Dale, just because I liked the sound of the name.

On our chosen morning, we woke early and briskly loaded our saddle bags with food and bike gear. The weather stayed fine and we expertly navigated along our route. We raced each other down country lanes, stopped for drinks when we wanted, and ate lunch at the edge of a field. It was a fantastic day, exploring without adults just like youngsters did in the comic book stories.

The escapade bolstered our relationship, but at other times, Leonard and I exploded into squabbles. He took little care of his own things and continually wanted to borrow mine. "Can I borrow your bike to go to the shop?" he asked one time.

"No, you can't! You leave that bike alone!"

I made it clear I never lent the bike to anyone. Looking back I realise how precious my bike had become, and how it symbolised an assurance that one day, things would come right for me.

Leonard was oblivious to all that, and one day he took my bike from the garage. In an impulsive moment, I ran to my cupboard for the Bowie knife I'd bought with Steve. I caught up with Leonard and flashed the blade. "Don't ever touch my bike again!" I said, trying to make him see I was serious.

I had no intention of using the knife. It was high play, like in the movies. I just wanted Leonard to get the message. He must have told Aunt Yvonne. Likely, the story came out of his mouth much worse. Aunt Yvonne asked me to give her the knife from my cupboard, which I did, and she didn't press it further. As there was no big reprimand, I thought the whole thing utterly unimportant.

It wasn't so. Without a word to me, Aunt Yvonne had asked for my removal. Within days, it was arranged. After school, she broke the news. "It's been decided you're leaving."

I collapsed inside. The ground wavered. I had no energy, no anger, no fight, just a hopeless world shrinking to nothing.

Surely, someone would say, *please let him stay. Just give him another chance, Aunt Yvonne. He'll come good.* But something told me it was a done deal. Challenging authority was futile. I sank into a torpid state, totally defeated, totally obedient. I vaguely remember a man coming to ensure I didn't run away or resist getting in the car. I had nowhere to run to, nothing to run for.

It was dark outside. Most of the other kids had gone to bed. Aunt Yvonne drove her black Morris Minor out of the garage and parked it by the front door. The tail lights glowed red on the tarmac drive, the exhaust smoking in the freezing winter air. I slipped into the passenger seat with my head down and a small bag of clothes at my feet. I had no idea where Aunt Yvonne was taking me. I didn't ask. I assumed it would be another children's home.

There was no conversation on the journey. I stared out of the cold windows at the darkness and the lights of the traffic. In my crushed state, I must have appeared drugged or hypnotised.

About an hour later, the headlights lit the drive of a large house beyond a dark outline of trees. The gravel drive under the tyres made a sound like rushing water. Aunt Yvonne parked the car short of the stone entrance porch.

Cold air rushed in as she opened her door. I opened mine and felt the full chill through my school blazer. I looked up at the night sky laden with stars. A huge wooden door was lit by a dim wall light. Aunt Yvonne sounded the metal knocker and another entrance light lit up before the door opened. A man stood in the doorway, clearly expecting us. "Come in."

The man's suit was well worn and his manner brusque. He was about sixty-years-old, medium build and almost bald. There was something creepy about him. We followed him to his office where he took up position behind his desk. I stood in front of it and Aunt Yvonne sat in a chair to one side. The man took my small bag, emptied the few items of underwear on the desk, then transferred them to a plastic bag and attached a label. "Empty your pockets," he said, tapping his finger on the desk in front of me. "Everything!"

I rifled my blazer and trouser pockets and placed the few items on the desk: sweets, a piece of string, some coins and the key to my bike lock. My hands nervously went into my pockets. "Hands out of pockets!" His eyes lifted to meet mine, looking for signs of dissent. I had none.

Papers were signed and Aunt Yvonne was shown out. Alone in the office, I heard the outside door slam. I remained standing to attention. The house was silent, as if nobody lived there.

Chapter 21

King of Spades, King of Hearts

"Follow me," the man said, without meeting my eyes. I followed him up a hefty, ornate staircase that doubled back on itself.

"Another boy for you, Mr Johnson," he said, handing me over to a man on the landing. Mr Johnson stood – his sleeves rolled up – directing numerous boys like a traffic policeman. He had dark hair, glasses, and his grey jumper fitted tight on his thin frame. Studying me through his thick glasses, I sensed Mr Johnson wanted me in his system with no fuss. The boys approaching Mr Johnson spoke few words, and each utterance ended with a military Sir!

Mr Johnson pointed. "Number one dormitory, take the empty bed." In the dorm, eight boys hurriedly readied themselves for bed. The room felt like a hospital ward with its tubular metal bed frames, identical linens, and clinical, disinfectant smell. The spartan decor and bare floors reminded me of Spennells.

"Show that lad how to fold his clothes," Mr Johnson instructed one of the boys. The boy did as he was told, but he was edgy and hurried, so I didn't understand too well. I could see that each item of clothing had to be placed in a neat pile exactly as prescribed: trousers at the bottom, then shirt, underpants, vest, and finally, socks. "Every fold has to be perfect," said the boy. I studied his own stack of clothes, trying to copy as fast as I could but fear ripped into my coordination.

I presented my folded offering to Mr Johnson. He barked loudly at the boy. "Get this one trained as quickly as you can!" My second attempt was better, but again I was sent away. "Get it right!"

I could tell he was stretching his patience for a new boy. Finally, another boy came to my aid and meticulously arranged my meagre stack of clothes so I would pass inspection.

Then it was wash, teeth clean, and into bed. No boy dared be caught still standing by *lights out*, hence the scurrying. Mr Johnson timed *lights out* to the second. No talking was allowed after that, and there wasn't any.

I lay on my back in the dark room, afraid to breathe too loud. Loneliness poured into the silence. *Maybe they had made a mistake,* I thought. *I was a technical schoolboy with the promise of a bright education.* But I was miles away from Ash Tree and no one here knew anything about me. Here, there would be no Mr Thomas trying to ease the ache in my chest; no Navy Tom smiling at me. I knew this move was a punishment, and I was sickened to the core with myself for whatever I had done to deserve it.

My heart continued racing from the intensity of the clothing procedure, and my hands gripped tight. The laundered smell of the sheets made me feel I was in a kind of sterilisation process. I knew I would have to learn the rules, act dumb, act grey, do exactly as I was told, and not show anything of myself. I tried to fall asleep among thoughts of Ash Tree House and the children watching television in front of the gas fire. I saw myself playing a Beatles record. I pictured Aunty Gaynor in front of the Aga stove, filling up the hot water bottles, and fussing over the girls. Sick with loneliness something told me I would never go back there, or anywhere like it.

The next morning, it was still dark when the light flicked on. "Everyone up!" the duty housemaster shouted. Boys burst into action. I followed their lead. Beds were stripped and coverings folded, all in a specified way. There was another fastidious inspection of bedding and then a strip wash, an all-over wash in front of the sink, in pants and socks only.

After another inspection, this time of our folded pyjamas, the boys lined up on the staircase. Two boys sat on each step, one each side, leaving a gap in the middle. Apart from scampering feet there was complete silence until Sir gave the order to the boy on the bottom step.

"Off you go!"

Boys silently filed downstairs and formed a queue outside the dining room. That first morning, I looked around nervously to see where I should sit. Keeping Sir in my peripheral vision, I took a place on one of the long wooden benches running each side of the tables. I followed the other boys' every move.

I spent the morning obeying instructions and helping with household jobs, mainly in the kitchen. In the afternoon we congregated in the day room, the large main room of the house. The linoleum-floored room had a table-tennis table, chairs lining the walls, and tables offering books or games. Toilets were at the far end of the room.

We were confined to this room and we played games or read until evening mealtime. Afterwards, we performed more cleaning jobs before our last hour back in the main room. Then the bedtime disciplines.

The routine was repeated every day and I soon perfected the folding of clothes and bed linen.

Mr Preston, another housemaster, came on duty. He was a thick-set man with a short neck. In his mid-fifties, with thinning grey hair, he had a permanent six o'clock shadow. Mr Preston was not a man to cross. His rough hands were the size of shovels. He wore a scruffy, dark brown cardigan that hung loosely buttoned as he swaggered around the house maintaining a tight ship.

A couple of nights into my stay, a boy arrived who had belonged to a biker gang. Greg was in his late teens, tall, with frizzy, shoulder-length hair. Shortly after lights out I heard Mr Preston raise his voice on the landing. I lifted my head from the pillow and looked toward the slither of light shining underneath the door. Mr Preston shouted. "Smart guy, are we?"

"No," said Greg.

Bang! I could hear him being pushed hard up against the wall.

"You little wretch. Tough guy are we?"

"No," Greg answered softly, without a trace of cockiness.

Whack! More words and punches followed. Whack! My muscles jerked, as if I were taking the blows. The sickening injustice shuddered through me. *Please, someone come and help him.* After more threats and more punches, Greg was finally allowed to go to bed.

Greg hadn't cried out or retaliated. I made a point of talking with him the next day, in the main room. "I heard it all last night," I said.

"Ah! I'm not bothered about him!" Greg said, as if he'd dealt with violent bullying before. I was drawn to Greg, in complete admiration of his lack of bitterness or anger.

I was also drawn to Christopher, a lad who arrived a week after I did. About sixteen, with short black hair, he towered above us all. Christopher was always calm, and his voice soft and low key. And unlike most of the boys, he never bragged about anything. Christopher and I shared a love of table tennis, and we played as much as we could in the afternoon competitions. Having played so often at Spennells, I always came out on top in my matches against Christopher. He thought it humorous that he was beaten by a twelve-year-old, and smiled and shook his head in admiration. Christopher gave a human touch to the place. I wanted to be like him.

During my years of group living, I had learned to categorize people into degrees of warmth or cold. If they showed some friendliness, I would interact; if I sensed indifference, I avoided them. Most grown-ups here measured at the cold to arctic end of my scale.

Mr Johnson, though, showed some degree of warmth and, although the strict rules remained, we felt less anxiety when he was on duty. One afternoon, Mr Johnson handed me a pack of cards. "See if you can arrange the cards so that when you count and turn them out of the pack they go like this:

One, this should be the ace of hearts.

One, this goes to the bottom of the pack. *Two,* should be the two of hearts.

One two, goes to the bottom of the pack, *Three* is the three of hearts.

One two three, goes to the bottom of the pack. *Four* is the four of hearts. And so on.

Each of the four suits has to come out in order starting with the ace and ending with the king."

I had never done anything like this, but I liked his challenge. "It's really complicated," Mr Johnson added. With paper and pencil I sat at a table on my own. Within an hour I had the puzzle figured out and arranged the cards in order. I could hardly wait to show him. "I've done it!"

"Let's see, then," said Mr Johnson, and called a couple of boys over. They pulled up their chairs and he explained what I was trying to do. Counting just like he said, each card emerged in numerical and suit order. Mr Johnson beamed. "Did you see that boys?"

Glowing inside and grinning widely, I lapped up his attention like a new puppy. I suddenly had something to like about myself, something warm.

Understanding . . . kindness . . . humanity . . . none of these was a priority in this place. Nothing drove that point home more than the shower incident. For me, and for most boys, it felt normal and easy to strip naked and shower among others. Daniel, a sensitive and slightly feminine thirteen-year-old, was terrified of the whole thing. While I was washing one morning, Daniel resisted taking his clothes off. "Go on. Get in the shower!" Mr Johnson ordered.

"Can I wait till I'm on my own?" Daniel pleaded in fear. I'm glad it's Mr Johnson on duty, I thought to myself as I dressed and took a place on the staircase amid the shouting. Suddenly, Mr Preston swept up the stairs. My body tensed rigid. That heavyweight thug loved to have a disobedient boy to deal with. He headed straight for the shower room.

"You little wretch!" I heard him shout. "Get in that shower!" It was obvious he was manhandling the youngster and pulling off his clothes. "No, no!" Daniel cried out.

Whack! "Stand still!"

"No, please no!" Daniel screamed.

Preston held the youngster down to strip him. Daniel wouldn't have stood a chance. But he managed to break free. I looked back to see a naked Daniel running across the landing with the brute pursuing him. Preston cornered Daniel in his dormitory. The boy's cries escalated into a terrified squealing, like the shrill of a piglet being slaughtered. My tears welled up. I wanted someone to beat the life out of that man, kill him. An urge to run for help coursed through me. But I knew everyone was scared of Preston, so I cramped my muscles tight and buried my head into my knees.

Daniel surrendered in a heap of tears. He was dragged along the floor back to the shower room. It was an ugly sight. Preston, seemed to take great pleasure in it.

Joshua was a sixteen-year-old street guy, bulky with a flowery mop of shiny, blond hair. Though not tall, he resembled Lennie in the John Steinbeck novel, *Of Mice and Men*. Like Lennie, Joshua was gentle and slow, and had passed through school with minimal education. Joshua's friend was helping him with some writing practice. Joshua wrote out, *Tong Park Remand Home*. "Where's that?" I asked. Immediately it dawned on me!

"That's here, Tong Park. Didn't you know?" they said laughing. Embarrassed I turned my face away from their laughter. For the first time in my two-week stay, I took stock of the bars on the windows. I hadn't given them a thought. Now they looked sinister. I had assumed I was in another children's home, maybe a Barnardo's home, just waiting to be sent to a new school.

Why was I here? How long would I stay? I pictured my former school and old school friends. I wondered if they knew where I was, and if I'd see them again. I winced at the thought of them knowing I was here. If they did know, I'd rather not return. And yet, I ached to get back to the academic life that had held some expectation of normality. I was shocked that I had let it all go so easily. I'd become used to life just 'happening' to me. Someone in authority said move, and move I did.

As I got to know the boys, it became clear they all had criminal records and were waiting for court appearances. They were from Liverpool, Manchester, Tyneside, London, as well as Scotland, Wales, and Ireland. One boy, only a couple of years older than I was, had stabbed two policemen. Others had raided shops or been caught breaking into houses. Lots were fighters and had been through all kinds of street crime, including mugging. The most shocking story was from the fifteen-year-old who, with little emotion, told how he had broken into an old lady's house and raped her. He seemed to want me to smile at his revelation.

Sean, a lean sixteen-year-old with a man's sideburns, came from a travelling family. He was a real hard nut and told me about his fights as a *vinegar-boxer*. Soaking his hands in vinegar apparently toughened his skin, making it more leather-like to avoid cuts. It was a practice the old bare-knuckle fighters used, Sean told me. This was unlicensed fighting and illegal, but Sean smiled and told how he made handsome money as the spectators wagered large amounts on the fights.

The blond-haired Joshua had also learned to box and was physically strong. He was easily led, and no doubt his fighting abilities were useful to some. I got to know Joshua well and grew to like him. He was easy to be with and he came to trust me. "Phil, come over here," Joshua called one afternoon. He was at a table deep in discussion with two other lads. "Phil's smart, let him in. He can help us."

Getting deeper into the conversation, I realised they were planning to raid a post office. "It's an easy target," one boy said with great enthusiasm. I listened thinking the whole thing seemed half-game, half-real . . . until I heard the boy say, "Josh, just whack the guy on the head if you have to!"

Joshua nodded without a care and I realised they were deadly serious. I kept clear of their discussions after that, and gravitated to a different table.

Twice monthly, on Saturday afternoons at 2pm, we boys sat expectantly in the main room for visiting hours. Over twenty boys looked at the door, wondering who might visit. When a family member entered, the boy would stand and they'd group themselves round a table. Visitors were also confined to the day room where a housemaster or two kept an eye on things. In the two-hour period, cigarette smoke gradually filled the air as family members lit up.

I found myself watching the visitors who came to see the boys I knew, trying to guess if a man and woman were his parents, or his aunt and uncle. *Were those younger visitor's cousins, or a brother and sister?* I wanted to know what my friends' home lives were like. "Are you having a visit today?" I'd ask if a boy were sitting alone.

"I think my mum might come, maybe my sister, not sure," was a usual reply. There was no advance notice of visitors. Some relatives didn't stay the full time and some arrived late. I would grab a book and engross myself in it by the window, but always glance towards the door whenever anyone entered. I sat with my same routine; watch the door, look at the boys and their families, and read a book to occupy my mind.

My dream was to see Dave; he had a way of making things better. *Maybe my mother would come. She had a habit of turning up unexpectedly. Maybe Aunt Yvonne or Mrs Greenwood would visit.* Anyone would have been good. Then it occurred to me; Mr Thomas might come. As much as I ached with longing to see him, I dreaded him seeing me here. I did not want to deal with his disappointed face. He would never have stolen anything. I was afraid of his rejection if he knew where I was, or why.

I had no reason to expect anyone would come, but I always looked. I looked every time there was a movement near the door, or even if someone glanced towards the door. I longed to tell someone I didn't belong here, but I don't think anyone in my family knew where I was. Dave was most likely away at sea. Even so, I couldn't help feeling hurt that he hadn't come.

No one ever came. And I was always glad when visiting was over, and the tension eased.

On a cold Sunday afternoon, I was surprised to hear Mr Johnson announce, "We're organising a football match on the pitch for you lads." *Wow, I didn't even know there was a playing field.* The chance for a full game of football threw my spirit high into the air. The beautiful game was here again.

"You lads put on these green shirts. You others, the yellow ones." The shirts were well worn and most of them badly ripped, but wearing them lifted the occasion. After a month of incarceration, it was a bite of freedom.

Patches of snow lay on the pitch from a recent downfall and the wind blew wildly across the field. The sun appeared on and off, but that wind made it bitterly cold. I wondered if the staff were concerned that one of us might run off. No one did. I guess most of the boys, like me, had nowhere to run.

I flew down the wing with the ball, and I was suddenly riding that magical wild horse again, galloping ahead of the world's problems.

Everyone played full out. Competing with the boys and watching them buzz felt exhilarating. Waves of bliss ran through me as I ran for every ball. To crown it all, I scored several times. Watching my shot fly into the back of the net was always a majestic feeling, but on that pitch it had a higher majesty to it, like it was the World Cup Final. In the middle of that game, hearing our banter, I felt like I belonged. I was alive again.

Chapter 22

Male Storms

After the euphoria of the football match I relaxed a little. Relaxing though was a dangerous thing among the Tong Park rules. At morning wash, the rule was to stand at the sink wearing both underpants and socks. On this particular day, I stood washing myself in my underpants only. I caught a glimpse of Mr Preston in the mirror. He's springing up behind me! His arm swinging wide!

Whack! He belted me hard.

A hot, stinging pain filled the side of my head. I was knocked sideways and boys scattered to get out of the way. I went dizzy as I held my head with both hands. *Whack!* A second blow struck the back of my head. It knocked me to the floor. I banged my knees as I went down. "You little wretch, where's your socks?" *Bang!* Another punch. My vision blurred. As I held my pounding head, I could make out Mr Prestons' brown shoes. I gulped to catch my breath. Hot tears filled my face and snot streamed from my nose. *Bang!* Another strike. Preston stood over me shouting about the rules while I steeled myself for more blows. *Bang!* A punch hit my shoulder. "Go get your socks on!"

I shuffled across the floor and scurried out of the washroom like a field rabbit. In my dormitory, arms and legs shaking, I fumbled for my woollen socks and pulled them over my feet. I made it back into the washroom, terrified to look anywhere but straight ahead. The other boys looked on, too scared to speak. "Get on with it!" Preston shouted at them.

Still trembling with shock my head throbbed for hours. I hardly said a word all that day, and no one approached me. I tried to bring myself to terms with what had happened but shame was biting lumps out of me. The other boys had seen me totally helpless and demeaned and I hadn't known what to do. I played the scene over and over: me scurrying off, almost naked, whimpering and not defending myself. I felt ashamed because I couldn't find a way to speak to anyone, and I felt ashamed because I was hiding away. I felt ashamed because I'd been on the receiving end of these assaults before, and I somehow felt Preston had the right to do that to me. I'd felt of little value before but now I felt a new level of worthlessness.

It's no wonder I made myself as small as possible when Mr Preston was on duty. Just hearing the sound of Prestons' voice made me shake. Several days after the beating I was shocked to hear him announce, "Get your coats and boots on, you lads. We're going for a walk." I was pleased to be going out, even though I dreaded being anywhere near the man.

Outside the air was arctic cold and our breath turned to vapour. Snow blanketed the trees and fields, and our faces looked brighter in the reflected light. We crunched the snow, walking through still woodlands and along frozen paths. It was such a joy to be in the open air for a second time; I felt I'd been canned in for years. I flashed back to that first winter at Spennells and the 'bigger playground' feel the expansive snowy landscape fed me. Hope was out there - somewhere.

On our return, half a mile from the house, Mr Johnson met us wrapped in a thick coat with his collar turned up.

"How's it going?" he said to Mr Preston.

"We've lost the little *nigger* back there somewhere," Preston growled. That word sounded sickeningly awful, especially the way he said it. I glanced back at the trail of footprints our group had left in the white landscape. I realised Bradley, the young black boy, had run off, probably into the woods we'd just walked through. A couple of years older than me, Bradley, was a small, easy going fourteen-year-old. I was glad to know he had escaped, but my chest pounded in fear for him. *Please, please, please, someone, take care of Bradley!* I pleaded that he'd get clean away, and find some kind of refuge. The thought of Bradley being brought back to face Mr Preston – *Please no.*

I yearned stronger than ever for someone with wisdom and authority to intervene at Tong Park. That night after dinner a group of us were talking. Christopher, the tall boy I played table tennis with, said his older brother would happily come and give Preston a good hiding. Hearing those words felt so good that I wouldn't allow in the reality – that such a thing would likely never happen.

It was a relief to have the regular tasks, to stay occupied. It stopped me endlessly mulling over Bradley's fate and my own situation. The jobs at least fed me with purpose. My new regular evening task was to wash the numerous cleaning cloths from the kitchen. As usual Mr Preston patrolled and barked orders to make sure jobs were done thoroughly.

The scullery, at the back of the kitchen, had a white enamel sink with a wooden draining board and a cupboard underneath. I had been shown how to scrub the dirty cloths on the draining board and prepare them for inspection. Most of the time I liked the work I was given; there was satisfaction in the immediate results. It was disheartening, though, to scrub those grey cloths with bars of soap, rinse, and scrub them again without seeing much improvement.

The remand home employed an assistant cook, a round-bodied woman in her sixties. One time, as she wrapped her coat around her ready to go home, she looked at me earnestly scrubbing away. "That's a thankless task," she said. I smiled back, grateful for her acknowledgement. She glanced around to ensure no staff was near, then came in the scullery and opened the cupboard under the sink. Grabbing a plastic bottle, she poured a little liquid into my dingy water, returned the bottle to the cupboard, and nudged the cloths below the surface. "That'll help!" she said.

Soon the grey cloths found a new sparkle. I was amazed how clean and white they came out, and how quickly! I offered my finished items to Mr Preston for inspection. "Very good," Mr Preston said. I hadn't heard him say anything like that to anyone! I could see Mr Preston had even surprised himself.

From then on I earned a reputation as the boy who could clean the cloths the best. Now, my heart beat fast every time I reached for the bleach, but by developing radar-like attentiveness, I could time it right. Cloth inspection always went well after that and when Mr Johnson moved me onto another job, I overheard Mr Preston complain, "You get a good lad on cloths and he gets moved on." *Good lad,* he said, *Good lad!* His words bounced around my mind like a pinball machine; they bolstered me. It was marvellous to feel useful.

And so, I was moved to floor cleaning. An awful, familiar, grinding feeling descended on me as I swept the darkened rooms and polished the hallway floors. *Spennells was back!* Those endless punishments on my hands and knees brought back another layer of self-loathing. I tried to put my heart into polishing the Tong Park floors, but energy bled out of me as soon as I attempted the old duty. I longed to be back on the cloths.

The last floor to clean was the quarry tiled floors of the kitchen and ancillary rooms; they required hand-scrubbing with hot soapy water. This, at least, was an enjoyable task, especially as I was left on my own to do it. I scrubbed the tiles spotless. When Mr Johnson once traipsed through and left his footprints over my clean floor, I seethed in silence.

Sometimes the small kitchen radio was left on and I could listen to music. I heard the song *Hey Jude* for the first time. There was a surety in the opening piano chords, solid and trustworthy. The aching sweetness of McCartney's voice sent a tingle up the back of my head. *Hey Jude, don't make it bad, take a sad song and make it better.* The song was feeding me. *Don't carry the world upon your shoulder.* The words leaned into me, and so did the melody. It sent waves under my skin loving me back into shape.

As the song played itself out McCartney let rip into primal screaming. I loved hearing him do that, it seemed to break me open, sparking me deep inside. It was easy to forgive Mr Johnson's careless footprints with that song swimming around my head.

There was something I liked about Mr Johnson, anyway. On occasion, he showed me warmth, stopping to talk while I buttered the dozens and dozens of bread slices that filled the deep, aluminium trays before every meal. The bleached-white loaves in their waxy paper and the big tubs of cheap margarine had an institutional smell, but I was glad of a job where I was on my feet. Mr Johnson asked me a little about my family, and he showed interest when I told him about my brother being at sea.

I appreciated these glimpses of Mr Johnson. I never saw him hit the boys and his sharp manner always felt a little unconvincing. When he ran the afternoon table-tennis competitions, they always felt more organised, and more fun. I also saw his patience when he sat by Joshua, tutoring him in reading and writing.

And so it was hard and disturbing, one evening, to see Mr Johnson stand back while Mr Preston belted the stuffing out of another boy for a minor misdemeanour. In fact, Mr Johnson laughed. It was a false, sickeningly loud, made-up laugh that tried to cover his inadequacy that he couldn't, or wouldn't, intervene.

Six long weeks had passed at Tong Park when I was called into the office to see the principal, Mr Brewster. The Dewsbury Children's Officer, Mrs Greenwood, was seated there as well, and I felt the reassurance of a familiar face. "Hello Philip," she said in her civil service voice, as if it were a normal day at the office.

I took up position standing in front of the desk. Mr Brewster told her I had behaved, done my tasks well, and shone in the afternoon table-tennis contests. But then Mrs Greenwood spoke about my recent behaviour and how some people were far from pleased with me. "You are *also* letting your mother down, Philip, and she has enough to cope with." It seemed a very strange thing for Mrs Greenwood to say. *What right did she have to say that?* And, I'd not seen my mother in ages. Anger growled deep inside me, but I kept it hidden.

"Philip, we are considering you for a three-year term in an approved school." Suddenly I felt dizzy, as if I'd been peppered with shrapnel. *Approved School?* I never, in my darkest hour, saw that coming. I had heard the boys talk about the prison regime of 'approved school'. My eyes fell to the floor. I swallowed hard as the images rushed in. Three years shut away feeling useless till I was fifteen, without a chance at life . . . that was forever!

I wanted to claw back a life that was slipping away in front of me. *All I want is to return to normal life and to my old school, can't Mrs Greenwood see that?* I ached for a champion, someone to tell her she was wrong. I didn't think of myself as rebellious or criminal.

"Philip, are you going to mend your ways and start behaving?" Mrs Greenwood said in her clipped, non-feeling tone.

"Yes," I said.

"Are you going to set an example for your younger brothers?"

"Yes."

"Do you not want us to give your mother a good report about you, Philip?"

"Yes," I replied, holding back my frustration at her stupid and meaningless questions.

I never felt much trust for Mrs Greenwood right from her useless Spennells visits. She had never once sat alone with me, and asked how I felt. In that room I could barely look at her.

"Off you go," Mr Brewster said. I left him and Mrs Greenwood in the office and slipped back into the obedience of the day. At least, I had an inkling of hope of another path. But approved school! I writhed in disbelief.

That evening, for the first time, we watched television. As a treat, it had been wheeled into the main room on a trolley and we boys gathered the chairs around it. The pop star, Barry Ryan, was singing his new song *Eloise.* It was about a woman that knew he was there, but was ignoring him, *I break my heart to please, Eloise.* It was a dramatic song, full of emotion that stirred my own jumbled feelings. The television screen looked brighter than I'd remembered it, as if reminding me that life had moved on and, as always, I was being left behind.

Two days later, I was summoned again to the principal's office. My possessions and my school blazer sat in a small pile on his desk, along with the contents from the clear plastic bag he'd filled on my arrival. "You're leaving. This man will take you in his car," he said, nodding at a man in a dark blue jumper with some keys in his hand.

Minutes later, I stepped out of the front entrance and followed the taxi driver along the gravel drive. The sky was overcast, but the air had lush, fresh life in it, like the first outing after a long bedridden illness.

I remembered the cold night when I'd arrived in the dark. It seemed years ago. I'd been outside only twice since then. My initial sense of being in a sterilisation process was more accurate than I had realised. I eased into the passenger seat and slammed the car door shut.

I felt a wave of sadness for some of the lads I was leaving behind – for the injustices that would continue being heaped upon them. I felt none of that for myself; I thought I deserved it all.

I knew that Mrs Greenwood and Aunt Yvonne would not agree to me going back to Ash Tree House, but I had no idea where I was going. I didn't know how much more numbed and cautious I was to become, but I did know that if I were to learn about life, it would not be from any adults like these.

Years later, my younger brother Matt also spent time in Tong Park. He told me one of the housemasters slipped on the quarry tiled kitchen floor, banged his head, and subsequently died. I never found out who it was - just as I never knew exactly how many boys were brutalised at Tong Park.

Chapter 23

A Dry Field

It was a shock to be joining the buzzing traffic. But the taxi driver sailed along, as professional drivers do, and made conversation in the same easy way. "Where are you from?"

"Dewsbury," I said, glad of his interest.

"I live in Dewsbury." The driver knew the Technical School, Savile Town where Ash Tree House was, and the Dewsbury Moor area where my mother lived. He was taken aback when I told him the size of my family.

"Crikey, ten of you!"

"Where . . . um, where are we going?" I asked quietly.

"I've been instructed to drop you in the town centre."

The way the driver spoke told me he wasn't to explain. I knew the council children's department was in the town centre, Mrs Greenwood's office. I guessed we were heading there. The journey took less than an hour. We talked about football and I told him about the game at Tong Park.

In Dewsbury we parked alongside the Town Hall and I followed the taxi man into a side entrance. He led me through reception and into a small room where two police officers relaxed at a table. The taxi man turned to leave. He hesitated in the doorway. "Good luck then," he said. I sensed he wanted to stay to support me, and failing that possibility, wanted a good word to land on me.

"Thanks," I replied, still trying to figure out what was

happening.

"Would you like a cup of tea?" asked one of the police officers.

"Yes please." Both officers were interested to know about me and my family. I explained the best I could and I told them a bit about my mother and her rough partner Stan.

"We know him," said one policeman, shaking his head. I felt comfort in their recognition of Stan as a known quantity. Just then, another man turned up, and introduced himself as a children's officer. He instructed me to follow him.

"Good luck," the policemen said, as we left the room.

I sat with the children's officer on a couple of hard chairs in a passageway. "We'll have to sit here until we're called in." I could tell he was a man just doing a job. At least I felt some comfort from being wished 'good luck' twice by others in the time I'd been in the building.

A uniformed man entered the hallway. "Come through." We followed him through some double wooden doors into a large room with dark, wood panelling. Solemnity hit me. The smell of wood polish and musty, aged timber matched the look on everyone's face. People scurried around clutching files and sorting papers. I was ushered into a panelled cubicle. The children's officer sat nearby.

I sat motionless and detached. A stern-faced man entered the room through a door in the panelling, followed by more officials. Everyone stood up and the uniformed man sitting behind me grabbed my arm and heaved me onto my feet. The stern-faced official took his place behind an elevated bench that separated him, and his other officials, from the rest of the room. Our eyes met: me looking up - him looking down.

I waited to see where they were sending me next. Various people stood and read out printed statements in clinical voices. Apart from hearing the sound of my own name once in a while, I may as well have been on Mars. I just stood up or sat down as directed by the man behind, with no idea who anybody was. Eventually the figure behind the bench spoke directly to me. "I'm told you are very skilled with your hands, Philip." I wondered how this person I'd never seen before could know how good I was at woodwork and metalwork. His expression clouded over. He repeated himself, "I'm told you are very skilled with your hands, Philip." The man behind poked a finger into my back.

"Yes," I said, responding to the prompt.

The stern face official behind the bench read out more statements and then consulted those alongside him. "Philip Barber, I'm giving you a two-year suspended sentence." He gave a long and elaborate explanation, but I must have looked confused. He leaned forward. "Do you understand?"

"Yes," I nodded compliantly. I didn't understand at all, but I was scared he would be irritated with me if I said 'no'. At this point, I finally made out that I was in a court and that man was a judge.

The proceedings ended and outside the courtroom, I queried the children's officer, "What does a 'suspended sentence' mean?" He explained that if I committed another crime in the next two years they would add this crime to that one. I was disgusted! I knew I was in trouble, but no one said, 'this is what you did wrong.'

What crime was he talking about? Was it the shoplifting? Was it my behaviour in general? Fury welled up. I wanted to go back and say, *you don't know me at all. How can you pass a sentence on someone you don't even know? And just what crimes do you think I'm likely to commit in the next two years?*

I was pleased with my thoughts, pleased with the strength of my opinion! But I felt injustice pointing at me from every person and every wall in that court room. Besides the good luck wishes the only thing that had a positive effect on me was the cup of hot tea from the policeman. The rest was a sick pantomime.

Outside the big stone building I walked alongside the children's officer to his car. Even though outdoors it was cold and grey, the blustery, fresh air was a tonic and I breathed in deep. "I'm taking you to Dryfield House," the officer said. Your two half-brothers, Matt and Mark are there."

I remembered seeing my brothers as babies, but knew nothing of their life since. I didn't know what or where Dryfield House was, but at least it held family connections. As relieved as I was that the idea of young-offenders school had been shelved, I again felt myself a piece of lost property on another pointless journey. I longed for a familiar face, for someone to tell me I was going to be okay and show me solid ground. I longed to see Dave; he was the only one I could be really open with without feeling swamped in shame. But I never knew where he was.

The car journey was brief. Light rain fell on the windscreen as we pulled into the drive of a large house with lawns and several outbuildings. Dryfield House was in the Batley area, a scant two miles from where my mother lived. In the drizzly air, the two-storey, blackened stone building had a familiar austere look. A row of tall broadleaf trees dwarfed the six-foot stone wall that stretched along the front of the house.

It was early afternoon: still school hours, so the house stood quiet. At the back door, I caught sight of a long, regimental line of shoes and Wellington boots. The smell of shoe polish hung in the air. So did an empty sound. It was the sound left behind in a room where disowned children congregate.

My heart sank. Immediately I knew I'd be just as lost here as I'd ever been. This place was another version of something I was weary of. A slight man in his mid-sixties greeted us. His grey hair matched his two-piece suit. It was the principal, Mr Fisher. After exchanging a few words, Mr Fisher said goodbye to the children's officer.

"Miss Patricia!" Mr Fisher called out in a cramped, nasal voice. He handed me over to a masculine woman with short brown hair.

"Follow me," Miss Patricia said. In military style, she showed me to my dormitory, and matched some clothes for me from a cupboard. Miss Patricia spoke just enough words to make her point. "Strip off to the waist," she said. "Put your head over this sink."

Miss Patricia's manner irritated me, but I did exactly as I was told. She washed my hair with a carbolic-smelling shampoo, a de-lousing lotion. Her fingers dug into my scalp. To break the cold silence I said, "My half-brothers, Mark and Matt, live here."

"Yes, I know."

She put a towel over my head. "I'll run the bath down the hall. You can get in it."

A few inches of bath water waited for me as I closed the

bathroom door. I lowered myself into the lukewarm water, and sat staring at the cracks in the white tiles. Hopelessness collapsed my chest. I was sick *of* something. I was sick *for* something. A despairing sigh released as I rubbed soap onto my arms.

Without warning, Miss Patricia came in. I was shocked at her blatant disregard for my privacy. She took hold of the flannel and started washing my ears. "Turn your head," she said. She twisted the flannel into a point and drilled deep into my ear. Anger surged through me - but I pushed it down, fed up with trouble. Eventually she went out, leaving the bathroom door wide open. I felt sick that I'd let her carry out her dehumanising tasks without saying a single word. Fury boiled in me again.

Scared to speak out, I withdrew and sat alone for the rest of the afternoon, feeling sterile inside and out. Clean and disinfected, I met Matt and Mark when they came home from school. Little was said between us; they had a routine and carried on with it without much curiosity about me.

I had assumed I would have a natural relationship with them and have lots to talk about. I did feel an affinity, but it was not grounded in any shared experience. My brothers and I had different accents, different fathers, liked different things and had different ways of seeing life. I felt inadequate that I couldn't find the words to bridge the gap between us, and dreadfully disappointed that we were not destined to be close.

The next day Mr Fisher called me into the front room. "I see you go to the Dewsbury Technical School. The children here attend a different school. What about changing?" I deadened at the thought. I had enough despair to cope with.

While detained at Tong Park, I had desperately missed the familiarity of my school friends and the normality they had given me. I had missed being called *Cobber*. The nickname felt personal and rang with affection and belonging. The Tech was the one thing that had contradicted the sinking feeling that I was a defective boy. Mr Fisher must have seen the fear in my eyes. After leaving the room for a few moments, he returned. "Let's try sending you back to your old school for a while."

Mr Fisher ran Dryfield House with the orderliness of a

watchmaker. There were rules about what to do with shoes, what to do with clothes, when to wash, where to sit, how to get up in the morning, and how go to bed at night. There were even rules about the way to eat meals. I followed as best I could, learning fast to stay ahead of trouble.

At the breakfast table one morning, a boiled egg stared up at me. *How should I eat the egg? What is the rule?* I panicked and my face turned red. *Do they slice the top off with a knife, or tap it with a spoon and peel the shell off?* A few of the kids stared at me, wondering what was wrong.

Eager to shift the moment on, I began tapping gently with the spoon. "What are you doing that for?" the boy next to me laughed, mocking my moves. The other kids turned their heads and it seemed the whole room was staring at my feeble tapping. Seconds hung like hours. I wanted to run. The boy beside me eventually attacked his egg with a knife, slicing the top off. I felt as lonely as I'd ever been.

Mr Fisher regularly appeared and was there most mealtimes, but his wife wasn't involved much with the children. We mostly saw the two female staff, Miss Dorothy – an older woman who was happiest doing housework – and Miss Patricia, the thirty-year-old cold fish I'd met on arrival.

One of the lads, Ian, snapped a shoelace getting ready for school. "Damn it!" he said loudly. It was the wrong thing to say around Miss Patricia. She was a devout Christian spinster who proudly wore a silver cross around her neck. "Ian, I've told you about swearing!"

"What's wrong with saying 'damn it'!" Ian asked.

"It does not please God!"

Miss Patricia was always telling us what does or does not please God, especially when she had no other reason for her disapproval. I craved feminine warmth, but Miss Patricia seemed to want to stone life to death.

Most of the children, including my brothers, had lived at Dryfield for some time and had moulded themselves to the staff and rules. I liked the other kids and wanted to get on with them, but there was little I could relate to. My identity seemed to belong elsewhere and I didn't know how to close the gap. In the other kids' eyes, I was clever, an intellectual. My school, my education, and my Midlands accent separated me. I was viewed as aloof.

Though I had no words for it, I sensed something was stunting the progress of the other kids. They seemed zombie-like, mindlessly shackled by the constant heavy rules.

As much as I sensed that Mr Fisher wanted to be helpful, he was as dusty as his grey suit and as rigid as his shirt collar. He did make some effort to give me a helping hand, as in the choice of school. And in the evenings, he would say to me, "You can do your homework on the kitchen table where it's quiet." No one else seemed to *have* homework and I felt strange to be singled out. At the same time, I was glad to take my time, study more thoroughly, and catch up on the schoolwork I had missed while I was at Tong Park.

The first days back at the Tech were painful. Inevitable questions came from my old mates. "Cobber, where have you *been?*" I'd prepared myself with a plan. It consisted of smiling, walking away and saying nothing! I quickly learned to bat off any prying.

I also had to deal with another item and my face dropped when I saw it: a black gabardine coat hanging on my peg at Dryfield, the same as the one at Spennells. I could not – and would not – wear it. Only children's home kids had that type of coat.

The long walk to the Tech meant I had to set off earlier than the other kids. I took the front path leading to the gate in the stone wall. Two stone pillars flanked the gate and I dumped the hideous gabardine in the hedge behind one of the pillars. In the chilly, wet days to come, I'd even walk in the rain without it. Only on very cold days would I bring myself to wear that coat, running to keep myself warm, and then stuffing it in my bag as I got near school.

Fear of my friends discovering the truth about me intensified. I built a wall of steel to keep my two lives separate; everything depended on it. But I was alienating myself from my friends and from myself and I didn't have a clue how to operate myself.

Sensing my instability, a couple of boys in my class began to push me around. I let one of them beat me up without retaliating.

Why didn't I fight back? Instead of challenging, I became more withdrawn. "It serves you right," one boy told me. "You used to bully others in the first year."

"Yes, you did," added another.

I was shocked! I didn't recall being that way. What I'd seen as playing about – at break and in games – had been bullying! It sobered me, and in my embarrassment, I didn't even reply. The familiar sinking feeling descended on me more and more. When I saw other kids in groups enjoying themselves, their laughter and easiness kicked at my increasing loneliness. The long walks to and from school were the only intervals when I felt free of shame.

Back at Dryfield, the single thing I looked forward to was a game of billiards or snooker. After changing into pyjamas and dressing gowns, we were occasionally allotted an hour on the table before bed. It was a brief time where my defences fell and loneliness dropped away. Apart from the beautiful clacking break of the coloured balls, only diving into my homework gave me respite.

Weekends were uneventful. Saturdays, I'd walk to the shop with pocket money, buy a large bag of wine gums, and deposit myself with the others in the television room to watch *World of Sport*.

Dryfield was living up to its name. I was turning dry, I was turning grey, and I ached for something more.

Chapter 24

Grey Stairs – Red Hair

Mr Fisher surprised me one Friday morning. "Do you want to spend the weekend with your mother?"

"Yes!" I said eagerly, wondering what had sparked the idea.

"I'll arrange for someone to take you there, tonight."

All day at school I was excited at the prospect of being out of the children's home. My last lesson was woodwork, a favourite, which added to Friday afternoon's thoughts of freedom. Apart from the week three years ago when Dave and Steve and I visited my mother and we'd all had food poisoning, I had never stayed with my mother.

That weekend I loved running errands, going to the corner shop, or bringing home a fish and chip order for her. I stayed up late watching television till the coal fire burned down, and in the morning, came downstairs only when I felt like it. My younger siblings, Alan and Emily, were there and it was good to be around them. But Stan was there too, sitting near the fire drawing on endless cigarettes. I couldn't bring myself to engage much with him, as I still loathed him for abusing my mother. My twelve-year-old mind was at a loss to understand why she stayed with him.

Stan was also wary of me and we avoided being in the same room. So it surprised me to have brief moments when I almost got to like him. "I'm going up the field to set a trap for a wild rabbit, I'll show you how to do it," Stan said on the Saturday morning. My curiosity had me follow him up the field behind the house. I watched how he carefully arranged several house bricks and used a twig as a trigger. Although I had no desire to snare a rabbit I admired his ingeniously simple trap, I'd never seen anything like that before.

The renegade in me was even more impressed with Stan's ability to pick locks. I marvelled as he took a pair of scissors and popped open the money compartment on the coin-operated rental television.

Ever since I'd known about Stan I'd disliked him. I hated his bullying nature. But here were moments of Stan as a regular man, free of the violence. It was confusing. Now I had to dislike myself for liking and admiring Stan in those moments.

I returned to Dryfield a little more contented than before the weekend. I didn't feel *at home* at my mother's, but at least I'd been free of Dryfield's relentless rules.

During the next Friday's woodwork lesson, I couldn't help but wish for word of another weekend stay. I looked for Mr Fisher as soon as I was home. "Am I going to my mother's this weekend?" I asked.

"If it is *arranged*, you can go!" Mr Fisher replied, like a recorded message. His lame, dismissive reply aggravated me, and fanned a fire in my chest that raged for hours. I longed for someone to take my side, for Mr Fisher to say, *I'll move the earth for you to go again*.

A month or two later, I decided to take matters into my own hands and go to my mother's house directly after school. I wanted to arrange a weekend stay, then return to Dryfield with permission. I ran at full steam to make up the time I'd lose on the detour. As I approached my mother's house, I heard Stan's voice bellowing obscenities from behind the closed door. "Shut up woman!"

My mother screamed back just as loud, "Where the bloody hell were you last night?" I stood stock-still. The shouting continued. It was not a good time to ask about a weekend visit. And I didn't want to see my mother battered about. I knew it happened, but I also knew she'd return to Stan no matter what.

Once I had asked my mother, "Why don't you leave him? You could move right away from Dewsbury!" But she had shouted me down, screwing her venomous face at me. "Oh, you know nothing!"

Now, standing outside my mother's house, I regained my breath from the run. Then I turned around, picked up my pace again and headed back to Dryfield. Not long afterwards, I gave up asking Mr Fisher if I were going to my mother's. I felt stupid for thinking it could ever happen. No more visits were arranged.

I started to bristle at Dryfield's endless regulations: the lack of privacy, the standard haircuts, the uniform clothing, and the degrading rules about washing and eating. We were being pounded and dumbed by useless rules, and no one said a word. The clinical, uncaring nature of it all made me want to scream.

Children had to use the steep and narrow, bare-tread stairwell, which was the original servants' stairway in times gone by. Staff used the ornate, central stairway that was wide and carpeted. A sharp feeling of injustice came over me every time I filed up the narrow staircase with the other kids at bedtime. It riled me more and more as the months went by. "We should all be able to use the same staircase as the adults," I said to the boys in my dormitory. Agreeable nods came back at me.

One evening my loathing broke loose. "I'm sick of these bloody rules!" As the other kids readied to clamber upstairs, I made a point of walking up the main stairs. Of course, I was scalded by Miss Patricia, but I argued my case. "Children don't use the main stairs, that's the rule," she countered. I half expected her to add, *and it doesn't please God!*

The kids were shocked at my assertiveness, but they were waking up to unfairness and their admiring glances and support bolstered my sense of justice.

The event released some pent-up steam in me, but that narrow staircase loomed every morning and every night, a symbol of Dryfield's oppression.

Soon hatred welled up in me again. After another disagreement with Miss Patricia, with her looking on, I took that wide carpeted flight again. I bore the consequences proudly. An early bed time punishment was worth it.

Doubtless, Miss Patricia reported the misdemeanour to Mr Fisher. I wanted change, and I wanted to get on with both of them, but I didn't know what to do with the hot energy that was taking me over. I felt bad about the sadness I saw in Miss Patricia, but her insistence on dreary obedience pressed on me with the weight of a lorry. I had to resist. Whatever had been done to her to make her that way, I sure didn't want for me.

I didn't dislike Mr Fisher, but any positive feelings I'd had for him began to whittle away. Walking around in his suit and tie like a headmaster, he demanded a neat conformity. He had little idea how to build a bridge of affection and understanding. I could not give him my trust and if I wasn't to lose myself I was trapped into battling with him.

On a few occasions, he watched me play billiards in the evening, or came into the kitchen and looked over my shoulder, wanting to know about my homework. My posture had become terrible and my writing often deteriorated into a scribble. "Your handwriting will neaten up if you sit more upright and have your book at less of an angle," he said. I appreciated his interest and, following his advice, I found he was right.

Sometimes in passing, Mr Fisher would ask me a question, as if he wanted conversation. I would answer, and then he would nod and walk off. I felt Mr Fisher liked me and wanted to be friendlier. But I was starving and he was giving me crumbs.

One Saturday after several months at Dryfield, Miss Patricia and I had another disagreement. Soon after, Mr Fisher came looking for me. I was sitting in the television room. "Philip, come out in the hall. I want a word with you."

In the hall Mr Fisher began shouting in his high, nasal voice. As he got louder and louder the freedom-fighter in me shouted back. Mr Fisher lost his composure. He grabbed me by the throat with both hands! My back hit the wall! I was choking. My heart beat with warrior energy and I pushed him off with all my strength! He fell back and stumbled. Disorientated by the attack, I didn't know what to do. I ran to the front door, flung it open, and took off down the path to the gate! I heard a shout from the house but I didn't look behind me. I had no coat, no proper shoes, and no intention of going back.

I dodged the traffic through the housing estates and galloped up to the Butchers Arms, a pub I passed on the way to school. I kept on running, turning left down the main road that led into Dewsbury. I kept up my pace until a mile or so later, descending the long hill into town, I slowed to catch my breath. The traffic flew past me and the sun came out from behind the clouds. I stopped and put my hands on my hips to rest for a moment. I looked behind me. *What was going on back at Dryfield?* My face flushed and my indoor plimsolls pinched my toes. A middle-aged couple stared at me. I didn't care. And I didn't care what would happen to me. The tidal wave of my breakout had at least swept away that greyness and made my heart beat loud.

I felt heady in the knowledge that wherever they took me, I'd find a way to run. *I've had enough of children's homes and their bloody crazy rules; I'll find my own way to make a life.* I had stood up to a grown man. I knew Mr Fisher was old and I didn't want to hurt him, but I had never done that before.

I had no desire to go to my mother's so I only had one place to go, Aunt Emmy's house in Eightlands where she'd moved back to. Number 2, Alfred Place. Dave had told me he'd stayed there once on leave. Aunt Emmy might know if Dave were home.

The front door was open, as usual Aunt Emmy was gazing into the fire. "Your Dave's home on leave, he's just gone down into town."

"Which way did he go?" I said, billowing with excitement. I ran straight to where she'd directed me. In the distance, I saw Dave walking towards me! *Oh, thank the stars* . . . All the strain in me melted away.

In snatches between breaths, I told him what just happened. Dave listened in his typically calm way. "I called up there to see you last Saturday," he said. "I came to the front door and the man in charge said you weren't there."

"I was there all along!" I said, furious at the revelation.

Dave asked me about Tong Park and I poured out the story as we walked back to Aunt Emmy's. Dave told me he had gone straight to Mrs Greenwood. "I told her I was disgusted with her. You should never have been sent to such a place." I could have hugged him, and hugged his words. *I should not have been sent there.* It lifted a dead weight off my chest.

"Mind," said Dave, "They might come looking for you here, so let's move on. I was going up to see Cousin Joey today, anyway. We'll go there."

Dave and I caught the bus together. I was glad to have a plan, even if it was just for the afternoon.

Like my brother, Joey was a sports fan and the three of us headed to the playing field with a football. The pitch was surrounded by trees, and we had the lush, green grass to ourselves. We played for an hour or so, passing, shooting, and controlling the ball. It was a bright, new feeling to be in a game with family, out in the open air.

Before we left Joey's house, Dave suggested we find our mother. "We can tell her what happened and see what might be the best thing to do."

A few hours later we eventually found her at a neighbour's house. I told her the story about Mr Fisher. "I'll go up there and knock his bloody head off!" she said. "I've never liked that fella. I'm not having him strangling any son of mine."

I was embarrassed by her talk. I did not want her visiting Dryfield, any more than I wanted to go back there myself. I'd seen her vicious temper and I knew it would make things worse. Then my mother changed her mind. She became excited about my escape. "I'll hide him from the authorities," she said to her neighbour friend. "I'll even dye his hair."

I pictured myself hiding under the stairs with my hair some awful, dark-red colour. I didn't want any of that. It was beginning to sound like a wild adventure for her. I wondered how to say no to her. I had little faith in my mother, and I wanted a say in what happened to me. I trusted Dave, but he was heading back to sea.

I wanted to set off to find Mr Thomas. I didn't know how to get to him; Wales seemed such a far-off place and he never did own a phone. Apart from letters, it was nearly a year since we had been in touch. Dave had not seen Mr Thomas since he left Spennells four years ago, and my mother had only seen him briefly. Then it hit me. *If he knew where I had ended up, he might not want me.*

Suddenly the running away didn't seem like such a good idea. I had no clothes, no money, nowhere to go and no plan except to take my chances with my mother. "What about you ring Mrs Greenwood and tell her I don't want to go back to Dryfield House?" I said.

"They're running out of children's homes for you," my mother joked. To my surprise, she took up my idea and contacted Mrs Greenwood.

Later that evening, a police car came for me. I was taken to Moorcroft Drive Children's Home where my brother Steve lived.

I thought myself fortunate to go to Moorcroft, especially after Mrs Greenwood's threats on leaving the remand home. Maybe at Dryfield House they were embarrassed about Mr Fisher's behaviour and wanted to keep things quiet. Maybe Dave's visit to Mrs Greenwood had made her think differently. Whatever the reason, I felt a little happier. I had seen Dave and felt his support, even if it were brief. I also knew that, if I had to, I was strong enough to run away.

Chapter 25

Old Chip – New Faces

After all I had been through on my own, I looked forward to being with Steve at Moorcroft. *Maybe it will be different now*, I thought. *Perhaps we'll get on better.*

Bill and Mary Clarke ran the Moorcroft Drive home. It was in a cul-de-sac at the bottom of a hill on a 1960s housing estate. Three semi-detached houses had been converted into one, and altogether housed twelve children. The Clarkes had kept their own home and once a month they made the thirty-mile journey back for a short break. Uncle Bill still worked an outside day job, while Aunty Mary ran the home with her assistant, Margaret.

The Clarkes had raised their own two children and the homely atmosphere at Moorcroft reflected that. Aunty Mary and Uncle Bill shared their sitting room with us kids, including the roomy armchairs and big television. I appreciated being given some choice about the food I ate and the clothes I wore. I was almost thirteen now, and it helped me feel a little more adult.

My brother Steve wasn't immediately friendly towards me; maybe he resented my arrival. Steve seemed to fit in well with the Clarkes. They liked him and treated him well. Between my brother and me, though, some essential piece was missing. In too many ways, we triggered unrest in each other. We continued to argue, and even though our skirmishes were over small things, I still didn't feel safe with him. Despite that, we did manage snatches of spontaneous fun, like at bath time when we timed ourselves to see which one of us could hold their breath longest under water.

When any antics ended up with me being in trouble, the shocking *unruly child* label I had earned within the local child-care system came back to haunt me. I could feel it in the small comments that came my way. Uncle Bill was the first to spit out the accusation. "You've got a great big *chip on your shoulder*, my lad." Every lecture ended with the chip on your shoulder remark. The chip was there alright, though Uncle Bill never mentioned how to knock the thing off, other than to do as he told me. His comments just worked the chip deeper into my shoulder flesh.

Around this time it became commonplace for those who got a shock or a surprise to exclaim, "Jesus Christ!" Many of the children said it. Margaret, the assistant, was a religious woman in her late twenties who looked very like Miss Patricia at Dryfield House. She had the same clinical manner and, when we misbehaved, the same lecturing style. Whenever Margaret heard the Jesus phrase she turned vicious. "That's blasphemy!" she'd blaze.

Her annoyance only invited the kids to say it more often, and Steve and I were no exception. We'd say it just loud enough so she could hear. *"Jesus Christ! It's cold outside!" "Christ, Steve, I didn't see you there!" "Jesus, what's that stink!"* Margaret complained to the Clarkes. Aunty Mary paid scant heed to her, but we got a dressing down from Uncle Bill. "Just eat a bit of humble pie you two, and say sorry to Margaret," he said, over and over like a broken record.

We hadn't meant any harm, and didn't feel we'd done any wrong. We felt it false to be forced to say sorry, so we stood our ground and refused. Most of us thought Margaret was petty and lacked understanding anyway, so a few months later when she moved on, none of us were sorry.

Standing my ground kept me from feeling a complete victim. I knew I was okay mentally, but my constant ability to land in trouble riddled me with self-doubt. *Why am I so defective?* Every move I made seemed ill-fated. I felt as if I had to voice myself loudly to the grown-ups just to keep functioning, but it was draining the lifeblood out of me.

My destructive thoughts dissolved, though, when I had a ball at my feet, so I jumped at any chance to play football.

Richard lived next door. He was my age and would come through the hedge from his garden and join in our game. He was a good footballer and easy to get on with, so I looked forward to our games after school.

I called over the hedge one spring evening. "Hey Richard, are you coming for a game of footy?"

"My dad says I'm not allowed to play with the kids from the children's home anymore." His words struck at the fragile place in my heart. My head went down. I couldn't battle against that. I never dared ask Richard again.

The six-week summer break of 1969 came around and we all took off for a two-week holiday at the Woodlands YMCA camp in Skegness, on the east coast. At least twelve other resident groups used the camp, like the Scouts, Cottage Homes and various Christian religious organisations. Our chalets were small and cramped, each with four beds and a sink in the corner.

Woodlands had a true, summer-camp feel and the holiday mood came over us the moment we arrived. There were organised games and, most nights, disco music in the function hall. Saturday was a big event night; a singer or a band would come in and play to a packed audience.

The huge, bustling dining hall was like rush hour at a city railway station. Scores of tables with brightly coloured, plastic tablecloths filled the room, with rickety, wooden folding chairs each side. Food was brought to the end of each table on huge metal trolley carts. The staff distributed uniform portions, conveyer-belt style, onto the white dishes piled high on the carts.

Each resident group took their turn clearing away the dishes and carrying out kitchen duty. I enjoyed the kitchen. The place was alive with helpers. The head cook was a tall, red-faced, cheerful fellow. "Come on, young man! Let's get stuck in," he said, showing me how to load the plates into the giant industrial dishwasher. Steam belched as we fed the pots in one end and stacked the trays of clean hot crockery from the other.

"He used to be in the navy on an aircraft carrier," Uncle Bill said. I wasn't sure if Uncle Bill was kidding us at first, but the way that cheery chef took charge of meals and cleaning up convinced me it was true.

The next day, Uncle Bill said to us three oldest lads, "You can go off on your own, now." The initial burst of freedom felt wonderful, but quickly gave way to confusion. I wandered around not knowing what to do, like I didn't belong anywhere. Not used to making my own decisions I was incapable of using my own freedom. When Uncle Bill said the same thing the next day, rejection ripped through me, as though he couldn't be bothered with me now.

I tried to blend with the other groups in the camp; but shyness blighted me, as though I had lost some huge part of myself. My *outsider* feelings didn't give me a chance.

I noticed how some groups kept themselves tightly closed, yet others invited everyone into their games. I felt free again as I was invited into a game of football.

A couple of days into the holiday, Steve said, "Let's go into town this afternoon." We had a good chunk of our holiday money to take with us. After a morning on the beach with our group, off we went. Just like at Scarborough, Steve and I gravitated to the brightly lit world of slot-machine arcades. Coin after coin was fed into the slots, until our pockets hung empty.

In town, Steve and I walked around looking in shop windows, but it wasn't long before an argument started and we split up. I felt the slot machines had made a fool of me, and now the quarrel with Steve was another failure. The two things sent me into a depressed mood and made it a lonely walk back to the beach. I spent the rest of the holiday hanging around the beach, swimming in the pool, or – when I felt welcome – joining in a football game.

Back at Moorcroft Drive, the Clarke's daughter, Helen, asked if I wanted to stay with her and her husband, Myles, during the school break. Helen and Myles had bought a modern bungalow in Barnsley, and needed some help with their garden. I agreed, and on the day of the trip, I moulded myself into the tiny space behind the seats of their old TVR two-seater sports car and off we went. I was happy to be useful in the garden and Helen paid me in pocket money. Myles, was fascinated by the size of my family. "Go on, name them all. From the top!"

"Dave, June, Steve, Phil, Matt, Mark, Alan, Emily, Adam, and Joe!" I said, glad of my entertainment value.

Helen was a big fan of the TV soap Crossroads and she was eager to own one of the new colour televisions. Helen and her husband were also considering fostering a child and, I found out later, were testing the waters with me. It felt good to be out of the home, and I enjoyed being taken to Barnsley football club, but our connection was thin and our relationship broke off that autumn when Helen's mum and dad left Moorcroft for good.

The Clarkes were replaced by Mr and Mrs Watson. Uncle Ken and Aunty Sheila were new to the children's home environment. Uncle Ken was well over six-feet tall. He was used to a simple life working as a council maintenance man, and was happy in shirt sleeves and cloth cap. But the physical work was taking its toll on his body and he liked nothing better than to retreat to his own space with a pack of smokes. When a salesman called one day with a home vending machine containing twenty packets of cigarettes, he happily had it installed in the corner of the sitting room.

Aunty Sheila was a former nurse. She was short, with a head of thick, black hair, and a way of looking at you that said, *I just want you to be happy*. The Watsons never had their own children and Uncle Ken struggled with the unruly and cheeky kids. I liked them both, but without meaning to, I pushed every one of Uncle Ken's buttons. When his temper snapped, he would shout his favourite phrases like, "I'm not letting him get away with that. He's taking me for a cuckoo!"

"I'll sort this out." Aunty Sheila said, always jumping in quickly. She would lead Uncle Ken away and try to calm him down. The last thing she wanted was to see him raging, especially as she was concerned about his health. A heavy smoker since boyhood, Uncle Ken's heart needed watching.

Despite his temper, Uncle Ken had gentleness in him. There was never fear of him hitting us, and he did at least let us speak our corner. Uncle Ken tried his best to sort out any conflict by getting to "the thing of it." This pet phrase was the signal that Uncle Ken's patience had reached its limit. *"The thing of it is, is this!"*

He would then go on to explain what *the thing* was, and that was to be the end of the matter. The trouble was, in his explanations to me, *the thing* was always - *my fault!*

Uncle Ken struggled with trying to be something of a father to twelve children who were not easy to love. We needed acres of patience, and Uncle Ken was often exhausted from his day job. He tried his best to take an interest in all our lives and make good things happen, but it was really Aunty Sheila's dream to be in that role.

She wasn't used to handling conflict either, but Aunty Sheila had a curiosity that made her search for a deeper understanding of our troubles. "I don't agree with the way the children's department labelled you," she said to me. Her words touched a tender place in me; I was not used to being defended.

Aunty Sheila also arranged for me to collect my bike from Ash Tree House, along with other belongings, which included all my letters.

On the brief visit to Ash Tree House Aunt Yvonne recounted the night she drove me to Tong Park Remand Home. She told me that earlier she had draped a blanket over the car engine, and placed a kerosene heater under it, to stop it freezing in the garage. She had forgotten to remove the blanket and on her return journey the car overheated and very nearly caught fire.

It was an interesting twist but I was more concerned to have my beloved bike back. It reunited me with something normal and good. I cleaned it up, pumped up the tyres and headed off for a burst of freedom.

Aunty Sheila encouraged my progress at school and even badgered the children's department to pay for technical drawing equipment for me. Moorcroft was a blessed fifteen-minute walk, much closer to the Tech, and I didn't have an embarrassing raincoat to hide anymore. And yet, reminders of institutional life were never far away. Every single Friday afternoon, I had to wait outside reception, next to the headmaster's office, for a receipt for my dinner tokens. I cursed the insistence of the children's department that I always collect it. It never failed; one of my friends would see me and ask, "Cobber, what are you doing outside the head's office?"

"Just need to ask something," I would say, turning away in raw embarrassment.

I was retreating into a solemn, secretive world that excluded friendship and closeness, just when I craved it the most. I was scared stiff of seeing any of my classmates beyond the school gates. My *left-behind* feelings kept surfacing with a vengeance. Other boys seemed to know how to hang out together and joke around easily. Some were partnering up with girls in my class.

The girls in my year seemed frighteningly grown-up. Some of them teased, "Would you go out with Denise? Would you go out with Sarah?" They all looked attractive, and were much smarter than I was. I never knew what to say. I felt crippled being naturally pulled to a girl and petrified of her all in the same moment. I longed to share life with them, but my yearning for them just led me into a fog of sorrow.

On a blustery autumn afternoon after our games lesson, a group of us thirteen-year-old boys were sitting on a grass bank eyeing the girls playing netball. The conversation steered around to sex. Without thinking I said, "Boys get a hard on. I wonder what happens to girls."

"Their nipples get hard," my friend Rob said.

"No way!" I said laughing, thinking he was making it up.

"It's true," said Rob. I was dying to know if this really happened, but I was too timid to pursue it.

Mr Cole, our headmaster, was far from timid. Outwardly cool, he was a small, fiery man with jet black hair, wearing a sweeping black gown. As we all filed into morning assembly, Mr Cole stood bolt upright with his head tilted back, peering down his nose at the rest of us. He was ever on the lookout for boys in mischief mode and girls who had hiked up their skirts or glossed their lips.

On occasion, my friend Alex and I were caught pushing each other in the line. "Come here, you two," barked Mr Cole. As we drew close, his weight shifted from one foot to the other. His eyes glared above our heads, his irritation too hot for direct eye contact. "Both of you. Report for detention tonight," he said, trying to keep a lid on his frustration. I avoided Mr Cole as much as I could. He kept a cane in his office and was one for using it.

Mr Cole's assembly speeches were also memorable. At the end of each crisply made point, he loosed a crooked smile followed by a nervous twitch that made his head shake from side to side as his eyes went skyward. No one dare laugh.

Our deputy head, Mr Murphy, personified a new and more progressive, friendlier manner. He wore a modern, light-grey suit and pale blue shirt. I was often reassured to see Mr Murphy's pained expression following one of Mr Cole's exasperating comments.

When our regular teacher went on holiday, Mr Murphy taught us English literature. He sat casually on the edge of the desk, holding H.G. Wells' *The Truth about Pyecraft* in one hand. He read from it in a most dry manner, never breaking into a smile. But Mr Murphy was a master at voices and the characters leapt off the page and into my imagination. He made me laugh, and when the bell sounded for break, I wanted to clutch hold of him longer. Encouraged by Mr Murphy's easy style, I found myself joining in discussions with him and jesting with ease.

On Fridays, Mr Murphy often saw my embarrassment while I was waiting for the dreaded meal chit outside reception. He made a point of saying hello to me. Then he opened the office door and called out, "Can you hurry up with this receipt?"

By the end of the 1960s, the wheels of change were turning. Social change was everywhere. The decade was coming to a close and it was time for new blood and shedding Mr Cole's fusty, old gown. When Mr Murphy took over as head teacher, you could almost hear us applaud.

Chapter 26

Stealing Moments

One crisp December morning, Steve and I walked the two miles to Number 2, Alfred Place, Aunt Emmy's back-to-back terrace in Eightlands. As we went in, Uncle Tommy was toasting a piece of bread over the coal fire in the Yorkshire range. The smell of coal dust and old, damp clothes was as strong as ever. Although the house was dark, we could see how worn and dirty the old settee, the chair and floor coverings were. We liked the open fire though. Most times, it was lit, and Tommy could take hot water from the kettle on the grate and use it to wash himself in the sink.

Despite the cold, Emmy's door was always open, and people called in when they were passing. Dave had decided not to go back to sea for the time being and moved into the small bedroom. Steve and I often walked or cycled to visit him there.

Aunt Emmy and Tommy struggled for food and clothing. Tommy would do all kinds of odd jobs to scrape money together for the week, but they seemed to have so little it was hard not to feel sorry for them. The more we thought about Tommy, the more we wanted to take him something, especially as Christmas approached. Back at Moorcroft the shelves of the walk-in-larder were stacked with food, and it was quite easy to sneak in with a duffle-bag and lift small items like butter, cheese, or tins of fish. It was good to see Tommy and Emmy's faces as Steve and I gave them the food. They were so grateful and it was an easy feeling to be useful to them. It didn't seem anything like the stealing from shops the detective back at Ash Tree House had lectured me about.

Steve and I really visited Alfred Place to see Dave. If he wasn't there, we never stayed too long. I found it hard to be with the poverty and lawlessness around the terraces. Conflict was common, and the mood at Emmy's could change at the drop of a hat. Across the street, a pimp was running a brothel and once I saw an old man held down with a knife to his throat. It affected me for days, and so did another incident when a man viciously hurled a puppy across the room into the wall.

Another time, Steve left his bike at the top of the stairs at Aunt Emmy's house while he walked into town. It was gone by the time he returned. The story was that our cousin had borrowed the bike to get home and was upset when, in turn, it was stolen from him. Months later, we found out the truth; our cousin had sold the bike.

One day, though, I called into Emmy's on my own. She needed me to run an errand. "Can you nip into town and get me a mop 'ed?" Aunt Emmy asked. I pictured a small motorbike and wondered why on earth this chair-ridden old lady would want one. She saw the confused look on my face and kept repeating the word. *"Mop 'ed,* Philip. You know a *mop 'ed."* To add to my confusion, she dropped some loose change in my hand. Eventually, a neighbour came round and seeing the impasse, acted out cleaning the floor.

"Oh! A mop-head!" I said. They looked at me as if I were an idiot. I was glad to be on my way to complete the errand.

I preferred visiting Emmy's on my own, as Steve and I increasingly grew apart. We each seemed to tread on every scrap of sensitivity the other owned.

Once, a lad from my school found out about the remand home and asked me about it. I was shocked anyone knew. Steve spoke up before I could gather my thoughts. "Phil's the only one in our family who's been to prison." I looked away, reeling from his words, my stomach burning with venom. I clung tight to the football under my arm, willing the moment to pass, and trying to pretend it didn't hurt.

I always reacted to Steve's jibes. I thought *him* the favoured one, the one who seemed to be able to do anything. But Steve would hit me or take things from me whenever he wanted and when the fight started, I would defend myself as best I could, throwing plates, pans, shoes, anything that was near to keep him off me. It's as if we were fighting for the family gold.

In the spring of 1970, the authorities found Steve a foster home about a mile away. It was only for a short while until he finished school. I heard the foster father took an interest in Steve and gave him much needed respect and admiration. At the end of term, my brother went on to the sea training school *Indefatigable* on Anglesey, where Dave had been years before. Steve wanted to join the Royal Navy.

A few weeks after Steve left, a new boy, Brian, was brought to Moorcroft. He was a thin, but good looking, a sixteen-year-old with thick, dark hair nearly to his shoulders. Brian was meek and gentle, yet he loved to mix with biker gangs, in fact, he belonged to the main gang in Dewsbury led by a guy called Jesus. Even though Brian was physically weak – and I couldn't imagine him hurting anyone – he was always smack in the middle of any trouble that involved the gangs.

The very night Brian arrived at Moorcroft, he ran off back into the town centre and re-joined the bikers. The police brought him back. "I won't run away again," he vowed to Uncle Ken. But Brian seemed physically incapable of staying home. To deter him from running off, the staff took the keys out of the doors, but to no avail. It became a game almost every evening, discovering which window Brian had climbed out of. Around midnight, we would see the flashing blue light penetrating our bedroom curtains as a police car dropped him off for the hundredth time.

One night after being brought back, Brian became seriously ill. He had overdosed on something and descended into a fit, groaning, and rolling on the floor. The look of pain on his face was awful. I shook with fear, thinking Brian was going to die. No one knew what to do. We were all out of our beds and the younger ones were hysterical. The ambulance seemed to take ages.

Eventually, the medics arrived and heaved Brian into the ambulance. I was shocked at their lack of care. A few days later, I was massively relieved to see our housemate back on his feet.

Brian had only one possession: a thick book that he carried everywhere and loved to read. "What's your book?" I asked him.

"Anti-Q collecting," he said, splitting the word.

"Antique collecting."

"Oh, yes," he laughed.

I was curious about Brian's connection with that book: *did someone special give it to him?* I was just as intrigued with his fascination with biker gangs. *Was it the adventure? The belonging?* Whatever it was, the gang offered him something Moorcroft could not. The next time Brian ran away, he never came back.

Colin took his place. He was tall with frizzy hair and, at first, he ran away, too, as his family and friends lived close by. Colin, at fifteen, was grown up in many ways. Though not academically bright, he had an ability to live with the flow of life, and just like Brian, Colin had a gentle nature. If Aunty Sheila asked Colin to do a job in the house he'd smile and get on with it happily, and had none of my defiance. I admired the ease he seemed to have around people. He wasn't interested in sports, like I was, but we would have great chats about family, about teachers and about sex. "Do you come yet? You know – masturbate?" he said calmly one day.

"No," I said, trying hard to hide an immature feeling. "What do you mean anyway?"

"I'll show you," he said, "tonight."

After bedtime, three of us younger boys congregated around Colin's bed for a demonstration. Holding onto his manhood his arm moved like a piston-rod. "It helps to think about a girl," he said, giving a running commentary like an outward bound instructor. For good measure, Colin included a few facts about what he did with one girl in a field. It looked a bit strange seeing him deliver a payload onto the carpet with a flushed, contorted face, but Colin had no qualms or hang ups.

"We'll date some girls at Skegness," Colin promised.

It would be my second summer at the YMCA camp in Skegness. Just like he said, Colin soon had a date with a girl who also had a friend named Linda. As soon as I agreed to the rendezvous, I was wishing I hadn't; fear consumed me. *How would I cope?* "Just be cool," Colin said easily, seeing my distress. *What the hell does that mean?* I thought.

It was dark when the four of us met up. Linda had blonde, shoulder-length hair, was at least two years older than I was and about a foot taller. Linda and I left the camp, walked across the road and onto a quiet path to the beach. She seemed to take a shine to me and was very kind, but it quickly became apparent I had no idea what to do. I stopped a couple of times to kiss her, but my moves were awkward and my conversation almost non-existent. I hated myself for not being able to find more than a handful of words. After about twenty minutes, anxiety increasing with every step, I walked Linda back to the camp. I was never so pleased to say goodbye to anyone. I must have made her feel awful.

Then came my mental review. *What the hell is wrong with you? What a useless idiot you are! Why didn't you speak?* As if to rub my face in it the pop song *All Right Now*, by Free, played over and over in the camp. It was a song about a boy talking a girl into a date. Girls leapt to their feet to dance to it. Colin was sympathetic and gave me helpful tips, but I had to concede he was streets ahead of me.

Summer holidays back home at Moorcroft stretched on and the memory of my embarrassment with Linda faded. Then, on a warm afternoon while playing football, I saw Sally, who lived in the next road. My attraction was instant. Sally was a year younger than I was, her hair was fairy tale blonde and her petite figure irresistible. Freshness and sweetness poured out of her, as if she'd appeared from a beautiful palace in a Disney film.

Just catching a glimpse of Sally lit up the moment, and my mind became intoxicated with thoughts of her. At night, when my head hit the pillow, pictures of Sally took me over. She had a boyfriend of whom I was extremely jealous. I wondered long and hard how on earth he'd managed to be with her. *What was his secret?*

Sally and I spoke briefly a couple of times, and though she was shy, she seemed to like me. When I found out Sally and her boyfriend had split up, I was elated. I sat on the wall out front, or kicked a ball around on the road until it grew dark, just hoping she would walk past. With renewed promise, I filled up with images of us being easy together and something wonderful happening.

I finally caught sight of Sally walking home one evening. Summoning all my courage, I called to her, "Are you coming out later?"

"Oh, I can't. I'm doing things with my family." She didn't stop. She barely looked at me.

"Oh," I said, almost to myself. All the threads of my tender enthusiasm collapsed. I took it as a brutal rejection. I pictured Sally with her family, sharing a warm meal with her doting mum and dad. With my glaringly obvious lack, all the inferiority I had ever felt being a children's home kid plunged down onto me. I cursed my stupidity. *What right did I have to think I could be matched with her?*

Try as I might to switch off any wish to be friendly with Sally or any girl in my class, my longing would not cease. My head spun. *Advance. Advance! No! Retreat – Retreat – Retreat.*

Relieved at the end of another confusing school day, I came home and changed out of my uniform. Sunlight brightened the bedroom. A tingling sensation ran through me, as if my whole body was in resplendent service to the fellow between my legs, which, by now, was pointing directly at heaven. Sensing the angels had arrived, I rushed to shut the bedroom door. The divine influx was powerful, but it needed a helping hand. Soon the whole, sweet glory of paradise coursed through me and burst into the world. My fertility was working its magic, just like Colin had said.

Minutes later, I locked myself in the bathroom with my body relaxed and bathing itself in loveliness. But I couldn't help worry that I'd be found out. A 'dirty' feeling of shame swept through me, but thankfully it dissipated after a while.

I thought about my schoolmates and their regular joking around about 'fetching'. I knew what they were talking about now.

Even if other parts of my life were not going well, bath times were a little more fun and I looked forward to stealing moments with my private angels.

Chapter 27

The Thing of It

At number 2, Alfred Place, my mother was sitting with Aunt Emmy, warming herself by the fire. She looked dejected, despite my having run an errand to bring her cigarettes. I turned to see a big, stocky man in a cloth cap walk through the door. My mother sprang to her feet and shouted in his face, "You're the bloody cause of it!"

Towering over her, the man growled back. "Get away, woman!" My mother let loose a string of accusations and oddly finished off by pointing at me, ". . . and this is my son." Like a volcano, the man's temper burst and he let fly his huge fist. It landed on the door next to her head. I panicked and ran out to the street! Frantic for help, I looked around as the shouting continued!

I ran up the road, desperate to find someone who could intervene. I was running up the hill towards Moorcroft Drive when I saw a police car coasting towards me. I waved my arms. Stop! The driver glanced at me – but carried on. I broke into a run again; this time without slowing until I'd covered the two miles back to Moorcroft with my lungs struggling to suck in enough air. I burst into the lounge and began – between breaths – telling Uncle Ken what happened. I stammered and tripped over my words. Uncle Ken was getting annoyed. "What do you want me to do?"

"I don't know! Call the police!" He dialled 999 and handed me the phone. I told a garbled story about my mother being attacked by a man. I just wanted someone to help, someone in authority to bring normality to my mother, to me, and to our family. I sat shaking with distress, waiting for the police to come and let me know my mother was safe.

No one came. I felt sick with myself for not being able to protect my mother against a thug. And I felt embarrassed, and confused, because I'd seen plain as day, the stupidity of my mother for provoking him.

Even on Sunday mornings I could not relax. I was thirteen, but it was compulsory for children in the home to attend church. The younger kids went to one church and Steve and I, when he was still at Moorcroft, would set off in our best clothes and walk to the morning service at St John's Church. The huge trees surrounding the old stone church had a reassuring effect on me. I instinctively felt that sacredness was present *outside,* not in damp, darkened churches where I felt stifled. The atmosphere felt more deathly than anything, and each service had the gravity of a penance. The hushed praying, the sullen voiced hymns and the sombre readings appeared to belong to an age that I knew nothing about. I always came away feeling there should have been something more, something to touch me - like music did.

One or two people at St John's were very friendly and spoke to Steve and me, although our conversation was a little stilted. "Come again," they would say kindly. It was nice to hear that, but I always wondered if one Sabbath something different might happen.

One gorgeous, bright Sunday morning after Steve had left Moorcroft, I set off for St John's on my own. As I neared the church, the sunshine compelled me to carry on towards the gates of Dewsbury Park. It was peaceful and quiet; the smell of cut grass lingered and birds were singing out. I continued down the long hill towards Eightlands. Of course, I nursed a hope that I would find Dave at Aunt Emmy's.

He was still in bed when I got there, but he woke up enough for a brief chat before I had to trek back to Moorcroft.

My Sunday morning visits became a regular thing then. Most times, Dave would still be in bed, so I'd wait for him downstairs or, make him a cup of tea and take it up. Often, Dave had been out on the town the night before, drinking heavily. Dave wasn't always filled with joy at seeing his little brother that early in the morning, but I was persistent. Spruced up in my best clothes, I would be bright-eyed, glad to have escaped church, and eager for a talk. Dave would be buried in the blankets, bleary-eyed and wanting to sleep off the effects of the night before.

If I couldn't get Dave to talk I trundled home disappointed, no one any the wiser I missed church.

On one of my visits, I perched on the chair at the foot of Dave's bed and noticed a large roll of bank notes curled inside an elastic band. It must have dropped from his pocket. I picked it up. There must have been several hundred pounds, more than I had ever seen. "Where did you get all *that*?" I asked in a bright voice.

"Oh, I won it," Dave said brusquely.

Though Dave had left the Merchant Navy, he still wanted the old excitement and the money he was used to. I had overheard snatches of talk about Dave hanging around with questionable friends. I had no idea how deep he was involved. Some of those late Saturday nights had been spent stripping lead from roofs or breaking into shops and warehouses. When the police came looking for Dave, there were stashes of items hidden around his room and under the floorboards.

A couple of weeks after I spied the bankroll, my mother called round to Moorcroft Drive. I knew it meant trouble. Even though she lived only a mile away, my mother never came to visit. "Our David's been sent down!" she said. "He's got six months."

I felt sick. My mother ranted about the people Dave hung out with, blaming them all. But I was tired of her troubles. *When will it ever stop?* I was sick of everything. I was sick of Dewsbury, sick of my mother, sick of my family, and sick of my whole life. No one could switch off the never-ending, bleak news. It seemed there was nowhere to build a better life, and no one was even interested in talking about it. I was stewing in a big melting pot of let-down, and now Dave had been swallowed up by it too.

Bad news was everywhere, and it appeared my mother enjoyed it that way. I knew she hadn't even talked to Dave. My mother had recently got married to Stan so Dave had cut all contact with her. I had felt hurt when Dave totally blanked out my mother, but in that moment, I wanted to do the same.

The news dredged up memories of the brutal coldness of the remand home. Somehow, I knew wherever Dave was, it would be much worse. I was terrified for him. I imagined men beating Dave, and dumping him in a bare cell, cold and lonely. I lay awake long after dark, terrorised by worry. I had nightmares about him suffering with no one to help. I desperately wanted to do something, but no one in authority could be trusted. No one could switch off the never-ending miserable news.

All I could do was fall deeper into a depressing silence and wish Dave could be back safe on a ship – he never had a bad word to say about his life at sea. His stories sounded thrilling, and they had been colouring my thoughts since I was ten. It seemed that all of life's brightness was where Dave had travelled to, and all of life's gloom was here, with me.

I found a way to distract myself from suffering, even if it were a temporary easement. I began to earn my own money. August passed and at newly fourteen, I was given permission to get a small job. My first day of employment, I gladly got up at 6am to start my newspaper round. I slung the bag of morning newspapers over my shoulder and set off on my bike. On the corner of the first street, an older boy jumped from an alleyway. *Bang!* "This is my round, you little shit!" He punched me twice in the face.

Badly shaken up and with blood pouring from my nose, I had to go back and tell Uncle Ken what happened. Uncle Ken had just bought a new car, and although he was annoyed about the boy punching me, he didn't offer to drive me on the round. Instead, he got me to sit quiet till I calmed enough to climb back on my bike and set out again. I gave the alleyways a wide berth from then.

Later, the newsagent told me she had sacked the boy for his unreliability. When I told Uncle Ken that the boy went to my school and I had to face him every day, he offered no advice and no encouragement. I took that as yet another injustice. I rubbed against Uncle Ken's authority again, refusing to do my jobs around the house. I dallied around in the evenings so I was late to bed. It wasn't long before Uncle Ken lectured me . . . *"The thing of it is, is this."*

A mule-like stubbornness in me grew more intense. It seemed it was always me that had to back down. Although Aunty Sheila showed some sympathy, I was told to stay in my bedroom till my bad attitude wore off. But it wouldn't wear off; it just hardened into ever more defiance.

After another heated disagreement, Aunty Sheila and Uncle Ken sent for a child-care officer to mediate. Those mediations became a regular occurrence and I'd stare at the floor, shutting them all out from my private world. Even my breathing seemed to shut down. The adults kept talking, *why can't you just do this, why don't you stop doing that.*

One Friday evening, an argument had broken out about which shoes I should wear for school – I was particularly stung by the injustice of not being heard. In that mood, it was a relief to get up the next morning at 6am and get stuck into my Saturday paper round. I seemed to be happiest working a job, and the money in my hand felt like progress.

Cycling back about 9am, I turned down the hill into the top of the cul-de-sac. My foul mood churned up again like bile. My brakes squealed as I came to a stop by a van parked outside the front door. The van looked familiar. I turned towards the house to see Mr Thomas waving through the window. My heart leapt! I picked up my bike, carried it round the back of the house, and ran inside bursting with joy. "Mr Thomas!"

"Hello, Phil," he smiled. Both of us glowed.

"I saw your van, and . . ." I was lost for words.

I could see Mr Thomas wanted to talk with Aunty Sheila and Uncle Ken, but I was still put out by them. My mood returned and I wanted to shun them. I imagined they would sound off about my latest bad behaviour. In typical stubborn mode, I marched outside and sat on the front wall by the camper van till Mr Thomas was ready to come out. I wanted him to take me away for good, *today.*

Mr Thomas took me to Knaresborough for the day. We took a row boat out on the river, which I loved to do as the water and physical effort of rowing seemed to calm me. Then we walked down to Mother Shipton's cave and later ate a meal in a cafe. I wanted the day to go on and on; the world seemed softer, gentler and easier with Mr Thomas. I relaxed as I felt held and heard. I felt things and said things that didn't normally come out of my mouth. He told me he hadn't given up hope of trying to persuade the authorities to let him foster me. But then I knew it would soon be time to say goodbye, and sadness pressed on me. Mr Thomas' next visit could be six months to a year away and the parting felt like I was being murdered again.

That night and over the next many days, I wrestled with the yearning for a gentler life with Mr Thomas and despising the one I lived. Nothing I did was right. No one I was with measured up to the brightness of Mr Thomas. I slipped back into my private sullen world hating the powers that be, while trying to pretend I didn't feel a thing.

There was no pretending a lack of feelings on Wednesday afternoons when we had a double lesson of chemistry, *double-death*, as we referred to it. We were all terrified of Mr Heale. He dictated homework at lightning speed and we struggled to comprehend. The heavy, red pen marks he left on our homework looked like spilled blood.

I had been on the receiving end of Mr Heale's temper too many times, but this afternoon he overheard one of the other boys exclaim, "Where the fuck is my book?"

Mr Heale swivelled on his heel. "Who was swearing?" he shouted. The class went silent. "Come on, who was it?" No one dare put up their hand. "How many of you swear?" A group of hands went up and, sensing safety, everyone raised their hand, including the girls. Mr Neale's face could have lit a bonfire. He screamed at us. "How *dare* you!" He glared at us and slammed a fist on his desk. "Swearing is a sin. You are a shame to your parents." The room was silent.

"Yes, I am putting THE FEAR OF GOD into you!"

We looked at one another in disbelief. Our chemistry teacher had seemingly turned himself into a vengeful hit-man for some mafia god in the sky. We were instructed to read from our textbooks as he walked the rows of desks to calm himself.

Having hated Mr Heale, I now felt a little sorry for him, and wondered to myself; *why do people who talk about God seem to behave like bullies?*

Mr Blackall, our woodwork teacher, didn't make references to God, but as far as working with wood was concerned, he thought he was God. He continued with his domineering teaching style and somehow we tolerated it. There was one homework task Mr Blackall set us that made me sink: to source wood not stocked at the school. "Get your dad to take you to a wood merchant," he said. As soon as he mentioned the word *Dad*, I froze. I also froze the task out of my mind.

The next week came round. "Where's your wood, Barber?"

"Couldn't get it, Sir."

It was obvious I hadn't tried. "What do you think you're playing at lad?" Mr Blackall screamed. As usual, the whole class stopped and my face lit up as red as a pillar-box. "Ay! What do you think you're doing?" With the boys staring and my face on fire, my heart hammered out of control. "Answer me, lad!"

"I don't know, Sir."

Mr Blackall eventually let me loose. I picked up a chisel and with my hands trembling I tried my best to do something meaningful with it on my work-piece.

Time stretched painfully slow until break. It was my turn to pack away the tools. Suddenly, I found myself looking at the six large classroom windows. They were above the wooden bench upon which were several wooden mallets, lined up like tomahawks. I looked at the glass panes. Flames leapt in my chest! Rage seethed out of me! I knew where I would hurl the mallets! I picked up the first one!

"Cobber! It's break-time!" my classmate shouted.

I felt the warm wood of the mallet in my palm. I then placed each of them in the cupboard - all in orderly fashion.

Chapter 28

Sacred Sycamore

The one and only time I'd seen my mother contented was the previous year when I'd stayed the weekend. I'd watched her roll out pastry for a meat and potato pie; she was actually humming. When I needed a new project for woodwork class, I hit on the idea of making a rolling pin and pastry board; it would make a perfect gift.

Despite Mr Blackall's criticism, I slowly became proficient at woodwork and was producing good work. I had made a mahogany bed tray with small hinged support legs. I was proud that we used the tray in the home.

Mr Blackall suggested I use sycamore for the rolling pin and board. He demonstrated how to make the board by planing strips of wood and gluing them together. The rolling pin would be my chance to learn how to use the wood lathe.

Over the next months, the pieces came to fruition and I sanded the wood till my fingers grew sore. One afternoon, Mr Bradford, the metalwork teacher, happened to come into the classroom. "Barber," he said, sweeping his hand over the silky smooth pastry board, "you've done a brilliant job with that." Mr Blackall shuffled on his feet in discomfort. I had never heard him give praise like that.

Mr Bradford's recognition went deep, and his comment made me glow as bright as the afternoon sun. I knew then I'd made something good.

I was thrilled to show off my pieces to Aunty Sheila and Uncle Ken. "Oh! How kind of you!" Aunty Sheila said, smiling.

"They're for my mother!" I said sharply, correcting her assumption. Aunty Sheila's eyes dropped. Just as quickly she composed herself. I went upstairs annoyed. *Why did she assume the gift was for her? Couldn't she see I was trying to support my mother?*

I protected the rolling pin and board in brown paper, and then wrapped them in coloured gift paper. My mother would be delighted! She would see they were so much better than a shop-bought set.

That weekend, the pieces tucked under my arm, I could barely contain myself as I approached her house. My mother answered the door. "I've brought you something! I made it at school."

"Oh, right," she said, her voice dropping. She tore the paper, looked for a second and plunked the gift on the kitchen table. She turned and went into the other room in search of a cigarette. My breath stuck in my chest. I looked at my treasured pieces on the table, the paper barely touched! After all the hours of strife, labour and care, they suddenly looked worthless.

"I've been making them for months," I called, hoping she'd come back to the kitchen.

"Oh right," my mother muttered again. Then I felt stupid for thinking she'd like the gift, for thinking she'd appreciate the aggravation I'd gone through, and how hard I'd worked. I was an idiot for believing I could make life better for her. I handled the paper back round the gifts trying to retrieve their sacredness, and pushed the pieces back on the table so they wouldn't fall. I followed my mother into the other room where she sat in her chair, smoking.

She picked up a few sheets of yesterday's newspaper to read. The rest were screwed up in the fire grate waiting to be lit. I slunk into a chair. Try as I might, I could not think of anything to say. My stomach churned with hurt.

"I'll put the telly on," my mother said. I sat for a few more minutes, but I couldn't settle near her.

"I'll be off now," I said, getting up.

"I'll see you later, then," she said, her eyes staying fixed on the television.

Some part of me wanted to stay, to find some normal, ordinary thing between us. But it was a relief to be out of there. By the time I dragged myself up the grassy slope at the back of Moorside Road, my chest felt like it was filled with wet sand. I was completely lost. My mother would never use the pin and board, I knew it. *But what should I do? How should I react?*

I thought about going back for the pieces and giving them to someone else – maybe Aunty Sheila? *No,* I thought, *I need to stay loyal to my mother.* Yet, as I walked back to the home, everything looked and felt stagnant; my life, my town, everything was dull, flat and bleak. Nothing had a chance to be good. Somewhere there had to be a road out.

My weekday paper round gave me promise, as well as being a refuge, so I took on a Sunday round as well. Delivering papers to the closely packed terrace houses was a speedy job, but I enjoyed cycling around the sprawling bungalows on one section of my round. I dreamed of owning one of those properties with a fancy gate, long drive, and cricket-pitch lawn. It spurred me on to work harder.

As I loaded my newspapers into the canvas bag one morning a front page advertisement shouted at me: *Your Passport to Adventure.* Underneath the headline was an illustration of a merchant ship and a smartly dressed ship's captain. It was a recruiting advert for merchant navy officers. I read the advert with fascination, especially the part that stated a captain's annual salary, £5000. "Wow, look at that!" I said out loud. *Adventure and money.* I was hooked. The dreamy notion of a life at sea turned into something solid. I knew £5000 was a mile above most men's wages. The life of a merchant navy officer could take me far from Dewsbury, and a world away from my situation.

The contrast between my working seven mornings a week for fifty-five pence, and a ship master's salary drove me to a new goal. I would do whatever I needed to be accepted as a ship's officer. The advert appeared over several weeks, and I deemed myself perfect for the job.

If I weren't spending my wages maintaining my bike, I spent it buying technical drawing instruments for school – in my mind, part of the necessary equipment for my future career.

As I was fourteen, Mr Parker, an officer from the council children's department, came to the home to talk about career prospects. Mr Parker was new and had been assigned to me. We sat down together and I boldly announced, "I'm going to be a merchant navy navigating officer."

Discomforted by my words, Mr Parker shifted in his chair. "It's good to set your sights high, Philip . . . but don't you think you ought to be more realistic about your prospects?" I looked away. I'd never thought about that. *Maybe he knew something I didn't? Maybe my plan is a childish pipe dream.*

"You're skilful with your hands," Mr Parker said. "You could be a tradesman. And if you work hard, there's electrical engineering." I tried to picture myself doing those things, but the pictures were dull; nothing like the colourful images Dave had fed me.

It was during this time I would hassle Uncle Ken on a Sunday to lend me his copy of the Sunday People. The newspaper was sponsoring John Fairfax and Sylvia Cook in their attempt to row across the Pacific Ocean. I felt sunk and dejected from my meeting with Mr Parker but reading the weekly running reports of the two adventurers, along with pictures of sightings of them at sea, set my adrenaline streaming again. It fuelled an eagerness to prove Mr Parker wrong. *Why should I listen to him? He doesn't know me.* As well as my own feelings, I had Dave's words rolling around my head. "Steve, Phil, never ever get a job in Dewsbury. I'll kick your arses if you do!" So I kept on dreaming, and kept on delivering papers.

Every Saturday, I handed over my customers' newspaper money from the Friday evening collection. After careful accounting, the newsagent, Mrs Crow, would give me my wages.

One Saturday, the eight pound total fell short by ten pence. "I'll have to take that out of your wages," Mrs Crow said apologetically. I felt the loss intensely and for the whole of the following week the incident wouldn't rest inside me. Then I realised what I was feeling. *Mrs Crow assumed I'd stolen the money!*

The next week, I double-checked the collection money and dutifully submitted every penny. When Mrs Crow slid my wages across the counter I looked up at her and politely told her I didn't want to work for her anymore.

I missed the pay like crazy, so I was on the lookout for earnings, eager for my own resources. When the chance came to pick potatoes, I was first at the farm the next morning with three younger kids from the home. Each gang was allotted a patch with a boundary marker. Being paid by the sackful, we picked the spuds in our patch with an unstoppable fervour.

One morning, to give us home kids a chance at more money, I slightly moved the boundary marker. "Leave that alone!" a lad on the next patch shouted, while moving back the marker. When I thought he and his older brother weren't looking, I moved the marker again. "What did I tell you?" He didn't wait for a reply, instead he slugged me hard in the face. I couldn't bring myself to fight him, especially with his brother looking on. Fighting him wouldn't solve my problems, or help my mother. I did feel weak in front of the other kids, which left me feeling hollow, but the truth was, all I really cared about was earning the money.

I loved working. I found I could turn my hand to gardening, painting, shelving, or any practical job I could find. When working I put myself into overdrive, grafting for each penny and feeling worthy as I accomplished each task. I ran myself like a machine, in my own world. Only when I worked, did I feel safe.

The next time I saw my mother, she was at Aunt Emmy's. She often gravitated there. My mother was raging about the police and the children's department. "Would you believe, they think Stan is a nice fella! Well, I'm getting right away from that bloody man. I'm seeing about a council house so I can have the kids on my own."

My mother ranted about the waiting lists for this and that, but I never really understood what she was saying. It was too complicated to grasp, and she didn't like me asking questions.

"What can I do without money?" she complained, reaching her arms to the air with a hopelessness that scuppered all thoughts of anything improving.

Back at the home, Aunty Sheila saw how dejected I was. She asked me if I wanted to do some cooking, which I liked. While peeling the potatoes, all my shame and confusion about my mother bubbled up in a jumble of words with no starting place. I got agitated and, yet again, ended up the wrong side of Uncle Ken.

Rage kept welling up in me and I was increasingly bullying some of the younger kids. After another dressing down from Uncle Ken one day, I stood on the road outside, my face rigid with defiance, refusing to come in. Suddenly, from behind, someone slapped me gently on the face. I spun round in anger! My brother Dave stood there laughing.

"What are you doing here?" I said, recovering myself to show how happy I was to see him.

"My girlfriend's sister lives at the top of this road," he said, pointing. He told me a little about Eileen, a local girl he met after getting out of prison. He was really serious about Eileen and she was fascinated by him, with his stories of travelling and his worldly outlook on life. Despite her devotion, Dave was ashamed Eileen would discover where he was living. He never wanted her to know he lived at Emmy's, in case she asked to go inside.

I saw Dave on occasion when he visited Eileen's sister's house. He was spending more time with Eileen and her family, so our encounters lasted only a few passing minutes. I saw how Eileen's family embraced Dave as a new son and, in turn, how much he cared for them. I longed to have more of my brother's kindness, his normality and stability; and the way he gave me a sense that I had something worthy inside me, waiting to unfold.

One morning, I spotted Dave as I rode my bike through Dewsbury town centre. "Where are you going?" I shouted.

"Up to the foundry to look for a job," he said, as I cycled close. "I've moved in with Eileen's parents."

"Hang on. I'll leave my bike at Emmy's and come with you." I hid my bike upstairs in Dave's old bedroom to save it going the same way as Steve's.

As we stood waiting for the bus I ventured the question. "Are you never going back to sea, then?"

"I just need some temporary work," Dave said abruptly. "Christmas is coming up."

I turned away from him and looked in the direction of our bus. Dave's caution about us getting a job in Dewsbury resounded in my head like canon fire.

Foundry work was hot and smoky. It was tough and often dangerous, but paid good money. "Good luck, then," I offered as we parted back in the town centre, trying not to show my disappointment he wasn't taking his own advice.

I called back to Aunt Emmy's for my bike. "Your mother's left word," Emmy said. "Stan kicked her out. She's in a home for battered women. In Leeds." The way Emmy spoke she may as well have been telling me about the weather.

"Did she leave an address?"

"No," Emmy said, turning away. I handled my bike back down the stairs and rode off, trying to blank out the latest, sickening news.

The next time I saw Dave, he told me he liked the hard work at the foundry, and the good wage it paid. Then he hit me with more news. "I'm going to get married." There was no doubt in his voice, just radiance.

"Really? Are you sure that's the right thing to do?" I said, spilling out the words before I had time to think. Dave thought it funny that his little brother should say such a thing. He was nineteen, I was fourteen. I had the notion, though, that each of us still had more growing up to do. And I still thought Dave would return to sea; he had never stopped talking about it. But now I knew he'd never go travelling again, and with my own eyes set on a far horizon, I felt us drawing apart.

In the back of my mind, I had nurtured a dreamy desire of us together as a team, we three brothers doing something wonderful and adventurous, like the three musketeers. But the dream was fading. Steve had long gone. Dave had his new family and was even saving for a house. Whatever mooring rope I had to Dave was being hacked away, and I felt fearful of being set more adrift and left farther behind.

The year of 1970 played out as a year of endings. It was equally memorable for hearing the last of The Beatles who had split among bitter arguments. They had released their final album, aptly named *Let It Be.* The film of the same name included a spontaneous concert performed on a rooftop in the middle of London. I loved the maverick way they just did that, belting out the music without permission from any authority. I was saddened the Beatles were splitting. They had always been there with new and fresh music that had a way of making my world seem right.

Christmas and the school holiday came and went; I needed school results and I had to get my head down to the serious business of schoolwork.

One early spring day I was walking home from school. Sadness had been welling in my gut all day, and now a hollow feeling was making my chest collapse. It worked its way up to my eyes, but I kept pushing it down. Winter was still in the wind, but earlier in the day, there had been a tinge of warmth in the sun and it had brought the girls outside to enjoy the breeze. In their school blouses, they looked soft and inviting; seeing them churned up more of my feelings. The urge to get home was strong, like rushing to be sick. Inside the house, I dumped my bag and locked myself in the bathroom. I crumbled and slumped to the floor with my head in my arms weeping and weeping, feeling a putrid sickness with myself, and my whole life.

In the privacy of my own room, I clung to Mr Thomas's letters. He would always ask about my mother, too, as I had confided snatches of her struggles with Stan. *She is always welcome here, Phil. She will be safe for a while.* I loved Mr Thomas even more for wanting to help, but he was too far away to have any real impact. Not only that, I also wanted to keep him well clear of the awful mess of my family life, lest he be tainted and brought down by its futile misery.

In the spring of 1971, Mr Thomas wrote to tell me he was going to ask that I stay with him for two weeks in the summer holiday. He wrote, *maybe if we are seen to be asking for less, we might get some success. The children's department is now called Social Services, but they are equally slow in their responses.*

I badgered Aunty Sheila to ask the authorities to release me for the holiday. Something was definitely in the air, as I hadn't been told *no*. Fired up by the prospect of me visiting Wales, the letters between Mr Thomas and me increased, crossing like arrows in the sky. Finally, Aunty Sheila broke the news that I would be allowed to go. It was hard to believe, it felt so unreal. "But you'll miss the Skegness holiday," she said. I didn't care, and, I could not contain my happiness about going to Wales.

It was about this time that Uncle Ken and Aunty Sheila talked about leaving Moorcroft and becoming foster parents. In fact, two other boys and I had stayed overnight at their modern bungalow just a few miles away, and I relaxed in the softness of a normal home. I had enjoyed helping Uncle Ken paint the outside gate and I noticed he did not tell me off for spilling the paint. But now, in the shadow of my joyful expectation of Mr Thomas, Aunty Sheila and Uncle Ken went quiet towards me. There were no more visits to their bungalow – and no more arguments.

The holiday tugged on every thread of yearning I had about a better life. I spent time making myself a calendar. I numbered all the days leading to the date in August. I kept the calendar in the drawer by my bed, and every morning I'd cross off the previous day. Coloured in crayon, I marked August 22nd, my fifteenth birthday. I would get to spend it with Mr Thomas.

On the arranged day, I sat with great expectations and a few packed belongings, looking out the window, ready for Mr Thomas to pick me up.

PART III

Chapter 29

250, Abergele Road

Gazing out of the sitting room window, I felt like a castaway scanning the horizon. The sun was hot when Mr Thomas's camper van rolled down the hill. I ran out to meet him as if he were a rescue ship. I had been seven years old when Mr Thomas first promised I could stay with him for a holiday in Wales. It had lived in my head ever since, like his home was my real home – the only place where I was wanted.

Mr Thomas slid back the driver's door and stepped out. He looked relaxed in a short-sleeved shirt and sleeveless jumper. Two boys scuttled out from the back seats. "Phil, this is Michael and Derek. I've been promising them a holiday," he said. I kept my smile wide to mask my disappointment at not having Mr Thomas to myself. He had planned a couple of days camping and exploring the wilds of North Yorkshire before heading back to Wales.

"We've got the locations of some crashed World War II aircraft," said Mr Thomas, hand at my back and leading the way to the front door of the home. "I'll show you on the map. We can go find them."

Over a cup of tea with Aunty Sheila and Uncle Ken, we all spread out the map with the grid references of the planes marked in red pen. I was excited to get going. After a quick goodbye we drove off. I sat proudly in the front passenger seat. I loved the vinyl plastic smell of the camper van; I loved its red vinyl seats, its elevating roof, and its long side windows dressed with short, pleated curtains.

In no time, we were far away in the countryside and parked in a remote, roadside spot. We packed some sandwiches and headed off, following rough trails over the moorland and scrambling up the sides of windswept hills in search of the wreckages. In the open landscape I felt released. It was new and electrifying to be with Mr Thomas for more than a day, far from the institutional homes.

We found three wrecks, including a Dakota that was mostly buried from its crash impact. Another plane was riddled with a line of bullet holes down one side of the fuselage. I poked my fingers in the holes. "I wonder how the fight in the sky went; if the pilot survived."

Mr Thomas looked at me. He placed a hand on my shoulder. "You're a different boy out of the homes, Phil."

Mr Thomas's words penetrated so deep my heart split open, and for the first time in my life, I allowed the possibility that the constant trouble circling me was not of my own making.

For the rest of that day and the next, new energy burst out of me. Every project we tackled felt fun – and funny. Every task we set upon felt easy. After each day's trek, I took over the job of heating up the baked beans and tins of stew on the small, built-in gas stove, and I joked with Michael and Derek like they were my younger brothers.

On the evening drive to Wales, the boys fell asleep in the back and I sat in the passenger seat sharing all my cares and worries with Mr Thomas. I wanted him to listen to it all, to show his horror and then have him tell me how to sort it all out. I tried to talk about my disjointed family and my life in the homes. I snatched at the most immediate memories of Moorcroft and the injustices there. I wanted to spill every detail of the arguments I'd had with Uncle Ken and Aunty Sheila. They were the most recent face of institutional care and I didn't have a good word to say about them. "They don't understand anything, Mr Thomas. I hate the rules they make up. They just shut themselves in the lounge, smoking and laughing. I hate both of them!"

"Hate is a dangerous thing, Phil," said Mr Thomas. He went on. "I struggled with it at Spennells, myself. The times I packed my bags to leave after rows with the Vaughans . . . It was usually Jo Vaughan that pushed me furthest. Then, right at the last minute, Charlie Vaughan would make her apologise."

Mr Thomas told me how sick he felt when Mr Vaughan attacked me in the hostel that evening after I had refused to pick up the towel. "That was the closest I came to blows with Charlie Vaughan," he said, staring ahead at the road.

I was stunned. Mr Thomas must have heard it all from his room. Mr Thomas was physically strong, but never moved to violence, yet, I couldn't understand. *Why didn't he help me that night? How could he have held back?* I looked away and stared out at the passing fields that were fading into the night. I was not ready to ask Mr Thomas why. Maybe, I mused, it was because Mr Thomas was soon leaving to foster me and punching Mr Vaughan could have put an end to everything.

Mr Thomas looked over at me. "The first year after I left you at Spennells, Phil, I didn't make much progress. I wanted to foster you, Steve and Dave. The authorities in Dewsbury and at Barnardo's were maddening to deal with. They kept me going in circles. So, I talked it over with the vicar at my church. He suggested I contact someone he'd read about at *The Sunday People* newspaper. Two reporters came to the house. They interviewed Jean and me and took pictures. They wanted to show what a welcoming home we had. Well, the article came out in the very next edition, challenging Barnardo's to release you to us. I'm afraid it got their backs up, Phil. Barnardo's sent word: I wasn't to contact any of you again."

Though I understood Mr Thomas's thoughts about hate I suddenly hated everyone but him. I wanted the drive to Wales to go on forever so I could empty every stupid rule of every stupid institution into the night. I wanted to clear my head of the idiotic authority voices that had been running my life. I wanted to be as far away from the agony of it as possible.

I told Mr Thomas about taking on my paper round, about getting punched the first day and how Uncle Ken had left me to deal with it all. And about Mr Parker telling me to be realistic about my prospects . . . But there was one thing I could not tell. I could not talk about the remand home; I couldn't be sure if Mr Thomas's understanding would stretch that far.

We arrived in Old Colwyn late that night. After dropping off Michael and Derek at their parents, the headlights of the Bedford van lit up the narrow lane at the back of the Thomas' house. Worn out from the day's trekking and the talking, I slid straight into bed.

The next morning, sunlight shone through the thin curtains. I had travelled a world away from the havoc of Dewsbury. I was finally at 250, Abergele Road. I had written so many letters to this address! Two whole weeks . . .

Mr Thomas had included in his letters the various children he and Mrs Thomas had fostered or hosted for holidays. Wrapped in my own problems, I had paid scant attention to their names. Now, I was overwhelmed listening to the stories about all the children who had stayed here. The Thomas's had given holidays to kids from London, Birmingham and Manchester, as well as from the local area. "One London borough was so needy for holiday placements, they asked us, *how many can you take*?" Mr Thomas recounted.

The Thomas's had tried to adopt several children, but their plans and preparations had fallen apart in the final hurdles. Parents had changed their minds, leaving the Thomas's bereft. Now they had two foster children, baby Marlon and nine-year-old Julie.

Julie had pigtails and thick round glasses. Her mother lived locally, but made no contact. Julie's panic attacks and bedwetting had slowly decreased in the two years she had lived with the Thomas's. "Jean has loved her back to health," Mr Thomas told me proudly.

Four-month-old Marlon was a West Indian baby. He was the prettiest baby I had ever seen. Marlon's parents had abruptly left him there one night and moved to London. They promised to pay for his keep but had sent no money. Mr and Mrs Thomas were crazy for Marlon, and were pushing for a legal adoption. I took to

Marlon quickly. He had a beautiful nature and would laugh wildly when I raised him in the air. "You're a little Muhammad Ali," I said, seeing how handsome he was.

Mrs Thomas was short and had cut her long, dark hair. I was trying to get used to her speech and struggled to catch every sentence. She smiled warmly at me and was generous, but still quiet, and shared interests for us were in short supply. Mrs Thomas let me do some of the cooking, which I loved to do. She let me make my own choices about simple things that used to be decided for me. But I could tell she was much more confident with Julie and Marlon.

The house was a tall, pebble-dashed mid-terrace in a row of twelve. It had seven bedrooms on three floors, plus a large attic and a cellar. There was a tiny front garden between the house and the busy A55 road that ran along the North Wales coast. I stood outside and read the house name on the front gate. "I named it Spennells so that if any of the boys from the home were passing, they might call in," Mr Thomas said, affectionately.

The air felt gentler and people seemed to smile more, even the tap water was softer here. Walking about later that first morning we stopped to talk to one of Mr Thomas's many friends from the church. "Bor-e-da," Mr Thomas said, keeping alive a Welsh greeting.

Over the next few days I tagged along with Mr Thomas wherever he went. We always saw someone he knew and always stopped to talk, as they each seemed to want to share endless news. Later that day, while sitting in the sitting room after tea, Mr Thomas told me what one of his friends, Mrs Williams, had said upon meeting me. "That boy's got troubles in him," she'd told him. "There's sadness etched on his face."

I reeled at the thought that people could see into me, but my mind soon shifted when Mr Thomas must have seen into me himself. "I could write to Dewsbury and ask if you can stay permanently, Phil." Mr Thomas leaned forward in his chair. "How would you feel if they said yes?" It was strange to be asked my opinion, and strange to think someone might take notice of it.

I beamed. Then, I thought about having to make new school friends. "I'd have to change schools!" I didn't relish that prospect. Also, I was a year into my two-year general certificate of secondary education (GCSE) exam course work and wondered how I would cope with getting the results I needed to go to sea. But sitting here with Mr Thomas, I was where I had always dreamed of being. "I don't want to go back," I said finally, "I'm sick of the homes."

"I'll write tonight," said Mr Thomas. "Let's not get fired up with too much hope, though. You know how they are."

Despite his warning, of course, I longed for a positive official reply. Before the day was out, I went with Mr Thomas to the post box, and pushed the letter in with a fervent wish.

In the middle of my two-week stay, Mr Thomas returned to the *Diamond Stylus* factory where he worked making gramophone needles. He disliked his job and missed an outdoor life, but the money supported his dream for a house full of children, growing up happy.

I was alone in the kitchen when I heard the postman push the mail through the letter box and land on the doormat. I placed the official-looking envelope on the table, knowing it was the letter we were waiting for. I itched to know its content. Mr Thomas wouldn't be home until evening, and the thought of waiting felt unbearable. I held the envelope up to the light in the hope I could see through it. I put it down again, made myself a drink of tea, and sat for a while. Suspense burned inside me. The flap wasn't fully stuck down. I pulled at it a little, and it came away. I took the letter through the kitchen into the outbuilding to hide myself away with it. I carefully peeled back the flap with only a small amount of tearing and held the paper delicately. And then I hardened myself for disappointment.

The letter started, *Re: Philip Barber and fostering arrangements.* There followed two short paragraphs in very formal language, but the message was clear: *I was to be allowed to stay!*

It was hard to absorb the words. I couldn't grasp the fullness of the news. With heart pulsing, I refolded the letter, gently reversing the procedure to place it back on the table. I licked the envelope flap and smoothed it flat on the table with my palm, and pressed down with all my weight.

I had to have something to do. I was told I could use the old bike in the garage, so I pulled it out, clicked the garage door padlock shut and pedalled off to the seafront. I raced along by the water with the wind in my face, thinking of all the new things we could do, the camping trips we could go on. Maybe we could buy a canoe or a boat and spend hours on the water. I kept peddling until all my gushing energy expended itself.

Back at the house, the Bedford van sat outside. Mr Thomas was smiling as I came through the door. He held the letter in his hand and read it to me. "Oh, son, after all this time, you're staying."

"I know," I said, "I couldn't help it! I opened the letter!"

Mr Thomas smiled at me, too overjoyed to tell me off. "I wonder what changed their minds. Maybe we've been so much trouble they were glad to see back of us." We laughed together and I felt brightness pouring into me as if we'd drawn back the curtains on a sunny spring morning.

We talked about getting my things from Moorcroft Drive, especially my bike. I showed Mr Thomas the small booklet I had brought with me about HMS Conway. "Can we visit there when we get chance?" HMS Conway was a training college for merchant navy and royal navy officers. The college was only forty miles away on the small Island of Anglesey. Not only was it close, but it was near the *Indefatigable Sea School* where my brothers had gone. Mr Thomas promised to take me. That day, I think he would have promised me the moon.

We were washing the dishes together a week or so after the letter arrived, when Mr Thomas turned to me. "I'd be happy if you want to call me Dad."

It was very sudden. I couldn't form words. I wanted Mr Thomas to be my father, but I had never used the word *Dad*. Many times in moments of affection, Mr Thomas had called me *son*, and I loved him for saying it. I knew the expression was something I would struggle with, and I knew it had come too soon. *'Dad'* had become a holy term, not to be spoken in normal conversation. After fifteen years of being fatherless, I had nowhere near enough trust in myself to use the word. I had never dared risk that kind of closeness.

I had been calling Mr Thomas *Mr Thomas* since I was six-years-old. He signed his letters 'Uncle Colin' and I wrote that in my letters to him. For the next few hours, in a cumbersome way, I imagined calling him Dad. I wanted to do it, for his sake. But my tongue would not cooperate. "Can I call you Uncle Colin, for now?" I asked. It was as much as I could give. I tried saying the word uncle in a closer, more affectionate way, but even that felt clumsy and uncomfortable.

As the weeks went by, I must have shown my discomfort. "Are you happy, Phil?" Uncle Colin asked me over and over again.

"Yes," I always said with a smile, but I was trying my best not to feel disappointed. Other things had begun to agitate me, like the room I slept in. It was large, with a high ceiling and a single bed either side of a central, boarded-up fireplace. An old china sink and an ancient wooden wardrobe stood against the opposite wall. The wardrobe opened with an ornate lock and key, and when I swung back the door a strong stale, musty smell hit me. Uncle Colin had the room decorated with cream-painted *anaglypta* paper and a utilitarian, nylon carpet. A clear, plastic carpet protector lay in front of the sink. There were no colourful, homely touches like rugs or cushions, and I was craving softness. The truth was, this seven-bedroom house felt like an empty creepy castle.

Uncle Colin had to make the rooms look clean and respectable for inspections from the *Social Services*. With little money, he was trying to create his own children's home out of this rambling house. I was old enough to understand Uncle Colin and Aunty Jean's dream of a home full of children. I wanted that for them as well, but I wanted it sometime in the future. Right now, I desperately wanted to be a young man in a family, not feeling myself an inmate with a mishmash of children.

"Are you happy, Phil?" Uncle Colin asked again. "Do you like living here?"

"I'd rather live in a smaller house," I said, grasping the opportunity. Mr Thomas laughed, but I sensed his disappointment. My empty feeling was accentuated by my bedroom being on the first floor next to three other bedrooms, each of them empty. Uncle and Aunty slept on the floor above. The only heating was the small gas fires in the two sitting rooms downstairs. When winter closed in, ice slicked the inside of my bedroom window.

For the first few months, I couldn't rest at night. I was too frightened by my own thoughts; I had always slept in a room with at least three other boys. I asked Uncle Colin to sit by my bed and talk to me until I fell asleep. He was usually weary, and had to wake early for work, so he would lie down quietly beside me. After some time, Uncle Colin would tire and leave. I begged him to stay. Eventually, I insisted he leave the stairway lights on and keep my bedroom door open. I was deeply ashamed for asking, but it was the only way I could settle.

I wanted Uncle Colin and Aunty Jean to sell the place and buy a normal, three-bedroom, semi-detached house, something that would feel like a normal family home in a normal street like I had seen many times on the TV. I didn't want to live in a house that felt like a children's home – or in any circumstance that had the slightest whiff of one.

Just like a fledgling needing a nest to grow its wings I craved normality, and I craved warmth.

Chapter 30

Pride and Protection

I was glad to have a visit from my new social worker, Miss Sanderson. Not having a phone in the house she just dropped in on us. In her late twenties she was tall and attractive with blonde, shoulder-length hair. In a pale blue tight-fitting sweater with her leather handbag slung over her shoulder she looked smart and confident. More importantly, she looked as if she would be more use than my previous social workers.

"It has been decided that you should go to Pendorlan School," Miss Sanderson said firmly. My face fell. *I'd been downgraded!* I had assumed I'd attend the more academic Eirias Park High School, and was annoyed that some authority figure thought poorly of my capabilities. It was a kick in the teeth for my chances of the grades to apply to HMS Conway.

I felt someone was stealing what little treasure I had. I wanted to ask Miss Sanderson to phone my old schoolteachers who, I felt sure, would tell of my academic achievements. But I never spoke up. I was tired of defending myself, and I shied away from making waves. After all, *wasn't I lucky to be able to stay in Wales with the Thomas's?*

Miss Sanderson next called at the house to drive me into town to order my school uniform. We talked a little in the car. I liked her, but I sensed an aloof professionalism. I told her my plan to be a merchant navy officer, but as the words stumbled their way out of my mouth my dreamy expectations sounded suspect.

"Mmm," was all she said, and kept her eyes on the road until she dropped me back home. "I'll come and pick you up for school on Monday. Ten o'clock."

On Monday I perched by the front-room window in my new school blazer. Miss Sanderson took me to see the head teacher. "I'll just have a word with Mr Evans, if you want to sit there, Phil," she said, pointing to a chair in the small reception room.

I sat obediently, but with a familiar sick feeling of grown-ups having private conversations about me.

I noticed how old the building was. An awful hankering for my former school washed through me. My defences were going up again, sensitive to starting over in a new environment.

Emerging from the headmaster's office, Miss Sanderson prepared to leave. "I will come and see you again soon then, Phil," she said. I didn't want to be left so soon. I looked up at her, hoping she would say *I can stay with you for a while, if you like.* Just as quickly I looked away, having long ago learned to hide my anxiety.

Mr Evans came out from his office and stood looking at me, one hand on his hip, the other scratching his head. His look was a mixture of sympathy and uncertainty. Finally he summoned a passing teacher. "Mr Williams, take this boy to Miss Parry's class, will you?"

Mr Williams was barely an inch taller than I was, and his heavy, tweed jacket seemed to both prop him up and devour him at the same time. He had the darkest six o'clock shadow I'd ever seen. "Where are you from, Phil?" he asked in the friendliest of manners, walking alongside me.

"Dewsbury. In Yorkshire."

"Oh, Yorkshire!" he said, "You've come a long way." He directed me to Miss Parry's maths class and I sat at a desk, ready to continue my education.

The school was a Victorian two-storey, red-brick building in a built-up area, with one small playing field a hundred yards up the road. My old school was a modern, glass building of four floors, surrounded by acres of green playing fields. Here, the Welsh accents swirled around me, and I could find little to match my life to the life of the other kids. My feelings of being *unwanted* and being a misfit seemed to follow me everywhere. I constantly wished I was somewhere else.

When the bike I'd borrowed got trashed in the first few days of school, my loneliness grew worse. Aching for a friend, but terrified of having one, too, I arrived at school dead on time, and left as soon as I could. In between, I kept myself bland and colourless.

Our headmaster at least kept my interest. Mr Evans was as Welsh as the local slate. His morning addresses were brief, but memorable for their flavour; he would repeat whole sentences in Welsh.

"What a bewt-ti-full day, children! It's one of those days when you want to . . . fill your lungs and say to yourself . . . it's good to be alive!" I sniggered inside at this slightly delirious Welshman's babblings about the weather. But his sentiments lingered with me all day. It was true! Cycling to school that autumn morning in full sunshine and a warm breeze, I had flung off my jacket and felt less worrisome.

Mr Evans loved his Welsh heritage and I'm sure he would have gladly dismissed all things English, including me. It was 1972 and nationalism was rearing up. The Welsh were kicking back, setting ablaze rural cottages purchased by prosperous English people as second homes. In those small communities, the Welsh language was in danger of dying out.

I saw Mr Evans' pride as he looked on at the kids practising clog dancing in the school's main hall. They were preparing for contests that culminated at the annual national Eisteddfod. Mr Evans earned my respect as he encouraged youngsters to perform in our assemblies. To my delight, we regularly had singers, dancers, and poetry readings.

It was during another assembly that I saw Mr Evans again in full gusto. "I keep hearing on the *ray*-deo about this so-called, *per-miss-sive sus-i-ety*, where you just *do* what you want! If you don't like someone, you can *smash* them in the face, *is that it?* Well! We'll have none of that in this school."

Something in the expressiveness of, '*smash* them in the face,' made me want to howl with laughter, as if it were a poorly disguised critique of English behaviour. But his reference to keeping order found a welcome place in me, even if his style was a bit odd.

Our games teacher, Mr Nott, was a giant of a man, six-and-a-half feet. Watching him lace up his boots twice around the soles like a rugby player, I couldn't help notice the most enormous feet I had ever laid eyes on. His enthusiasm for football, though, had a springtime effect on me.

For the first time in what seemed like ages, on a football pitch in a full game, my troubles evaporated. The big Welsh lads on the opposing team regularly switched languages as they shouted instructions to one another. Ours was the weaker side, and to save us from getting completely hammered, Mr Nott played on our team. Holding the final line of defence, he launched into the ball like a tidal wave, sending it cruising into orbit way above our heads. I tried my best to get on the end of his passes, but they came at a cracking pace. Finally getting one at my feet, I went for goal. But instead of slipping around defenders like the wind, my body held back. *Where was my swiftness?* I felt like I was carrying an injury, as if my mind told my muscles, *don't play too well, you'll stand out.*

My speed came in snatches, and so did the odd goal, but I felt second-rate. I came away disappointed. To bat off depression I told myself that I was concentrating on my academics, and being clever.

That view was bolstered by the arrival of a package and personal letter from Mr Murphy, my previous head teacher in Dewsbury. Mr Murphy wished me luck in my new school and sent me my previous year's course work. I could see it was good. More importantly, Mr Murphy's personal wishes in the letter brought back a much-needed inner glow.

That evening, I pulled the black and white booklet for HMS Conway out of my drawer. Looking at the pictures I imagined that it was me there in uniform steering the boat into the dockyard. Then the weather in my head came as bright as day.

The belief that I was clever was a protection; it was never supposed to stray into arrogance. But it did, as I was too proud and too scared to ask for help. I kidded myself that I would excel come exam time. My confidence in my school work began to suffer.

I was surprised, though, when our history lessons struck a chord inside, as if they were meant for me. Our teacher, Mr Davies, was a masculine man with a deep, resonant voice. Every so often, he would stop lecturing and take off his glasses to put one end in the corner of his mouth as if he were smoking it. He would look straight at us and emphasise the reason behind some important event. Instead of a history lesson it was as if he was dissecting family squabbles, and he would scan our faces to see if his words landed.

I was drawn to his lessons where we learned about the Second World War, about the invasion of Poland, about the tenacity of Winston Churchill. I was also learning about India's struggle for independence after the war, and about the personal power of Mahatma Gandhi.

I paid attention to these great turning points in history as if I were divining secrets. There was something I needed to know about how great swathes of humanity were dominated by only a few individuals. The stories sparked an interest in how people overcome struggles and, though I had yet to realise it, my connection to recent Polish history.

Chapter 31

Sunday People

I loved being up in the loft where Uncle Colin had installed a work bench. There were woodworking tools, screws, nuts and bolts, and stacks of wood offcuts. From the first time Uncle Colin took me there, my hands itched to make something. I poked around among the wood and tools alone most days, imagining the day when Uncle Colin and I would build a useful item for the house - like a stool or a table. To keep my hands moving, I refinished an old school desk I found up there.

But as Uncle Colin never came up to join me, the excitement started to fade. Though I felt undeserving of his time, I had assumed we would do some things together. Boredom and feelings of being let down began to take root.

At a loose end one time, I stood on a chair to reach the sloping skylight and admire the view. The skylight hadn't been opened in years, but I managed to release the catch and poke my head out. In the distance, far over the rooftops, I could see the hills, brightened by the sun. As I pulled the frame back into place, a pane of glass broke loose and slid down the roof to the ground. *Crash!* I flew down the four flights of stairs, praying no one got caught by the falling glass. As I collected the shards from outside the back door, I thanked my lucky stars no one was in the way.

Uncle Colin was furious when he came home. "Why don't you leave things *alone*? I'll have to pay a builder to put in new glass now!" The scolding shook me to the core. He had never said a cross word to me before. I felt like a pane of glass myself, crashing to the ground.

It soon became clear that Uncle Colin's spare time revolved around St John's Church. He sang in the choir, and for years had shouldered full responsibility for keeping it alive with youngsters. Three evenings a week, Uncle Colin walked around Old Colwyn dropping off newsletters and encouraging fickle choirboys and girls to attend evening practice and Sunday service. He made sure they were paid properly, and if they needed a drive to church, often went to collect them. Uncle Colin also delivered cards on choir members' birthdays and took them all out on special weekend outings. Through the Royal School of Church Music, he entered the St John's Church Choir into national choir competitions, which motivated the boys no end.

At first, I walked with Uncle Colin wherever he went, hanging on to his coat-tails. His mind was always on his tasks, though, and when he had to make "just one more house call," I most often walked back to Old Colwyn's 'Spennells' on my own. After a while, I just stayed home, watching television or spending idle time in my room.

On Sunday mornings, Uncle Colin set off thirty minutes early to prepare the choristers. "See you there!" he would call out. Later, spruced up in my good clothes, I walked the mile to church, wishing Uncle Colin would sometimes take time out on a Sunday to enjoy other things. The first time I went to St John's, Uncle Colin introduced me to Idris, the verger, and asked him to take care of me.

Idris, with his balding head, walking stick and black robe, looked like a monk. I stood with him in the stone entrance porch welcoming people and handing them a red hymn book and a blue prayer book. The congregation was mostly elderly; they came in their Sunday-best and smiled indulgently at me. Some hovered in the arched porch-way to talk with Idris, chewing over the week's events in their native tongue, or in a florid Welsh accent. "How's the gaaaar-den Missster Davies." Each greeting was more animated than the last.

"Helloooo Misses Joooones," Idris said to yet another person named Jones. Idris' sing-song voice embodied each parishioner's news with long, extended vowels, and he opened his arms and swayed his body this way and that in sympathy.

I was feeling a little out of place, so I was happy to keep busy handing out books. But I faltered a little after twenty minutes of steady greetings. Idris became annoyed with me. "Give these people a welcome, won't you," he said in his thick tongue. I was annoyed and wanted to say, *well, you quit jabbering in a language I can't bloody well understand, then*. But I was far too polite.

During the service, I sat alone in a pew at the very back. As the choristers left the vestry two abreast behind the vicar, I looked out for Uncle Colin. Dressed in cassock and surplice, he'd be near the back of the procession. I'd catch his eye as they all glided past me and up the nave to the choir stall.

Uncle Colin didn't force me to attend church, but I knew he wanted me to share his enjoyment. I wanted to please him, and I felt I had signed a contract of attendance. I tried my best to like it, but the services still felt dull and meaningless. I couldn't connect the hymns, prayers and sermons with anything in my own life.

One Sunday morning, my mind drifted during the service. The Beatles' song, *While My Guitar Gently Weeps*, kept playing in my head. Without realising, I started singing the words to myself: *I look at you all. See the love there that's sleeping.* The people in the rows ahead turned and stared, and I looked away in embarrassment.

If Aunty Jean weren't working, she sat right up in the front pew with Julie. Sometimes she visited the Pentecostal church a stone's throw from our house. I would pass by that church and hear joyful singing bursting from the open windows. I always wanted to go in, but Uncle Colin wasn't keen.

By the end of the service at St John's, my feet needed to move. I gladly collected the books and, preparing for the evening service, changed the numbers in the wooden hymn boards. I waited for Uncle Colin, but most times he had a meeting, or wanted to make house calls, so I walked back on my own. I wandered home in the fresh air, often detouring down by the front to look at the sea for a while, feeling glad the whole thing was over for another week.

All through that first autumn, Sundays began to feel like lost days. I felt disorientated and couldn't help sensing a clock was ticking and precious time with Uncle Colin was being wasted.

Christmas Eve was different. I'd never been to a midnight mass before and it seemed the whole of Old Colwyn turned out for the service. I stayed in my greeting role right up till the minute the service began so I could welcome in the stragglers. Many *were* straggling – straight from the pub. With the whiff of spirit on their breath and a glow in their cheeks, I delighted in inviting them all in. The church was alive and people sang full out. Afterwards, I hung around doing my own jabbering, in English, to lots of new people, my cheeks warm with the same glow.

Uncle Colin had a good friend, Albert Roberts, who really was a monk. Known to all as Father Roberts, he was earnest and amiable. I remembered Father Roberts from a Spennells summer-fortnight in Old Colwyn when I was six. We had camped in St John's church hall, and Father Roberts visited us in his black monastic robes. We crowded round him as he entertained us with stories of his travels, and tricks with cards and matchsticks!

The year before I arrived at Uncle Colin's, Father Roberts suffered a heart attack. He'd collapsed and died. Uncle Colin was devastated, they were such good pals. Jean had been close to him, as well, and they grieved together.

Uncle Colin showed me the bedroom he'd kept just for Father Roberts' visits. Furnished with only a bed and a writing desk, the room was sparse. "It's the way he liked it – he called it his *cell*," said Uncle Colin. "Albert's only vice was cigarettes, but he smoked like a factory chimney!"

Father Roberts' room wasn't needed for anyone else, so his *cell* remained untouched, as if it were a loving shrine.

Father Roberts' monastic home was *The Community of the Resurrection*, coincidentally in Mirfield, Yorkshire, near Dewsbury. Uncle Colin took me to the monastery on a return visit to Dewsbury in the camper van. When we arrived, the Head Father happened to be walking the grounds. He was a tall, soft-spoken man with a bushy beard and, as he made us tea in his office, Uncle Colin told him about me, and how I had come to live with him and Aunty Jean. The Father's warmth was evident, and he made a point of asking me about my original family in Yorkshire. He listened with curiosity and intent as I told him about my brothers, and about my plans to go to sea - his expressive face easing the words out of me.

"Come on, I'll show you around," the Father said. Walking down the main corridor, buoyed by his genuine nature, my questions bubbled up. *What made him wish to be a monk? What was a monk's life like?* And then I heard the monks chanting. We stood still to listen. I was moved. Their singing beckoned to something achingly deep in me. It were as if the beautiful sound were carrying the very nutrients of life.

We visited Father Roberts' grave in the monastery grounds. Aunty Jean had instructed Uncle Colin to carry a kiss from her, and I watched from the path as he bent to kiss the triangular wooden headstone. I was moved to see Uncle Colin's affection for his friend.

Later on, Uncle Colin asked the Father about one of the monks he had met when Father Roberts was still alive. The Father said the monk had recently taken his own life and it had come to light that he had been ridiculed by some of the other monks. As we drove away down the gravel drive, Uncle Colin looked back across the lawns at the stone building. He shook his head with sadness. "I thought this was one place where people actually loved one another."

We found a place to park the camper van for the night. After hearing the news of the monk, I wanted to be of the most help to Uncle Colin, and fixed a dinner of tinned stew and toast. I cleaned up and made two cups of tea as I kept thinking about Uncle Colin's words: *a place where people loved one another.* I had never heard anything like that before.

The next day, we planned to get my bike from the Moorcroft children's home, and pay a visit to my mother. I had a lot to reflect on as we bedded down that night.

At Moorcroft, I collected my bike, but there was sad news. Uncle Ken had passed away. The years of cigarettes had finally claimed him. Aunty Sheila looked lost. I felt for her and didn't know what to say. I was glad to have Uncle Colin's kindness speaking for me.

We went on to visit my mother but, not surprisingly, she had abandoned Moorside Road. It looked like I wouldn't see her but, quite by chance, later that evening as we drove through Dewsbury town centre, there she was walking along the pavement.

We picked her up, parked the van and made her a cup of hot tea. My mother was in a state again, reeling off all her recent conflicts in a voice that pierced the little van. She had been in endless confrontations with Stan about the younger children who had been returned to care homes. "I'll never to go back to Stan again!" she snapped.

"You know Annie," said Uncle Colin, "our offer of a place to stay is always open, if you ever need a break and feel like coming to Wales."

"I know I'd be glad to get out of Yorkshire for good!" she barked back. But my mother was never one to listen to reason. After twenty minutes, she said goodbye and walked off into the night. Watching her leave made me feel wretched; like watching a tiny raft being swamped by hostile waves, disappearing into the blackness.

"Where will she sleep tonight?" I asked Uncle Colin.

He sat still and stared out of the window. "She'll walk the streets till she finds one of the shelters."

In silence, we drove off to find an overnight parking place. As I lay my head down, my eyes watered up. My impotence made my heart bleed. I prayed hard that my mother would be safe.

Father Roberts' mother lived in a small cottage in Llysfaen, a hamlet in the hills above Old Colwyn. Hers was the darkest house I had ever been in. The heavy curtains on the small windows allowed only a sliver of light. Old dark paintings of stags and owls hung on the walls.

Mrs Foulkes had a different surname to her son, Father Albert Roberts. I asked Uncle Colin about that one time. He and Aunty Jean looked at each other, and said little, but I picked up that Father Roberts was likely born out of wedlock.

Every Friday night, Uncle and Aunty, Julie, Marlon and I would go and visit Mrs Foulkes, and she was always overjoyed to see us. In mourning for her son, she lived in black clothes, including a black hat. She frequently broke into the Welsh language, sometimes mid-sentence. "He was here again last night, Colin," she said, referring to Albert. She said it time and again, and I felt for her as her eyes welled with tears.

Uncle Colin and Aunty Jean never missed a Friday visit, and though I found Mrs Foulkes' house deeply depressing – even scary – I always went along so I could be with Uncle Colin. It was my only chance to sit with him for two hours. Eventually, as their conversation drew to a close, I was granted a reprieve from the darkness.

After I had my bike back, I was allowed to bring it along in the camper van, then, after sitting at Mrs Foulkes' for thirty minutes, I could cycle along the country lanes and down the long steep hills back into Old Colwyn. What a ride it was! I reached terrific speeds going downhill, fearlessly sweeping round the corners with the wind rushing in my face.

I always made it back home in time to watch a TV series called *Budgie,* starring Adam Faith. The main character, nicknamed *Budgie*, was a likeable, young ex-convict desperately trying to make money from petty crime. He thought himself smart, but in every episode, he failed to make anything come good.

Some Saturdays, I'd tag along with Uncle Colin if he were visiting his mother, Dorothy, in Min-y-Don Avenue just half a mile away. Dorothy was short with white hair and thick glasses. She lived in a 1920s semi-detached house. It was the house where Uncle Colin and his sister had grown up and been teenagers during the war. I liked that cosy, solid house with its bow windows, green and white paintwork and lawned back garden. It was the kind of house I would have liked to live in.

It was on one of those Saturdays, walking home together from Min-y-Don Avenue, that I found myself fishing for details about my own mother. *"When my mother married my father - "* I opened in curiosity.

Uncle Colin butted in sharply, "But your mother never married your father." My face must have sunk. "I'm sorry I thought you knew that Phil," he said, in an effort to recover the moment. Hurt rushed in, I couldn't say anything else. He didn't *sound* sorry, and I felt ashamed that I wasn't aware of such a significant detail. It was a long time before I dared get curious about my roots again.

On Sunday nights, Dorothy came round to our house for the evening meal. She dressed smartly and wore heaps of face powder. Dorothy always disapproved of something, though it was never quite clear what. Some things slipped out though: she would have liked her son to have continued his early career in the bank, a job she could at least fathom.

Uncle Colin explained to me, "Mother never could understand our impulse to care for children. She thought Jean and I were washed up in a crazy world of mess and heartbreak."

Uncle Colin also told me that, years back, his mother had been hostile to his taking the housemaster job at Spennells, pleading with him to stay in Old Colwyn.

Friction sprang up between Dorothy and Aunty Jean at times. Jean was reserved and meek, whereas Dorothy could be fiery, speaking her mind full out. On several occasions, after some trivial disagreement, she announced, "I'll go home early tonight, Colin," her voice growing shriller as the sentence progressed. She'd kiss Julie and go off looking for her coat. Uncle Colin would try and calm her, but she wouldn't be swayed.

When Dorothy did stay, she liked to sit with me and watch my favourite programme, *The Onedin Line*. It was a drama series about merchant shipping in the days of sail. She could never pronounce the name Onedin. "Shall we watch On . . . Ondin . . . On . . . What's it called again?"

"Onedin Line." I clipped in reply, half wanting her to have one of her tantrums and go home, and half liking the fact that she shared an interest with me.

I sat glued to the TV, relishing another unfolding sea adventure. The weekly opening scene was compelling to me. The bowsprit and foresails came into view first, gradually revealing a three-master ploughing through the waves with sails billowed. The violins stirred, rose in volume and reached a crescendo before releasing into the long notes of the melody as the camera scanned the topsails. The camera panned and the proud vessel was seen from above in all its majesty, rallying all my spirit with it. I looked on in rapture at that beautiful ship heading for open water to some exotic destination. My heart leapt with desire for my pending life at sea. Freedom never looked so enticing and I couldn't get enough of it.

The Onedin Line was based around the life of James Onedin, a man yearning to elevate his lowly status by building his own shipping line. The storylines tapped into his thirst for success, his dubious methods to achieve it, and the many difficulties he encountered. I was absorbed, but Dorothy continually interrupted. "What was that he said?" she would ask. "He won't get away with that, will he?"

Dorothy always volunteered James Onedin some advice. One evening, Dorothy's comment came just when a crucial piece of the drama unfolded. *"Bloody hell,"* I said out loud. *"I missed that!"* Dorothy turned knowing I'd said something, but deaf to my words. She smiled at my enthusiasm for our programme and turned back to the screen.

Just before the programme started, Uncle Colin would set off for evening church. He had made himself indispensable there and, bound by his duties, he felt obligated to never miss a service. He never did. As he opened the door to go, there was always a moment of knotty, awkward silence when our eyes met. I looked on at him, unable to express the collapsing of the hope I had carried all those years before.

There was a lost infant in me that craved nurturing, and to be given personal time. That infant could have killed him stone dead for walking out so many times like that.

Chapter 32

Music, Money, and Love

I looked along the rows of acoustic guitars in the music shop. They were expensive, and I knew Uncle Colin and Aunty Jean were stretching themselves to buy me one for my birthday. A guitar leaning against the back wall of the shop caught my eye. "What about that one?" I said, pointing.

The shopkeeper looked surprised. "That's just come in. It's not new." I picked it up and caressed its curves. I smiled when the shopkeeper said we could have it for ten pounds.

"It's okay," I said to Uncle Colin. "I like it." Uncle Colin paid extra for a PVC case. I was pleased it didn't cost too much, and it looked as new as any of the others to me. I emerged from the shop radiant with pride. Uncle Colin looked just as pleased, knowing he'd bought me what I really wanted.

Owning the instrument renewed me; as well as its feel and shape, its sounds were gratifying. Then there were the grown-up smells; traces of wood, glue and strings. It all gave me the feeling of stepping into an adult world.

We found Jeff, a guitar teacher who lived in town. I eagerly strapped the instrument onto my back every week and cycled the mile to his house. Around forty-years-old, Jeff was tall and balding. "Oh! I forgot you were coming," he'd say, holding a cigarette ready to light up. He quickly cleared a space in the untidy lounge, and fell back into the settee to hear my beginner's progress.

It was an adventure going to Jeff's house. Sometimes he was in mid-argument with his wife, or desperately trying to care for his infant son, for which he frequently left the room. Keen as mustard to learn from Jeff, the disruptions didn't bother me too much. It was all quite entertaining and, in a way, a more normal household than 250, Abergele Road. His wife was always very kind to me, on the few occasions when she appeared.

Being with Jeff, and seeing his talent and dedication, was good medicine for me as I struggled with believing I could do anything half as well. "Phil, I just got my head down, and worked at it," he kept reminding me, insisting I learn musical notation.

Jeff could play anything, and he spiced my lessons with stories of his time in Liverpool as a session musician in the early 60s. That was the heyday of the Cavern and The Beatles, and Jeff had played on the same circuit. He set me challenging homework – pieces by Strauss, as well as Dylan and Chuck Berry, which he demonstrated on his beautiful, red Gibson semi-acoustic. I followed on my instrument, my willing fingers stretching themselves into new patterns on the strings.

I always felt welcome at Jeff's, and the lesson often ran over time. "You're the only one I'm teaching now," he told me six months later. "All the others stopped coming." Jeff's unreliability likely had something to do with that, but I was hungry to play, and he liked me for it.

I liked him and I liked watching his easy style that made the music jump off the page and on to the frets like child's play. Every week for an hour, I forgot my troubles. "Keep taking the pills," Jeff would say, waving me off home.

As well as chord shapes and rhythms, Jeff was teaching me dedication in pursuit of excellence. I felt as if he were pulling important pieces of me into shape, and I never wanted to go home.

In between visiting Jeff I practised from a book of Beatles songs and kept up my diet of music from Thursday night's *Top of the Pops.* When I saw Rod Stewart singing *Maggie May* I was hooked again, not only by the song and guitar playing, but seeing Rod cheekily playing football mid-performance.

In our front room, we had a piano and an old, ornately carved reed organ. That room was seldom used, so in the winter it was damp, and a musty pong took over. Despite that, I regularly took myself in there to play the two instruments, tinkering and learning as I went. Transposing my guitar learning to the piano, I soon had a range of chords to improvise with. There was satisfaction in seeing the notes laid out in a line and freedom in playing the strong one-to-four chord progression, C to F, as powerfully as I liked.

The organ had a pair of foot-bellows that you had to pump to get sound and dozens of pull-out stops that enabled numerous orchestral sounds. I liked the way the organ could produce a more empathetic and forgiving tone. The noises I made on both keyboards were likely awful to everyone else's ear, but it alternated between supplying an outlet for my aggression and answering my search for sweet and pleasing sounds.

Uncle Colin came in one day in an enthusiastic mood. "What about piano lessons, instead of guitar?"

"I'd rather keep on with guitar."

"But you could do your grades with piano, and take your exams."

It sounded like an order. "I don't want to do any bloody exams!" I spat out. Then I stood up and yelled, "Why does it always have to be about exams?"

Uncle Colin looked sick. The pride in his face broke, and his eyes dropped away from me. A few quiet words fell from his mouth, and he left the room shutting the door behind him. I could hear his footsteps on the stairs as torment twisted in my gut.

I hated him for walking away. I wanted to talk it through, explain what I meant in a reasoned way. Left to wrestle with the ferocity of my own hatred, I felt lost. My rage felt ugly and repulsive, and my body ached for a comforter. This was not how it was supposed to be, and I thought it entirely my fault.

Maybe Uncle Colin was seeing possibilities for my playing in church. Whatever his thoughts, the incident never got mentioned again, but the sourness of it lingered. Another sign of the defectiveness I carried.

The back of the house carried its own defects. The old lean-to extension was leaking, the wood was rotting, and rats had made themselves comfortable under the floorboards. Uncle Colin had hired a local builder to knock it down, extend the kitchen and add a bathroom, all to the end of accommodating more children. Work on the extension started just after I arrived. The builder, Mr Harding, was a local man, short, but agile and wedded to his craft. He was never far away from a cigarette and a cup of tea, and always parked a pencil behind his right ear.

As the foundation went in and the walls grew from the ground, I took to hanging around and watching him work. It fascinated me how he knew just what to do, how the masonry and windows appeared, all perfectly in line. "I can give you a hand, if you like," I said, keen to be in the thick of it.

I started doing an hour here and there, mixing cement and carrying for him. Seeing I was skilful, it wasn't long before Mr Harding let me saw and plane the wood – and, I tucked a pencil behind *my* right ear.

I was thrilled when Mr Harding started paying me. As time went by I worked with him on other jobs as well. "That lad wants to know everything," he remarked to Uncle Colin.

But our extension became an aggravation for Aunty Jean and Uncle Colin, as Mr Harding had underestimated costs and the price kept rising by thousands of pounds. The project was swallowing Uncle Colin's regular factory salary, so he worked overtime many evenings.

Diamond Stylus was only a small factory but it was the biggest supplier of record-player stylus needles in the world. Uncle Colin was bitter about his already stressful workload there, and the way he was treated by the factory boss.

Mixing diamond powder, and carbon powder, other workers on the shop floor relied on Uncle Colin's output to keep their own performance high, lest they lose money. Under pressure he started working through his break and lunchtime as well. He was afraid to protest in case it jeopardised his job, and his ability to keep the house. So, he only complained at home.

An awful hurt came over me seeing Uncle Colin slave in that

job. I knew how conscientious he was, and that the factory owner trusted him above others with the valuable diamond powder. "Why don't you just ask for a pay rise?" I said as I saw his forehead crease with despair, yet again.

"It's not as easy as that," Uncle Colin said, dismissively. I went away scowling at whatever stupid system was the cause of the situation, but I still soaked up his worry.

Uncle Colin was always on the lookout for extra income. He eagerly checked his premium bond numbers each week hoping for a turn up. "George has won thousands on the football pools," he said, speaking about his brother-in-law in thinly veiled envy and disgust as his own bonds never turned up a penny.

"Why don't you have a go at the Pools? I can help," I offered, knowing I knew far more about football than he did.

"That's gambling, Phil. It's against my religious beliefs." he said, closing the conversation.

Late one night, a family with young kids knocked on our door, desperate for accommodation. The bed and breakfast two doors away was full. "Wait a minute," Uncle Colin said, skipping off to find Aunty Jean. Seeing the children, Jean readily agreed to take the family in. Uncle Colin took them up to their room, while I made tea and biscuits. "Its money for old rope," Uncle Colin said to me, glad of the easy earnings.

Our seven-bedroom house on the busy main road was tailor-made for that trade. Aunty Jean was having none of it, though, and put brakes on the idea. Uncle Colin's frustrated face was a sad sight.

There was great promise of extra income, however, from an advertisement that had begun running in the newspaper: *Make Money Growing Mushrooms under Your Stairs.* Having a cellar, and bursting to get the money-spinning project under way, Uncle Colin bought a sizeable kit.

When the kit arrived, Uncle Colin sorted through it and ran up from the cellar. "I'm going to write to that company and give them a piece of my mind," he said maddeningly. I tried not to laugh as he added, "What they don't tell you in the advert, is you have to buy 112 pounds of straw, and rot it down for five days with eighty gallons of water. One can hardly do that under the stairs!"

Aunty Jean wasn't interested in money-making schemes. If she wasn't helping Julie with reading and writing, she was doting on little Marlon. He was easy to love. It was a joy to make him chuckle, and I crawled around the floor with him at every opportunity. Marlon carried the torch of harmony for us all. He was, really, my only connection to Aunty Jean, as we seemed to have little else in common and neither of us knew how to bridge to the other. Aunty Jean seemed to have a fear of being near me. "You're Colin's lad, Philip," she said. I never knew what to do with that statement. She didn't intend it, but her comment distanced me even further.

I was polite. We coexisted. Around Marlon though, Aunty Jean was more alive and easier to be with. If I were Uncle Colin's lad, Marlon was hers. Uncle Colin relaxed as he watched the two of them together; adoption papers were under way and he must have felt things were finally coming good after so many disappointing adoption attempts.

One Saturday, just after breakfast, I was playing my latest guitar chords for everyone when there was a knock on the front door. A lady in her mid-twenties with beaded hair stood on the step. She was a relative of Marlon's father. "I've come to collect Marlon," she said. "His father asked me to bring him to London."

Her words tore at the belly of our house. Aunty Jean didn't stop to talk or reason. She marched into each room, frantically scooping up Marlon's clothes and toys.

"But we haven't had any notice," Uncle Colin protested to the young woman.

"Don't say anything else, Colin!" Aunty Jean said in a strangled voice as she put Marlon's possessions in the hall. Within minutes, she had found every last thing that was attached to Marlon and brought it to the front door. The young woman stood still, not daring to speak.

Aunty Jean was shaking as she handed over little Marlon. The lady clutched the baby with one arm, while picking up as many of his things as she could with the other. She was eager to leave. The door closed behind her and there were still clothes and toys in the hallway.

Aunty Jean wailed. "That's the end of it, Colin. We're not having any more!" Tears flooded her eyes and Uncle Colin tried to put his arms around her. She pushed him off. "No more, Colin, no more!"

Uncle Colin stood still, looking at his wife. The burden for building hopes of keeping Marlon, and all the children before, piled on Uncle Colin's shoulders. His face looked as feeble as I had ever seen it. I wanted to sob for him. I wanted to fight for him. I wanted to rescue their dreams.

Aunty Jean's grief was too unbearable to look at. Grief poured into every corner of the house. I took a long walk to the seafront and sat alone watching the waves batter the concrete slipway.

Jean stuck to her word. Other children would come to stay but there were no more attempts to foster or adopt any of them.

Chapter 33

"Rumble, young man, rumble."

Uncle Colin was excited that I would soon be confirmed into the Christian faith. "The Bishop of St Asaph is conducting the ceremony," he said proudly. I wasn't sure what it all meant, but it appeared to be a coming-of-age ceremony. *This is what people my age do,* I reasoned.

I took the day off school and, dressed in my smart, brown blazer, I hopped on the bus into Colwyn Bay for the midday service at St Paul's. As I entered the church, the organ was already in full throttle, and the congregation was neatly settled in their seats. I checked my watch. I was punctual. *Maybe there's been a mix up with the times.* I didn't see anyone I knew, but I briskly took a seat in the pew behind the others. I followed along with the service and stood on queue to sing the hymns.

"All those to be confirmed, please stand," summoned the warden. Oh no! I was horror-stricken when I saw the others boys dressed in dark suits, looking like public schoolboys – and me in a brown blazer! Not only that they all stood together in a tidy group, ten rows in front of me. I wanted to implode. *Should I move forward? Should I stay put?* I tried to appear calm, but I felt my face heating up. As the organ accompanied them, one boy after another peeled out of position to approach the bishop. Several older people turned their heads to look back at me, fuelling the embarrassing fire in my cheeks. I felt sure someone would usher me forward.

More people turned around. I stood rock still. After the last dark-suited boy received the sacrament and returned to join the others, the warden took the staff and Bible from the bishop and, robes swishing, the bishop glided off to the side.

The congregation was instructed to open their hymn books. I felt sick. *Why hadn't someone helped me? How on earth will I explain this to Uncle Colin?* Then, a man whispered to the warden, who, in turn, spoke to the bishop. The Bishop of St Asaph returned to his place front and centre, and I was motioned forward. I felt an idiot. I knelt in front of him and our eyes connected. Stony annoyance scored the bishop's face as he looked down at me.

I felt the glaring eyes of the congregation as I shamefully returned to my place. I didn't feel confirmed, I felt mortified. My blessing came when the service ended, and I stepped back into the fresh air. In a concoction of irritation and sadness, I headed for the bus stop. Then, not wishing a chance meeting with anyone from the church, I decided to walk most of the way home.

I was glad to get home, and to release myself from collar and necktie. I was fed up with feigning a liking for the church. I longed for a place where I didn't have to fake meaning. If the day confirmed anything, it was that I needed faith in something true to me.

When Uncle Colin came home, I explained what happened. "You told me the wrong time," I said, only half disguising my anger. He didn't say much as his eyes dropped to the floor, disappointed that I hadn't been enthused by my day. Seeing Uncle Colin's face, I mellowed, and went up to my room feeling sorry for both of us.

To keep faith with Uncle Colin, I carried on attending St John's, and even once took Holy Communion. Still, nothing moved in my heart. But I was glad when the regular vicar of St John's called out to me after one Sunday service. "I'm doing a Sunday school class this afternoon. Why don't you come along?"

I was pleased he asked me. I was joined by another younger boy and three neatly dressed, well-to-do girls around my own age. The girls looked a little aloof with their coats buttoned tight to their chin and their pretty, woollen gloves, but they were talkative and friendly.

The vicar, the Reverend Derbyshire-Robert, was tall and walked with a severe limp. He was the one who, all those years ago, had suggested to Uncle Colin that he contact the Sunday papers to facilitate my being fostered. Although the reverend's sermons rarely touched me, I liked him. We exchanged conversation several times when, in cassock and surplice, he was outside church presiding over a well-earned cigarette after the service.

He was likeable, and his Sunday School lessons were lively and interesting. Reverend Derbyshire-Robert thought on things deeply, like I seemed to do, and he stretched us all with his searching questions. The vicar relaxed with us, and the way he referenced scriptural stories and then hung questions in the air gave encouragement to us to share our opinions. There were no suffocating lectures on what we were supposed to believe, no spoon-feeding *this is what the Bible says,* and no insistence that we reject other people's ways of life.

He asked each of us in turn, "And where were you born?" He told us interesting information about our various birthplaces, as if each city or town or village had something special. "Dewsbury," the vicar nodded at me, "is one of the textile mill towns that grew up in the Industrial Revolution. It was a centre for the Chartist movement." Not only was I wildly impressed with his geographical knowledge, I felt strangely secured as he told me more about my birthplace than I knew myself.

"Do you know the meaning of your name, Phil?"

"No," I said, amazed that it even had a meaning.

"It means *lover of horses*," he smiled.

"Do you like horses?" the girls asked me enthusiastically.

"Yes, I suppose I do," I said, wondering when the heck the last time was I'd even been near one. And then, I felt something new inside me, telling me that – in a way I couldn't quite grasp – my name, and where I came from, stored meaning.

Reverend Derbyshire-Robert's classes extended into the spring, and I was very disappointed when they ended. We were told the vicar had to restrict his workload for health reasons, and I wondered if it had something to do with his bad limp. I never did learn what was wrong with Vicar Derbyshire-Robert's leg, but I asked Uncle Colin to tell me if he ever started up his Sunday school classes again.

If there was a faking towards an established faith, there was no faking the truth about my inspiration. There was one person, above all others, who roused a fire in me: *Muhammad Ali.*

I had been in awe of Ali since 1964 back in Spennells, when he beat Sonny Liston to become the youngest-ever heavyweight champion. Ali was a seven-to-one underdog against Sonny, the man they called Godzilla.

"I am the Greatest!" the new champ chanted after his win. "I shook up the world! I shook up the world!"

Ever since then, I'd heard Ali's critics. "He's arrogant," they said. "He's just a bighead," they said. "Ah, the big mouth's at it again. He'll get beat soon." I read such comments in many newspaper articles, and heard them from staff in the homes as well as people at school.

To my way of thinking, Ali wasn't bragging; there was too much humour and poetry in the way he spoke. I saw it for what it was: flair, theatrics, a performance, his way of injecting vitality into the moment. Ali captured my attention, and the attention of the world. The price of ringside seats rocketed. And, as Ali said, "It isn't bragging if it's true."

Not only had Ali *shook up the world* by winning the world title, he shook up middle-America by denouncing his handed-down slave name Cassius Clay and proclaiming his ancestral African Moslem faith.

For the next three years, Muhammad Ali remained unbeaten, and became one of the rallying figures for American blacks still trying to free themselves from racism. Every time I saw him on television he spoke from his heart and I felt compelled to listen even when I didn't understand the details.

In 1967, Ali was thrust into the heat of the major political issue, the Vietnam War. Refusing to be drafted, the American government stripped him of his world title, his boxing licence, and his passport. It was the biggest fight Ali had ever been in, one that would test his character and convictions to the full. As he said to the television cameras, "I ain't got no fight with the Viet Cong. My fight is here. I'll die here in America fighting the oppression of black people." His words struck a chord in me, because he was fighting for a cause.

Overnight, Muhammad Ali went from being the highly respected champion of the world to the most-hated man in America, receiving death threats and hate mail. The civil rights movement was roaring and Ali's defiance against the army draft meant he stood deeper in the fire. He was now a champion for human rights, and he was prepared to give up all his success, his right to travel, and endure a prison sentence for that cause. "I have lost nothing. I have gained peace of heart," he said.

I didn't fully understand the politics or the issues, but I knew what it felt like to be denied a title, a licence to operate, and a passport for life. Something in Ali's story was calling me awake, and my heart answered like a drum. I had yet to find my own heart, but he showed me what it could look like. Ali acted and sounded like a liberated man, and I loved his playfulness, his generosity – and most of all – his self-belief.

My brother Dave had loved boxing and was a big fan of Ali. It was another thing we had in common and we'd follow the fights together. I never followed any other fighter though; I was inspired by the man and would go to bed in fine spirits when he'd been on the evening news.

The ban meant Ali spent three-and-a-half years in exile. In that period, he was invited to deliver lectures in universities where he spoke with eloquence and humour on equal rights for black people. Slowly he turned the hate to respect; respect for his actions and his dedication, and it became clear there were millions like me who were inspired by him.

By the time I arrived in Wales, Ali had come out of exile, beaten two top-class heavyweights, and then been defeated by champion 'Smokin' Joe Frazier. Frazier was a tough fighter who had clawed his way up from the streets. I had followed the media for the fight build-up like an addict, and was devastated by Ali's defeat. But Ali kept his dignity and carried on.

My eyes filled with water when I saw him on TV. "Rumble,

young man, rumble," he sang out with one of his corner men. "Float like a butterfly, sting like a bee," they sang. They were rallying calls, mantras to keep his energy fresh.

I bought the *Boxing News* with my pocket money just to read about his upcoming fight. Time after time, I soared with hope as I prepared to watch my hero step into the ring. I couldn't get enough of Ali, craving every last detail about how he designed his own training schedules and fight tactics – his unique style of boxing so contrary to the orthodox way.

Ali's contests ran like sacred milestones alongside the road of my life. He brought life to the very edge. He wasn't just a boxer; his fighting transcended the ring. That's what made him so compelling to me.

I was so aligned with Ali that I was nervous every time he fought. Uncle Colin was usually out, Aunty Jean doing housework and Julie in bed so I had the lounge to myself. I couldn't just sit in front of the television during his fights, I was on my feet copying his footwork. I sat down between rounds, and then got back up on my feet dancing and whipping out the Ali-style left jabs. I only relaxed when the fight was over.

Everything that I ever wanted was around me: friends, girls, warm families and the sea to go sailing. But they all felt out of reach, and I was giving up hope on so much of it. Then, when Ali was fighting, hope was everywhere. I felt free of the mundane back and forth to school, or church, and free of the criticisms that fought for space in my head. When Ali was fighting, it was like the air around me split in two, and the warrior in me showed himself saying, "Stand tall. You were born for something worthy!"

My heart was with Ali from the very beginning and right through it all. Little did I know that one day, I would get to see my hero in person.

Chapter 34

Loving People

"Look at this youngster, Phil. He's got no legs and only one arm!" Uncle Colin said clutching a newspaper article about a young boy named Joey. The article included pictures of Joey in London meeting Douglas Bader, the famous WWII fighter-pilot amputee. "He doesn't have a Dad. I'm going to write and invite him and his family for a week's holiday."

Joey's mother, Helen, wrote back, gladly accepting and relishing a break in Wales. I welcomed the sparkle when outsiders came to the house. The place shone when Helen arrived with her twelve-year-old daughter, Angela, and ten-year-old Joey, a mop of blonde hair in a wheelchair.

Joey's mum had the kind of irreverence that could have started a war. Helen seemed to make a joke about everything, starting on Wales. "You don't speak that funny language do you?" Aunty and Uncle's faces were a picture. "Just kidding!" Helen said grinning.

She saw the ridiculous in ordinary things, and laughed at everyone's mistakes, including her own. I loved Helen and her lack of courtesy, and I felt closer to real life when I was around her. I noticed how much she made Uncle Colin laugh, too. Helen brought fun and a much-needed ordinariness into our house. On Sunday Uncle Colin mentioned we normally attend church. "We can go out for a drive in the afternoon," he said.

"I'll come to church if its communion, I like a drop of wine. Any good-looking blokes there?" Uncle Colin couldn't help but laugh. Sometimes, his religious morals and beliefs sucked the life out of him, and it was glorious to see his rigidity blown away with this Atlantic gale of a woman.

Joey, despite his condition from birth, was also a lively and fun character, although he sometimes despaired of his mum's outrageous comments. "Just pulling your leg Joey, Oh we can't can we?"

The seven of us crammed into the camper van for days out. We took picnics into the mountains above Conway, and into the Snowdonia National Park. As ever, I brought along a football and was kicking it around with Angela one morning, when Joey bounded in like a puppy. Strapped into his false legs, he awkwardly balanced himself with only one arm as he chased the ball.

For Joey, his disability seemed little more than a minor irritation. I smiled in amazement at him. Joey never stopped smiling, even when his faced flushed bright red and he was covered in sweat.

At the end of the week, as the time drew closer for our new friends to head home, a familiar empty feeling grew in my stomach. It was the same wrenching loss I had felt whenever Uncle Colin had to leave after visiting the children's home. Uncle Colin must have felt it too, because he offered to drive Helen, Joey and Angela all the way back to Leicester in the camper van, a seven-hour round-trip. I was really happy when they accepted; it meant we got to spend another day with them. Aunty Jean and Julie decided to stay at home and do some baking together.

Helen's home was an ordinary, semi-detached house on a council estate, and their small lounge was cosy. Joey and I sat on the floor together playing board games. I overheard Helen explaining to Uncle Colin that Joey was not a *Thalidomide child*, as the press had stated. There had been a national campaign to gain compensation for the thousands of Thalidomide victims, a drug given to some women during pregnancy. Helen said there was another drug involved which had not attracted so much publicity and little monetary compensation for Joey.

Sorrow crept through me as we prepared to finally head back. I didn't want to return to Old Colwyn. I didn't want Uncle Colin to go back to the factory, and I didn't want to be alone again with those same old lost feelings. I noticed Uncle Colin was not rushing to push on, which was unusual for him. At first, I assumed it was little Joey he would miss, but as we made the long journey back home, I twigged that Uncle Colin liked himself a little better when Helen made him laugh.

In my first year in Old Colwyn, a child, or sometimes a group of children, stayed with us during the school holidays. Three brothers and a sister, ages seven to twelve, came to visit. They came from a deprived area of Manchester and as always, Uncle Colin took us on day trips. He was happiest scrambling up the side of a hill, surrounded by a gaggle of kids. We never went to sit on a beach; Uncle Colin would not have looked right doing that.

Back home in the sitting room watching television, the four children huddled on the settee like a litter of puppies. They were so friendly and, as I was older, they showed a real interest in me and asked me lots of questions. I taught them how to play the few chords I had learned on guitar. The second week of their stay, I returned to school, and when I came home at the end of the day, they danced about and all talked to me at once. It gave me such a warm feeling, I felt slightly embarrassed. The eldest, Rebecca, snuggled up to me on the settee whenever she could, a bundle of affection I really liked but struggled to be easy with.

I knew I would miss them when it came to their leaving. I cycled home from school at lunchtime so I could wave them off. They clambered into the car and their smiling faces looked back at me through the window. I saddened. They looked so tender and vulnerable as they drove off, frantically waving. My heart felt as if it were being pulled from my chest.

Back in the house that had emptied of energy, I tried mightily to push my feelings away. Eager to keep moving, I cycled back to school, but my muscles weakened and my pace slowed down. In class, I tried to concentrate on the history lesson, but I couldn't focus. Images of my new friends and our fun together refused to lie down. When I thought about going home and them not being there, I had to gulp to catch my breath. I had never missed other kids like this before, not even little Joey. It seemed so awkward, and foolish. I felt fragile sitting at my desk in the front of the class trying to strap down my tear-filled feelings.

I made it to afternoon break, but I could not sit through another lesson. I hauled my bike from the rack and cycled off to the seafront. Like so many times the expansive open sea was pulling on me. I watched the shifting winds disturb the water and the never-ending tumble of waves crashing onto the sand.

The crisp horizon seemed to nurse my emptiness. It was as if, where sea met sky, there was something calm and friendly trying to help me. I wanted to shout out, *I'm missing you like crazy, please find a way to come back.*

I drew a little comfort knowing my new friends would be missing me, too. But they were gone, and although I hoped differently, I knew I wouldn't see them again.

It was more than gloom that swept through me at these partings. A dark melancholy took hold and I felt its gravity pulling my chest down as if it were an iron weight. Though I craved a companion at such times, I also wanted to be alone.

The sense that I had irretrievably lost something, or someone, had lived in me since I first saw my mother, head bowed, walking away from Hallow Park meadow. The feeling of wandering around lost had grown familiar, but sometimes it grew with a force that made me feel a complete alien.

Uncle Colin never talked about what to do when you miss people. Maybe that's why he had attended the spiritualist church in Kidderminster when he worked at Spennells. He had become good friends with Mr and Mrs Townsend from that church. Mrs Townsend was a gifted medium and back then, when Uncle Colin was still Mr Thomas the housemaster, he had taken me to visit her. Mrs Townsend was delighted to see us both, and was interested to know about the children's home. I remember the way she asked me about my mother, and the good feelings that came when she did.

Even though our visits were short, there was something in the way Mrs Townsend looked at me that told me she was a woman of great depth and caring. It drew me to her.

Through the Kidderminster church, Uncle Colin met other spiritual mediums, like Mr and Mrs Bartlett from Sutton Coldfield in Birmingham. Mr Bartlett would tour around the churches, and once, Uncle Colin invited them to stay with us.

Over supper that first evening Mrs Bartlett recounted an event that reflected the suspicions of many people. "In a hotel late the other night," said Mrs Bartlett, "we had a knock at the door. 'You'll have to leave,' the owner told us. He'd found out we were mediums."

We held two meetings where Mr Bartlett went into a trance and allowed entities to speak through him. I don't recall much of what was said, only that his voice altered as a girl named Mary-Lou spoke through him. I was a little scared, at first, hearing that strange voice. Then I tried to figure out if these were spirits of people who had died, or something else.

Afterwards, I asked questions, and Mr Bartlett explained about life after death, life before birth, and astral travel. I would have liked to enquire more as I knew that I wanted that kind of deeper education, and to be exposed to different ways of understanding life.

Mr and Mrs Bartlett were a lovely and interesting couple, and I felt bad that some people did not respect, or even tolerate, their gifts.

I was learning more about prejudice. I met Gary, who lived farther along the A55 towards Colwyn Bay. Gary was highly intellectual and – unusual for the early 1970s – he was open about his homosexuality, something that was only decriminalised in 1967.

"When I lived in Liverpool, I was a friend of Brian Epstein, The Beatles' manager," he told us when he came around for a meal. Massive Beatles fan that I was, the connection fascinated me. I hadn't known that Brian Epstein was gay, and was forced to lead a secret life in the 1960s because of some people's discrimination.

After Gary left Uncle Colin told me, "Gary has a long history of suicide attempts. He's lucky to be alive." I soon wished he hadn't told me as I was disturbed by images of Gary trying to hang himself, and lay awake at night worrying for him. But I loved how Uncle Colin gave time to vulnerable people, and how he accepted them for their differences. I always remembered his compassion and offers of help to my mother, it moved me deeply.

I was surprised then by his intolerance of a television programme I happened to be watching one evening. It was about an interesting and aristocratically spoken man called Quentin Crisp.

"Excuse me, I don't want that on," Uncle Colin said, switching the television off abruptly. Quentin Crisp was the 'Englishman in New York', a famous gay writer and entertaining speaker.

Aunty Jean and Uncle Colin often helped our neighbour who lived in one of the flats next door. Margaret was a middle-aged woman, and a long-time alcoholic. She always tried to get me talking, but I couldn't understand her slurred speech. One time, she vomited all the way down the outside metal staircase leading up to her flat. Aunty Jean went over to help. On days when Margaret felt too ill to pick up groceries, Aunty Jean would shop for her.

"You've got to help people, Phil," Uncle Colin stressed to me during many conversations. Uncle Colin was a lifelong blood donor. He donated at every opportunity and proudly wore the donor badges on his blazer. He viewed it as his gift, ever since his time at a military hospital in his post-war, conscripted military service years.

Uncle Colin's helping nature sometimes dropped him in the soup. When the family across the road fell on hard times, Uncle Colin loaned them a thousand pounds to start a business. "I haven't seen a penny of that money back," he told me, with hurt in his voice. The neighbours never spoke of it, in fact, they avoided him altogether. It made me angry to think they'd taken advantage of Uncle Colin so easily, I knew he needed the money.

One evening, there was a knock at the door, and after a moment's chat about religion, Uncle Colin welcomed in two extremely polite and well-dressed lads. When he invited them along to St John's Church, they didn't seem keen. They did ask if they could come back and talk some more.

The following week, I sat with Uncle Colin, Aunty Jean, and Julie in the front room as we joined the two boys in prayer. We listened to them read from the Bible and talk about the Mormon Church. I couldn't help admiring the boys' tenacity, knocking on doors and talking to people so openly, like that. But it wasn't long before they ushered in a more serious mood, erasing the colour from our friendly chat. Something in the way they spoke felt very robotic. Their sentences sounded stiff and well-rehearsed, as if they owned a blueprint for how to live life. They didn't seem to want to know our opinions, or anything about us.

"What lovely boys!" Uncle Colin and Aunty Jean agreed after they waved them off. But I saw the confusion on the two boys' faces as they looked back from the road. They had maintained impeccable manners, yet I recognised the cracks in their smiles - just like my own.

Chapter 35

Summer Fruit

"Why don't we build a boat together?" I asked. "If we clean out the garage, we could build one in there!" Uncle Colin smiled at me as if I were fantasising. He never really answered so I assumed he was thinking about it.

Uncle Colin was skilled with his hands. He had built many go-kart style trolleys in the loft using old pram wheels, and then given them to various children. I still liked being among the tools in the loft, and I couldn't help but hold on to my desire to build something. Living by the sea kept my love of boats alive, and the idea of building one felt like a beautiful project, one Uncle Colin and I could share.

I had sent off for drawings and photographs of a newly designed racing dinghy I'd seen in a magazine. The Mirror 14 was designed to be constructed from two large sheets of marine-plywood. As well as the step-by-step building instructions, the photographs showed a completed craft flying across the water. I pinned the pictures to my bedroom wall so I could study the details and gaze at them at every opportunity.

"Why don't you join a sailing club?" Uncle Colin suggested one May evening. "There's one in Rhyl." My heart gladdened in anticipation of being on the water. Uncle Colin had asked around and got hold of some contacts at the sailing club. He handed me a short list of names and phone numbers. I didn't mind the idea of calling one of the members from the phone box down the street, but the thought of arriving alone at the club paralysed me. My head played scenes of being left with strangers and not having a clue what to do. Days later, I had yet to make a single phone call and I berated myself for my lack of courage. Finally, I asked Uncle Colin to take me, and stay with me till I felt at ease.

"I'll take you the first time," he said. "Once you meet people there, Phil, you'll be able to make your own way."

I was knocked over by his response. I felt abandoned. My bursting desire to go sailing was not enough to overcome the fear of being left on my own. And while I knew sailing didn't interest Uncle Colin, I had imagined at least he'd be enthused about helping me build a boat.

As time passed we were spending even less time together and the whole idea slowly drifted away. But a stormy bitterness towards Uncle Colin lingered.

My connection with Aunty Jean continued to be equally unsteady. I thought myself a disappointment – feeling I was letting her down by not bonding with her, especially after her support in fostering me. "You're Colin's lad," she said, again. It was a painful truth that we never talked further on; it just floated along the surface of our relationships. Uncle Colin let it all ride.

Aunty Jean was a trained nurse and seemed happiest when she went off to her part-time job at a local nursing home. When she worked a late-afternoon shift, she would prepare a sandwich meal for us, leaving it covered with a cloth. My craving for warmth extended even to food. I cursed under my breath when I sat down with Uncle Colin and Julie for a cold meal. The bread and tinned meat felt like the indifference I had so wanted to leave behind. If the temperature dropped, it was worse: cold food in a cold house.

The next time it happened, I couldn't contain a violent sweep of emotion. "Hell, not again!"

Uncle Colin looked at me, shocked. I sighed heavily before sinking into embarrassment.

"What's the matter Phil?" Uncle Colin said.

"I can easily cook something warm for us," I said, trying to pull back my outburst.

"I don't want to upset Aunty. She's doing her best," he said, "but I know how you feel; I miss a hot meal especially after my days at the factory." I felt more supported hearing that. *But why hadn't he voiced it? Why did he leave it to me to erupt in anger, and then feel ashamed?* As usual, Uncle Colin cleared the dishes, went upstairs and was soon on his way out.

Uncle Colin's mother's house felt much cosier and warm food was more certain. I loved to go there, and as spring came round, I helped Uncle Colin cut the grass and trim the privet hedge. Dorothy thanked us in her usual way. "Thanks for doing the lawn. Well, I can't call it a lawn; it's a grass patch, really." After we had spent hours labouring in the garden to get it looking good, Uncle Colin would lift his eyes in disbelief, and I'd smile.

I noticed how Dorothy loved to feed us after the work, preparing something we liked. It was either hot soup, or a favourite of mine – warm rhubarb served with homemade shortbread. It felt so welcoming, and seemed to restore some order into my internal chaos. Dorothy hovered with her china tea-pot retrieved from under a quilted cosy. "Have a drink of tea. All your troubles go away when you have a cup of tea."

Sitting in Dorothy's lounge after garden work one day, I noticed a pair of swastikas carved into the wooden fire surround. "Why are they there?" I asked.

"Well, that was there long before it came to symbolise the Nazis. It was originally a good luck symbol," Dorothy said.

"What was it like here during the war?" I said, pouring myself more tea.

"Well, the beach was covered in barbed wire, and we dug up the garden to grow vegetables, because food was rationed," Dorothy said, liking my interest.

"Dig for victory!" Uncle Colin chimed in the war time slogan. "I will never forget the ringing of St John's church bells marking the end of war," he said, retrieving the moment in his head.

Dorothy pointed to a wood-veneered wireless set with Bakelite tuning dials. She switched it on. *Clunk.* The dial moved a marker behind the calibrated window panel. "This radio is the one we gathered round when Chamberlain declared war." I knew the speech, I had learned of it in history class at school. *"Unless we heard by 11 o'clock that Hitler was prepared at once to withdraw his troops from Poland, a state of war would exist between us. I have to tell you now that no such undertaking has been received, and consequently, this country is at war with Germany."* I marvelled as I pictured Uncle Colin with his mother, father and sister sitting around the radio hearing that announcement.

Uncle Colin had never ever spoken to me about his father. Walking back to 250, Abergele Road that day, I asked about him, "Would I have liked your father?"

"Well, there was nothing to *dislike* about him," Uncle Colin said. I went quiet, thinking on his strange answer. *What kind of person was that?* His father sounded invisible! No more was mentioned.

Whenever Dorothy wanted Uncle Colin to do an extra job in the house, she would quietly mention her dead husband. "Bill would want it done." Sometimes, Uncle Colin caved in to the subtle pressure. Usually, he wanted to be off and onto the next task.

If history lessons like the ones we had about Neville Chamberlain and World War II intrigued me, current wars seemed to spark up from nowhere and envelop me. One of them happened towards the end of my first year at Pendorlan. I liked my art teacher and enjoyed Mr Chilton's lessons. After giving a final brush stroke to one of my paintings, I put my paints away and sat back on my stool. "It's finished," I said.

"No." Mr Chilton said. "Complete it like I told you to."

"It's finished," I said, annoyed he wasn't listening to me and unwittingly raising my voice. Mr Chilton flared and slapped me hard on the side of the head. My classmates looked on in disbelief as my face burned hot. The same terrifying helplessness flooded me just as it had at Spennells and Tong Park Remand Home. With my body shaking, all I could do was walk out. I headed for my bike and set off home. I didn't tell anyone. It's a miserable and lonely feeling, to be beaten and harbour a feeling you deserve it.

Nothing was said the next day at school. I couldn't fight Mr Chilton but I refused to just go back into his lessons and went home each time instead. Something of the Muhammad Ali warrior spirit was rubbing off.

Eventually, Mr Chilton approached me. He apologised and quietly asked me to come back. I eventually returned to his class wary, but curious. *Why had conflict suddenly erupted between us?*

An identical incident occurred when a temporary games teacher struck me. I had developed a cobra-like reflex to defend myself, a flash of defiance burst from me when I was aggressively ordered around. I said something provocative; I was powerless to avoid it. Again the delayed apology, and again it left me searching.

It was a different kind of powerlessness I felt when I came home one spring afternoon. I'd detoured to cycle down the seafront and watched the offshore wind whipping up spray and forming small rainbows. Uncle Colin was already home sitting at the table with a newspaper on his lap. Aunty Jean was frying sausages for tea and looked over to me.

"I'm afraid I've some bad news," Uncle Colin said, holding up the paper. "HMS Conway is to close. They've run out of money. They won't take any more recruits."

"What! What do you mean . . . how could they do that?" It didn't make sense. "How can a college run out of money?" I was gutted. I felt my dream being stolen. All my efforts had been to that end.

I didn't feel like eating. I went to my room to be alone. I took out the booklet about HMS Conway that had held so much promise. Lying down on my bed I looked at it one more time, not wanting to accept its worthlessness.

There were other navy colleges, but none near *Indefatigable* where my brothers went, so they didn't hold the same draw. My enthusiasm for schoolwork tumbled as summer came and my year at Pendorlan School ended. I thought I had done well enough in my exams. If my results turned up good, I would have a chance to apply to a shipping company once I turned sixteen.

I learned about a recruitment presentation to be given by the British Petroleum Shipping Company. A dozen young hopefuls, including myself and a couple of boys from my school, gathered in a hotel in nearby Llandudno. The presenter was articulate and impressed us with facts about the BP Shipping Company that had a fleet of one hundred and twenty ships. He showed us lots of pictures of ships and ships' officers wearing tropical uniform.

It was a local BP captain who mostly impressed me. Captain Roberts was a short man, round bodied with a deep voice and a gentle confidence. In his dark navy captain's uniform, he enthused about his own life at sea, and his journey as an apprentice. I trusted him and felt safe. As I came away a voice in me said, *if it's good enough for him, it's good enough for me. All I need are those results.*

When the school term ended, I was in the middle of a woodwork project making a coffee table. The teacher told me I could continue using the woodworking room during the school holidays. The caretaker let me in and even turned on the radio for me through the public address speaker. That summer of 1972, Elton John's *Rocket Man* played almost every hour. I loved that song – the story about a man in lonely outer space, missing earth, and admitting he wasn't the man people thought he was. I felt moved by the music while working on a project with sunlight streaming through the windows, instead of hanging around in my bedroom waiting for Uncle Colin to come home.

If I weren't in the school workshop, I was riding my bike along the narrow local roads, or cycling into Snowdonia until I tired myself out. Mostly, I headed for the town of Conway, only six miles along the coast. Riding over the bridge into Conway made me smile, like being welcomed into a sacred valley. Conway is strikingly beautiful. The medieval castle with its circular turrets sits alongside the river, guarding it like a granite bulldog.

The river was teaming with boats, and beyond them was the open sea, the estuary widening like a gateway to the whole universe. I cycled along the river, trying to get close to the small cabin-boats moored to the shore, and imagining myself a proud owner whenever I saw a *for sale* sign on one of them.

There was loneliness in my solitary excursions, which I swallowed down with great lungfuls of fresh air. But at least I could point the bike in a direction of my own choosing, and I was learning how to survive on my own.

My exam results were poor, claiming only woodwork, art, and

geography, just three GCSE passes. I needed five to apply for merchant navy entry and they had to include maths, english and a science pass. I was bitterly disappointed. I would have to drag myself into another school year, and have to change schools again, as there was no retake facility at Pendorlan.

Whatever cleverness I thought I possessed had yet to show itself. After the news about HMS Conway I still felt myself a victim of a serious theft, and I wallowed in it. Other than my dreams of going to sea I had no other plan, just a prayer and a good deal of anger. With that, I signed up and readied myself for a year at the nearby Eirias Park High School, and in the school holiday I continued working for the builder Mr Harding.

"Come on, Betsy," Uncle Colin said affectionately as the van strained up the steep hill out of Old Colwyn. The two of us stole into the hills one Saturday afternoon in search of blackberries. We parked on a quiet road and wandered in the sunshine, filling bags and bags of fruit from the wild bushes that seemed to go on forever. Working together to get the out-of-reach berries, one of us pulled the thorny stems to bring it closer for the other to pick. Released from the stresses of work, Uncle Colin loosened up.

Like we had done years ago back at Spennells, I propped myself on a gate and clambered onto his shoulders to reach the higher fruit. Uncle Colin nearly fell over laughing. We bathed in playfulness, making a joke of everything we talked about. We laughed at the same things and blended like father and son; food for me, and food for him.

It was a snatched afternoon, timeless and blissful. I felt Uncle Colin and I had walked into another world where my father figure could see right into me and understand and admire every little thing about me. No man ever stood so close to my heart. I glimpsed a feeling of belonging I hadn't known before; the bushes, the berries, the fields all came alive – as if my eyes had opened for the first time. Radiance flowed through me and every scrap of trouble I'd known dropped away. It was enough to teach me that somehow, inside me, I carried something ageless.

We collected more berries than we could eat, so we dropped off the bounty to some of Uncle Colin's church friends. I remember the delight of one woman, and how her face lit up when she saw the plump, purple-black fruit. "How kind of you to think of me," she said, swooning. It put a gilt edge on our day.

There were more golden moments when I helped Uncle Colin mow the grass at the vicarage for extra money. The Reverend Derbyshire-Roberts lived at the vicarage, near St John's Church. It was a lovely old grey stone house with sprawling lawns on three sides. Mature shrubs softened the high boundary walls. The stone outbuildings at the back were stuffed with old harps in various stages of renovation waiting for the vicar to have more time. I loved being there, working amid the smell of freshly cut grass and whiffs of petrol from the beefy mower.

Uncle Colin and I drank tea in between the mowing, and the moments spread out like tree branches in the warm sun. We talked about a recent trip to Anglesey. "Would you like to have a house there when you retire?" I asked him.

"My factory pension won't get me much," Uncle Colin said, tossing the last bit of his tea on the grass.

"I'll be looking after you when you retire!" I said. My spontaneity and boldness surprised me. But I was sure that my future wealth would be more than enough to buy him a home of his choosing. Uncle Colin crossed his arms over his lap, his teacup loose in one hand. He smiled to himself and gazed into the distance. I could see he was moved. It was one of those moments that passed so fleetingly, yet also seemed to hang in the air.

We packed away the big petrol mower and garden tools so Uncle Colin could move on to the next thing. Uncle Colin also ran errands for old people he knew, and gave them lifts if they were struggling with transport. He never did like saying *no*. I registered a worry for him – that his life would be lost in responsibilities and he'd become ill. I wanted him to slow down.

"Right then," said Uncle Colin, "I must get on."

Chapter 36

The Face of Life

Over the next school year, I would have to cram in two years of learning. It was a tall order being faced with a completely new curriculum for each subject at Eirias Park High School. I needed maths and english, plus a science, for which I chose physics. I must have prayed for divine help, as I was fortunate to meet a teacher named John Kindle, who taught maths and physics. To boost my learning, I also attended Mr Kindle's evening class at the Llandudno College.

Mr Kindle was my first long term encounter with a natural teacher, one that loved his work, *and* was brilliant at it. Nobody misbehaved in his class. Engaging and attentive, Mr Kindle was the kind of person I wanted to be. Other instructors had shamed me for not *getting* their teaching. In their classes, I felt like I had brain cells missing; in Mr Kindle's class, I felt like Albert Einstein. "It's easy," he said. And he *made* it so. He turned calculus into child's play. When Mr Kindle told me he had taught maths at HMS Conway, I felt even more connected with him. "Oh, closing that place is a real shame, Phil." It was hugely affirming to hear him share my disappointment.

So many times, Mr Kindle just appeared alongside me, and pulled up a chair. He would pick up a pencil and slowly illustrate each step to find where I was stuck, and would not leave me until the light bulb in my head was glowing. I walked out of Mr Kindle's class with my chest swelled and my head high. With John Kindle on my side, at least I would have a chance at those exam results.

I wished my growing confidence in maths and physics would extend to girls. Joyce was my age. I noticed her at my new school, and sometimes she sang in St John's Church Choir. Her vitality and tomboyish looks turned my head every time. I nursed a dream of Joyce as my girlfriend, and my head played out scenes of things happening between us. My dream ignored an important reality; that I was running scared of girls.

Still, the fantasy seasoned me with hope and I rode my bike past Joyce's house at every opportunity in case I caught a glimpse of her and could say hello.

After one Sunday church service, I was changing the hymn numbers in the display board when Joyce appeared from the vestry. She was smiling and radiant as she approached. "Hello, Phil. I've got something to ask you. Have you got a girlfriend?" she said in her easy way.

I was thrust into exhilarated panic. "Er . . . no, . . . not at the moment," I said, my legs barely supporting me.

"Well, my friend Linda fancies you. Would you meet her?"

I stumbled for breath. I was eager to talk, but crumbling at the closeness of Joyce's bright face and confidence. My heart was leaping and I had to turn away. I fidgeted with the wooden hymn-board numbers. "I could do," I managed to reply, dry as old toast.

Joyce's curly, fair hair was brushed back off her glowing face. Three feet away, I could smell her fresh skin. How I wanted to kiss that face! But my entire body was wincing in discomfort, and I could see I was unsettling her.

"Linda lives near you. Let me know if you want to meet her," she said, and turned to go.

I watched Joyce walk away; she looked puzzled and dulled. I must have appeared arrogant, but inside I was being slaughtered as my head compared her beauty to mine. I looked down at the pieces of wood I had been shuffling in my hands. I slotted them into the hymn board, despising my uselessness. Hopelessly attracted to her, hopelessly petrified of her, I knew then I had no chance with Joyce.

I was equally afraid of meeting her friend.

I sidled home and collapsed on my bed. Furious with myself for my gaping weaknesses, I descended into a miserable hole. It was as though Joyce possessed the entire world's joy, and I possessed none. My mind endlessly replayed the embarrassing encounter over and over. I got the message: *don't you ever dare dream like that again!*

Everything about Joyce was completely desirable, but absolutely nothing about her was familiar. Nothing had prepared me to meet that kind of female warmth. I had not the faintest idea how to act or how to talk. I came from a different planet than Joyce and the desolation of it tore me to pieces.

Whenever I saw Joyce after that, I felt ugly and inept as I remembered my failure to speak to her properly. My thoughts sped into top gear. *She's thinking awful things about me.* I ached to tell Joyce I was sorry, and that really, I idolised her.

Later, I thought about Joyce's friend Linda, and my vulnerability triggered again. *She probably wouldn't be right for me, either, I told myself - someday I will sort it all out.*

I really missed Dave, and kept in touch with him by sending him the latest John Lennon and Paul McCartney albums. I bought them with my pocket money and recorded them onto cassette tape so I could play them in my bedroom. I felt closer to Dave sending him the records. It gave me a good feeling knowing we were sharing the music.

Dave was not one for writing back, but as 1973 rolled out, he did write to tell me his springtime wedding date and that he wanted me there. He also said Steve would be away at sea and not able to go. Uncle Colin was busy that day, so I wrote back to Dave telling him I would take the train.

On the morning of Dave's wedding, I dressed in my best clothes and, with a small present and card tucked under my arm, caught the bus to the railway station. The platform was empty and the train seemed to take ages to arrive. When I inquired, the ticket agent explained that the train had been taken off-track because of flooding. The next train wouldn't get me to Yorkshire until Dave's wedding was over! Tension filled me. *What should I do.?* I imagined myself looking stupid turning up after the ceremony was over. I felt as lonely and incompetent as ever. Eventually I decided to walk back home, feeling foolish carrying the card and present, and all the while imagining my brother on the lookout for my arrival.

I discovered later that Steve had attended the wedding after all, so Dave did have some family support, but I felt huge guilt at not being there with him.

Around this time, I had some notable visitors. The first arrived in the middle of an April night. I awoke to see a man standing near my bed, looking at me. Light emanated from him as if he were a solid, luminous block. The man didn't move; he just stood and watched me, as if he were giving me a message, but without words. Something about him looked vaguely familiar.

The next evening, I saw pictures of Pablo Picasso on TV, as the famous artist had died the previous day. Immediately, I recognised him as the person I saw standing over me. Whatever it was I experienced, I didn't find it frightening, but personal - and intriguing. I wondered what Uncle Colin's spiritualist friends, Mr and Mrs Bartlett would have made of it!

Not long after my visitation, two old boys from Spennells Barnardo's home landed on our doorstep. I remembered Randall Paul and his older brother Terry from the home, even though they were much older than I was.

The two had started a business together and were doing well. Uncle Colin fished out some photos of Spennells, and we shared stories about life there. I pointed to the boys wearing the black 'uniform' gabardine. "I used to hide that blessed thing in the hedge on the way to school." They laughed.

We talked about the house itself, Basil the dog, Pickles the horse, the stream, and the lake known as Spennells Pool. As we skimmed the pictures, I could not bear to look at the photographs of Matron and Mr Vaughan. Back in those troubled years, I felt my very presence irritated them, and here, all this time later, I had to turn away to deflect the intense discomfort at seeing their image. I was relieved when the pictures got put away and the brothers invited me for a drive.

I smiled as I perched in the passenger seat. I was impressed with their brand new, yellow Ford Escort. I directed Randall and Terry to the seafront, around Colwyn Bay and out to Rhos-on-Sea, as if I were a local guide who had lived in Old Colwyn all my life. The boys asked about Dave and Steve, about my intention to join the Merchant Navy, about music, and the things I liked to do. The drive and the talk felt wonderfully close, as if Randall and Terry were two older brothers.

I was reassured, too, knowing that they enjoyed material success. It gave me much-needed confirmation that boys from children's homes could achieve things. I had already figured out that kids like me often struggled when they entered the adult world.

The brothers stayed for a meal, and I admired their easy manner, it seemed calm and mature. They joked around with Julie and helped Aunty wash the dishes, and then, too soon, they had to head home.

"Come see us if you're in the Manchester area!" they called, as we waved them goodbye. I watched the bright yellow Escort disappear down the road, and felt loneliness descending.

That same evening, Uncle Colin and I argued over something minor. He lost his temper. "Why can't you be like those two boys, polite and helpful?" Hate for Uncle Colin seared through me. I slammed the kitchen door as hard as I could, and marched up to my room. Like a torpedo into a ship's belly the comparison sunk me. I could not defend myself, and Uncle Colin did nothing to smooth our conflict. I distanced myself even more.

Chapter 37

My Face

The world seemed hostile before, but that conflict with Uncle Colin added a new depth of antagonism. I had brief respite on Thursday nights watching Top of the Pops. Music always brought me back to life but people like David Bowie, Slade and Marc Bolan also dressed wildly. They always looked like they were having fun and I was pulled towards them.

The early 70s brought a fashion for bell-bottom trousers, flowered shirts, and platform shoes. I had started to buy my own clothes and desperately wanted to fit in with styles other teenagers were wearing. But whenever I even approached the shops in town, I had to push down panic. While I could venture into the bigger stores and lose myself in the crowd, the clothes there were often less fashionable than in the smaller specialist shops. And in those more personal shops, I dreaded the approach of a sales person.

"Can you come to town with me?" I asked Uncle Colin. Even asking him was a struggle, but I was desperate.

"Why do you need me with you? You're a young man now. You need to learn to cope on your own." But it all felt too much, and I didn't want to expose myself to ridicule.

I gathered my strength. I decided to go to Llandudno where there were more shops and I could be more anonymous. On the bus, my head filled with images of returning with just the right clothes. After a brisk walk on the Llandudno seafront, I wandered around window-shopping. And there it was! I stared through the glass at a trendy, orange-coloured shirt with fashionable round lapels. Inside I could see the staff buzzing around the counters.

I strolled along the street to give myself breathing space to make a decision. I walked back, peering in the window and studying the shirt from every angle. It was a quality shirt; well above what I expected to pay. *Was it worth that much money? Would it suit me?* I carried on walking, hoping time would come to my aid, but becoming more and more annoyed at my stupid inability to make a decision.

Three hours later, I checked my watch. My bus was due soon and I had walked past the shop thirty times. Not only was I further away than ever from making up my mind, I now had the added worry that I'd been seen thirty times by the shop staff!

I cursed my pathetic indecision, pacing up and down in ritual self-loathing. Sick to death of it, I took a deep breath and strode into the shop. "Can I have that shirt in the window?" I said, in a monotone voice. I handed over the money and was outside again as quickly as my feet allowed.

I sat exhausted on the bus, inspecting every detail of my purchase, longing for someone to tell me the shirt was okay.

My next shopping trip came when Uncle Colin planned to visit town one afternoon. I had wanted to look in a newly opened shop, and this was my chance to have his support. Buoyed by Uncle Colin's presence, I remained in high spirits even when he suggested we go our separate ways. Uncle Colin headed off towards the bank.

I walked into the shop plucky and resolute. "I'm looking for a shirt like the ones folded in the window." The salesman, a small man smiling widely and wearing a pale blue shirt and tie, took me to the shirt section. He opened some drawers, took out a selection, and arranged them neatly on the counter.

"These are similar to the ones in the window," he said.

"They're not quite the same," I said, not liking what he was showing me. I tried to explain that the fabric was different.

"Hang on. I think I know what you want." More shirts came down from the high shelves.

"Not really," I said, looking back at the window.

"Let me fetch one out of the window display for you," said the salesman, patient as ever.

"Can I look at those other ones again?" I asked. None of the shirts seemed right, and as I struggled to articulate what I wanted, I noticed the counter and a good deal of the shop floor was now covered in shirt boxes. I had taken over the place! In my hesitant state, I felt completely exposed. The salesman, eager for a sale, must have wondered what to suggest next. I tried to hide my anxiety, but my meagre reservoir of confidence was fast evaporating. I could feel my face heating up.

"I'll come back another time," I said, turning to leave and stepping over the shirt boxes, but not before glimpsing a look of disbelief on the salesman's face.

Everything I had looked at had flaws in it, just like I did. "How did you get on?" Uncle Colin asked. I daren't tell him.

I never went near that shop again. Even thinking about it made the fear of *getting it wrong* wash through me. I couldn't understand how other people could shop and know within minutes what they wanted. It seemed that a crucial piece of me was missing, as though something important had been denied me.

As well as my discomfort in entering shops, I had developed a fear of going into urinals. I harboured a fear of being attacked. Standing in front of the open urinal, I found it impossible to pee when someone was standing anywhere near me. I had to wait until they had gone, or find a closed cubicle. I felt safe only in an enclosed, private space.

I was convinced that my fear of people, my shopping fear, and my anxiety around public toilets – all my troubles – would ease if I had a girlfriend. I blamed my miserable failure with girls on my facial appearance, and I became convinced the shape of my nose was the reason for my lack of confidence. I studied photographs of my younger self. My nose looked smoother, and had no kink in it. I reasoned that my nose must have become misshapen from taking punches to the face. The more I dwelled on my looks, the more I convinced myself that if I got my nose fixed, my confidence would increase.

I had heard about plastic surgery on television, and I mustered the courage to go to the doctor for a referral. Nervously, I told him I wanted my nose changed.

"Are you sure there is something wrong with it?" he asked.

"I want it straightened because that's how it used to be."

Seeing my persistence the doctor offered up details of a plastic surgeon in Liverpool, and told me it would have to be a private arrangement, not covered by the healthcare system. I had no idea how much it would cost, or how I would pay for it, but I knew I would find a way. That same day, I wrote to the Liverpool surgeon asking for an appointment. Two weeks later, without telling a soul, I caught the train to Liverpool and found my way to his office.

The white portico entrance displayed a brass plaque with the surgeon's name and numerous letters after it. I felt small walking into his grand reception room. "He'll call you through in a minute," the receptionist informed me.

I sat in one of the generous chairs, quietly swallowing the gulps in my throat, wondering if I could explain myself. But at least I was taking steps to sort out my problem.

The surgeon was a short man in a dark suit and tie with round spectacles. His eyes widened as if he were surprised to see me. He listened sympathetically as I told him I wanted a straight nose. He sat me down and held my head at various angles to take a good look at me. "What makes you think there is something wrong with it?" he said in a calm voice. I told him the kink wasn't there when I was younger. He looked again. "Do you have any trouble breathing?" I told him I didn't. "There's really nothing wrong with your nose, Philip. I can't do anything." The meeting lasted barely ten minutes.

I retraced my route back to the station feeling a little foolish for coming and glad I hadn't told anyone. As the homeward train hugged the coastline, I gazed at the sea, the surgeon's words running through my mind. *Could it be possible? Was my nose okay? Maybe he's just another grown-up who doesn't understand.*

If the surgeon were right, how had I got it so wrong? I didn't give up the idea of having plastic surgery. And I didn't give up the notion that my difficulties were related to how I looked. I continued to envy those boys who seemed able to attract girls without giving it a second thought.

That envy, and the fear of being close to females, brought excruciating pain. I couldn't even stand still and talk with a pretty girl. I hid. Whenever I saw Joyce at school, I pretended I was headed somewhere, never stopping to make conversation. Then I would pour curses on myself for being so feeble.

Towards the end of the school year, I fell for another girl, Sue Roberts. Sue had dark hair and the prettiness of a young Elizabeth Taylor. She turned out to be the daughter of Captain Roberts, the man I had met at the BP recruitment event. In time, I came to know Sue better, but the whole cycle of allure and rejection started up again.

It was August and I was about to turn seventeen, and receive my exam results. I was confident as I opened the envelope. Physics and maths: good passes! *Thank you John Kindle!* His patience, powers of explanation, and belief in me had a remarkable effect. I got my five GCSE passes. But english - failed! *Damn the thing, I needed that one.*

I had always struggled with that subject; with putting words together and with grammar. Maybe I viewed it as pointless, or maybe I didn't have a teacher who made it seem even remotely interesting. Luckily, there was a re-sit facility for the english paper in the autumn. Until then, I would need to get work to tide me over.

"I'll ask if they have a job at our place," Uncle Colin said.

Chapter 38

So Much Dust

Along the North Wales stretch of coast jobs were not easily come by. Apart from the *Hotpoint* washing machine factory, *Diamond Stylus* was the only major employer, employing about two hundred people. Diamond Stylus was a noisy, dusty place, with rows and rows of men and women in turquoise coats sitting at their desk-mounted machines grinding gramophone needles. Huge fans sucked the dust-laden air and vented it through a maze of overhead ducts. Uncle Colin worked in his own section making items the machinists required to keep their machines running.

"There is a job going, you can start on Monday," Uncle Colin said.

That first day in the factory, I noticed some youngsters had gone straight to Diamond Stylus from school to sit all day grinding needles. It was good money. I was shocked when Uncle Colin told me the size of their wage packets. It was more than *he* earned.

"Why don't you work in that section?"

"Not a chance," said Uncle Colin. "At least I can move around doing my job – not chained to a machine like a prisoner." That put me off any thoughts of joining the machinists' lines.

My job, in the subsidiary company, *Elgin*, was making aluminium and Bakelite cylinder blanks for the lathe turners to fashion into a cutting wheel. A skilled worker added the diamond cutting edges. I mixed the powder for the blanks, filled up the twelve-inch-tall steel moulds, pressed on the steel lids and baked the whole thing under pressure in a heated hydraulic press. I was glad of work that produced a regular wage, but the novelty only lasted into the second week. After that, I found myself becoming enthused about toilet breaks, just to break the monotony. I longed for my sea career to get underway.

Elgin consisted of me, two lathe turners and three staff finishing the cutting wheels. Having learned to use a lathe at school, I asked if I could operate one. This change of pace made the work tolerable. I was becoming over-confident using the huge lathe until one day, I saw a man get his coat snagged in one. I heard a scream and turned my head. He was being pulled into the machine with the jaws still rotating at high speed. He just managed to knock the power off before he broke an arm, or worse! I was more cautious after that.

At the end of the working day, it was lovely to breathe fresh air and rinse off the dust at home. Even though the fans ran continually, dust lined my nose and soiled my clothes.

1973 was the year the coal miners' union embattled themselves with the Conservative government. Raging inflation was devaluing pay-packets, and in protest, the union bosses told the miners to slow production. Coal reserves dwindled and threatened power supplies. In a stand-off, it was clear that conserving coal stocks was crucial if the government were to avoid a complete blackout. At midnight on December 31st all commercial premises were restricted to only three days of electricity supply.

The Diamond Stylus Company had bought a state-of-the-art computer. It was so big it was housed in its own room. To keep the computer and the electrical machines running, the owner purchased a six-foot-tall generator that stood outside the front entrance. Cables ran into the main power board and the generator supplied enough electricity for the main factory to operate during the day, and for our section alone to work at night time.

At night it could not supply the heating system. Not only that, the heavy motors on the lathes frequently overloaded and tripped out the generator. The grouchy faced factory owner appeared every so often holding a torch and cursing under his breath, but being plunged into darkness many times in the night made work quite entertaining for me. Alas, January turned bitterly cold, and Diamond Stylus became a miserable ice-box to work in, even inside my layers of thermals and jumpers.

At the factory, people on occasion urged me to be thankful to Uncle Colin for all he had done for me. I guessed they meant well. No doubt the workers knew all about Uncle Colin's efforts to foster and adopt children, and heard of the trials and tribulations he'd endured as a result. But their comments had a depressing effect. To my ears, it sounded like they thought our relationship was all one way, that I was valueless and Uncle Colin received *not a thing* from fostering me. Sometimes it churned up anger and I felt like shouting back, *what the hell do you know about it?* But I kept the angry feelings inside.

I would watch Uncle Colin in his green factory coat, hurrying around his section, operating presses, regulating ovens and mixing various powders. He often worked through his tea breaks to keep up – and my heart raged for his freedom. The owners treated him with scant respect and I watched it wear him down. He grew tired and, much of the time, short-tempered.

Sitting on stools together at lunchtime in the middle of his work section, I remembered the day at the vicarage when I told Uncle Colin I wanted to take care of him when he was older. *I wished I could change things for him sooner.*

The factory was a far cry from our simple time together back at Spennells with its huge open grounds, woods and playing fields. Something of the two of us was still back there, in the landscape, like buried treasure.

It was a harsh thing to have all these things flowing through me, and at the same time, feel totally powerless.

Chapter 39

Something to Lean On

Captain Roberts discovered I was interested in joining BP. He sent word for me to visit his house for tea one Sunday, in late summer. I was eager to meet him again and looked forward to the day. Dressed in my best clothes and shoes, Uncle Colin dropped me at the Roberts' house near the Old Colwyn Golf Club.

The large, white-fronted semi was pleasing to the eye with its bay windows and tended front garden. A warm breeze swayed the branches on the trees that sheltered the driveway. I pressed the doorbell, trying not to feel nervous about visiting this normal family home and his daughter Sue. Captain Roberts' wife, Pat, answered the door and broke open a welcoming smile. "You must be Phil." I liked her instantly. Captain Roberts appeared and welcomed me inside with the deep voice and confident presence that I had admired upon first meeting him. I shook the captain's hand firmly, hoping madly that he would like me.

In the lounge, Sue relaxed on the settee. Her brothers, Richard and Chris, sat on the carpeted floor. "Hi!" Sue said, her lovely eyes reflecting her bright smile. We talked about school and I mentioned I was resitting my English paper. "How can you fail English?" she teased, "it's your own language."

I shared her joke – but couldn't help making a mental note that *I would pass that bloody English exam this time, if it killed me.*

"Sue, lots of people struggle with English," Captain Roberts came to my aid. But I hadn't minded his daughter's comment at all.

I felt warmed by her teasing me. I liked Sue's honesty, and it gave me a chance to laugh at myself.

"Come on, Phil. You sit here," Pat said, as we gathered in the dining room for a meal. She was singling me out for special care, no doubt sensing my nervousness. I loved it, and wanted more. Sitting at the table amidst this beautiful family was shaking me inside, but I held on tight and joined in the conversation as best I could.

It turned out that Sue was travelling to London that very evening, and was taking the 6.30 train. When it was time for her to leave for the station, Captain Roberts turned to me. "We can drop you on the way, Phil, if you like." I would have said "yes" to anything he said. I wanted to soak up every bit of his kindness, his knowledge of the world, and what I viewed as manliness.

The whole Roberts family was going in the car to see Sue off. Her two brothers, Sue, and I bundled into the back seat. Thrust so close together, I felt myself in the arms of a family; their casual intimacy filling me with warmth and melting my barriers.

We pulled up outside 250, Abergele Road. I clambered out among the goodbyes. "Let me know how you get on," Captain Roberts said. They all waved. I stood on the pavement, my emotions churning like Atlantic rollers.

In the house, despite Aunty Jean and Julie's presence, loss bit at me, swamping my composure. The rooms felt cold and empty. I climbed the stairs and locked myself in the toilet closet. On my knees I broke down. I sobbed as if my head were breaking apart. *What is wrong with me?* Wave after wave, the tears would not stop. Something deep was wrenching my heart. I stayed in the safety of my small hideaway till my weeping released me.

Crushed and confused I slipped into bed and, lying on my side, I curled my knees to my chest like I did back in my dormitory at Spennells.

The next day, I was still churning from the impressions that the Roberts family had made on me. I thought again of Sue's playful taunt and pushed myself to knuckle-down for that English exam. I poured over the sample tests I borrowed from Eirias Park School. Uncle Colin had mentioned to the Reverend Derbyshire-Roberts that I could do with a helping hand, and the vicar gladly offered to read and comment on one of my essays. The Reverend had a love for language, and it showed in the generous remarks and helpful suggestions in the margins! Where I'd written *I cycled through the countryside,* he added, *don't forget the gently rolling hills.* Why didn't I write that? I got it: it's about adding colour and expressiveness.

Living in survival mode, my mind had dulled. But with six words Derbyshire-Roberts punched daylight into that dullness. Two months later I opened the white envelope: English Language, passed!

I rushed to tell Uncle Colin and then get his help filling in the *British Petroleum* application. I was thrilled, one week later, to be awarded an interview in London. The company would pay my travel and arrange an overnight stay at Anchor House, a Seaman's Mission in East London.

On the morning of the interview, I took a bus and the tube, making my way across London and double checking my instructions on each leg of the journey. I arrived spot-on 9am at Britannic House, BP's headquarters in the centre of the city. In that enormous building my small and insignificant feelings pressed hard on me, though I kept my feet moving.

Along with four other boys, I absorbed briefings, watched slide shows, took all kinds of aptitude tests, and underwent a full medical examination. Finally, our group zipped to the 32nd floor to marvel at the view over the whole of great London town.

The journey home from Euston station gave me time to digest all I had been through. I was in awe at the size of Britannic House, with London itself, and with the prospect of travelling abroad. Dave's travelling stories flooded in: the friends he'd made, the exotic and sunny places he'd been to – the Persian Gulf, Rio de Janeiro, Venezuela and Texas.

Within days, my letter of acceptance arrived, together with a formal agreement. It would bind me to BP for four years training to be a navigating officer, four years sea service interspersed with stretches of college attendance. Self-assurance was bursting from my chest; I knew I would do well with this chance.

I received a list of uniform items to get in readiness for my first ship. The uniform was to be purchased from a specialist merchant navy outfitter in Liverpool. The fifty items on the list included a peaked cap, tropical whites for warm weather, 'blues' for colder climates, deck shirts, a marlin spike for splicing wire, and a deck knife for rope work. The dark blue uniform jacket and trousers had become familiar to me. In contrast to the old gabardine, they were clothes I would gladly wear.

My uniform braid and cap badge arrived in the post. As I carefully unfolded the tissue paper wrapping, I glowed with pride. I asked Aunty Jean to sew the braid onto my uniform. "Of course Phil, show me where it should go." I was overjoyed with the result and thanked her for the care she took in doing it.

My next instruction was to attend the merchant navy college in South Shields, near Newcastle, for two weeks of basic seamanship training.

On a wintery day in February 1974, another lone train journey took me back into the industrial North of England. Looking out at the rows and rows of terraced houses as we approached Newcastle reminded me of my first train journey with Steve seven years before. It churned up miserable feelings of my time in Yorkshire, and my mother's despair. The tangled mess of my roots snapped again at my heels, and my body riddled itself with shame and worthlessness. Although I tried to deny it, I felt deeply ashamed of my unfathomable mother. But I would not give up trying to help and protect her.

Uncle Colin wrote to me at the college. "It's quiet here. I miss hearing your Beatles cassettes. We all miss your guitar twanging and your falsetto voice piercing the atmosphere. This afternoon, Julie said to Aunty Jean, 'It's just too quiet without Phil here!'"

Uncle Colin had enclosed a letter from my mother. She thanked me for the scarf I had sent her for Christmas, and mentioned a younger brother. *Matt has been sent to an approved school for three years, and was asking about you.* An approved school! I was sickened to my core. When will it ever end? *Stan is in prison, and I finally have my four younger ones at home. Mr Gibson, the social worker, told me you were joining a ship. I'm glad you have been accepted for BP, it's what you wanted. I hope that it won't be long before I see you again.*

Sorrow always accompanied word from my mother.

At college, though, the sorrow was curbed among a flurry of instruction. I thrived as I learned to identify ropes, tie scores of different knots, handle lifeboats, and launch life rafts.

The college had a forty-foot sailing vessel, St Hilda, on which sixteen of us cadet officers spent a damp February night. Among the cramped rows of bunks and the constant lapping of water, I didn't manage much sleep. The next morning on the St Hilda we took a trip up the River Tyne with the ship masters running a commentary on the proud history of the river's shipbuilding yards. I listened with awe and appreciation.

Most of the lads at college had been allocated ships. By the time I took the train home, I still did not have mine, which afforded me time to break my journey and visit Dave and my mother for a couple of days. Dave was delighted to see me, especially as I missed his wedding. He was proud to have his little brother stay in his newly bought house. And out drinking in a local pub with Dave that weekend I noticed the fear of peeing did not occur. As he'd done for many years, Dave afforded me some safety.

I took a bus to see my mother, alone, as Dave still refused to speak with her. She seemed to be doing her best to give her four younger ones a period of steadiness during Stan's absence. But the same old struggles were there.

Just before I left, the young ones were gathered in the small kitchen, asking for Saturday pocket money. She had told them 'no' but as children do, they kept asking. In temper my mother marched to the door, snatched her coat from its hook and rummaged in the pocket for her purse. She raised it above her head, and turned it upside down. A few small coins skittered along the kitchen floor. "Look! That's all I have!"

A gaping hole opened in my heart. I had to leave before my tears showed. *Money was the answer,* I was surer than ever.

The next day I boarded the train back to Wales, Dave waving me off at the station. My brother was pleased with his life – full of optimism about his marriage and buying his first house. We never hugged or touched, we just joked around like kids to mask the discomfort of our affection for each other.

"I'll see you as soon as I get back," I said, in the absence of words to tell him just how much I wished him well. I sat thoughtfully on the moving train, feeling my deep affection for him coursing through my heart.

My own plans had momentum now. I was eager for news of my first ship, but first I needed to make another trip to Liverpool. This time, not to change my face, but to have it confirmed on a passport and a merchant navy discharge book that would record the details of the ships I would serve on.

All this preparation was stoking a fire in me. For the first time in my life, I felt merited. I had done well to get myself to this point.

My joining instructions finally arrived. I was to fly from Heathrow airport to the Persian Gulf to join British Confidence, a 68,000 ton crude oil carrier. The letter, together with my one-way flight ticket, made my shoulders broaden. I could almost feel the chip that had ridden there for so long shrink a little.

Finally, I had something good to lean on, and something I could talk about, not just a handful of ashes.

After living under so many clouds I felt closer to blue sky. Though I lacked female warmth and love, imagining my travels warmed me, as well as the promise of a life where I wouldn't have to bow and scrape for recognition. I sensed the same wild-horse spirit that freed me back on the Spennells football pitch, flying me above the mundane and carrying me somewhere good. No one ever mentioned the word destiny, but I certainly had faith in it.

The name of my ship, British Confidence, sounded solid and proud. It was ironic as it seemed the only confidence I had ever owned was a brash, outward conviction that I could keep myself moving.

Running alongside my own movements I'd lapped up the press reports that Muhammad Ali was heading for a crack at regaining his world title that year. *Rumble young man rumble.* Could my hero shake up the world again?

Chapter 40

Growing Heart

My first ship would take me away for four-and-a-half months. In my bedroom I looked down at my bulging suitcase. My uniform jacket and trousers would not go in it, so, as it was cold, I decided to wear them. Documents and papers I carefully tucked into my jacket. Lastly, I slipped my guitar into its soft case, complete with a spare set of strings.

My London train that evening, for some reason, was not stopping in Colwyn Bay station, I would have to go to Bangor, twenty miles away. I asked Uncle Colin to drive me. He had appointments that evening and sounded irritated with me at having to go the extra distance. I didn't react, but I felt again the *nuisance-child* feeling that was so familiar.

While Uncle Colin revved the van I loaded my bags and ventured back into the kitchen where Julie was helping Aunty Jean with the dishes. We said goodbye to each other. It was brief; more pleasantries than our hearts speaking.

On the drive to Bangor, Uncle Colin talked about the recent low-tide that had allowed parts of a wrecked paddle-steamer and a wartime aircraft to show above the water. In the two weeks I'd been at college he'd risen early one morning to walk the beach at Rhos Point to look at them. I told him I'd wished I could have gone with him. The talk of the wreck took me back a couple of years to those first days out of the children's homes, and the freedom I'd felt being with Uncle Colin while searching for crashed aircraft.

I talked about buying a car and having driving lessons when I was home in the summer. There were tense silences in the camper van as well, which pushed me into reflecting more on all the years I'd known Uncle Colin.

It was dark when we got to Bangor station and on the platform were no more than six people. It was not a parting with any finesse. Uncle Colin put one hand on my shoulder and shook my hand with the other. "Write as soon as you can, Phil."

"I will," I said. We did not have words to match the moment. Anyway, manliness seemed to mean *covering* one's heart. I boarded the train. We waved and both smiled as it pulled away.

In spite of the lost years, so much crushed hope, and bitterness that grew in places where things couldn't happen, Uncle Colin and I had stood shoulder-to-shoulder. I grasped the notion that, together, we had beaten down the world until it gave us a human shape. We hadn't shared a religion; we had something much much deeper, far more enduring, and way more important than that.

I didn't need him to tell me he loved me; his visits, his letters, and all his plans were enough. He loved me when others gave up. In our time together, I had built an altar to him in my heart. It was easy for me to keep a father-son fire burning between us.

As the train picked up speed into the night, the interior lights flickered, the carriage rocked and clattered on the rails. I looked down the long carriage I shared with only three others. I felt lonely again.

My busy head tried to match itself to my journey. Like the wind that drives majestic sailing vessels, there was a force pushing me into another life.

I was leaving the coast, not with my hands gripping the wheel, or my arms masterfully trimming the sails. It was more my hungry spirit urging me to scramble up to the bowsprit. With the rush of the bow wave below me, I was striving to peer out into the wide ocean and fill my lungs with new air. From there I hoped with everything I had, that I was at the leading edge of a wondrous adventure.

Afterword

Looking back on these years I owe a great swell of gratitude not just for those who supported my progress, but also for those who appeared to do the opposite. All of the people in this book helped to create the timely experiences from which I learned the most precious life lessons. Some are dead and some are still living. As I grow, so I remember each character with growing affection.

About the Author

Phil Barber lives in Devon. He has two daughters and two grandsons. Phil works as a Life Coach, Speaking Trainer and Writer.

Website: www.philbarbercoaching.co.uk

Front cover
My grandson Calum posing as my eight-year-old-self

Back cover
Top - My eight-year-old-self with bow and arrow at Spennells
Below - My first Barnardo's home Hallow Park

Names
Where I have needed to change names I have used names from the crew and passengers of the Mayflower, the ship that carried the Pilgrims across the Atlantic.

Printed in Great Britain
by Amazon